Reading Race in American Poetry

Reading Race in American Poetry

"An Area of Act"

Edited by Aldon Lynn Nielsen

University of Illinois Press
Urbana and Chicago

© 2000 by the Board of Trustees of the University of Illinois
Copyright to chapter 4 is retained by Charles Bernstein
All rights reserved
Manufactured in the United States of America
⊗ This book is printed on acid-free paper.

Library of Congress Cataloging-in-Publication Data
Reading race in American poetry : an area of act / edited by
Aldon Lynn Nielsen.
    p.   cm.
Includes bibliographical references (p.   ) and index.
ISBN 0-252-02518-0 (alk. paper)
ISBN 0-252-06832-7 (pbk. : alk. paper)
    1. American poetry—20th century—History and criticism.
2. Race in literature. 3. American poetry—Afro-American
authors—History and criticism. 4. American poetry—White
authors—History and criticism. 5. Afro-Americans in literature.
I. Nielsen, Aldon Lynn.
PS310.R34R43   2000
811'.509355—dc21   99-6417
CIP
1 2 3 4 5 C P 5 4 3 2 1

In Memoriam

John Sekora

Contents

Acknowledgments ix

In the Place of an Introduction: Eating Jim Crow 1
Aldon Lynn Nielsen

1. Prospects of AMERICA: Nation as Woman in the Poetry of Du Bois, Johnson, and McKay 25
Felipe Smith

2. "Darken Your Speech": Racialized Cultural Work of Modernist Poets 43
Rachel Blau DuPlessis

3. W. S. Braithwaite vs. Harriet Monroe: The Heavyweight Poetry Championship, 1917 84
Lorenzo Thomas

4. Poetics of the Americas 107
Charles Bernstein

5. "The Step of Iron Feet": Creative Practice in the War Sonnets of Melvin B. Tolson and Gwendolyn Brooks 133
Maria K. Mootry

6. Black Margins: African-American Prose Poems 148
Aldon Lynn Nielsen

7. Bob Kaufman, Sir Real, and His Revisionary Surreal Self-Presentation   163
   Kathryne V. Lindberg

8. Decolonizing the Spirits: History and Storytelling in Jay Wright's *Soothsayers and Omens*   183
   C. K. Doreski

9. From Gassire's Lute: Robert Duncan's Vietnam War Poems   209
   Nathaniel Mackey

Contibutors   225
Name Index   227

Acknowledgments

The initial planning for this collection was done from a desk at the University of California at Los Angeles's Center for Afro-American Studies during a fellowship year that allowed me, for the first time in my career, the time and resources to conceive of such grandiose projects. This is the third book to have emerged from that one year of scholarly fellowship, and I am particularly grateful to the staff of the center for their help and encouragement. That, though, was some years ago. From conception to publication, this project has trailed me back to San Jose, to Los Angeles for a term visiting in the English department of UCLA, back to San Jose, to Boulder, Colorado, during the term of a fellowship from the National Endowment for the Humanities, back to San Jose, and, finally, to Los Angeles again, where I am now at home with my new colleagues at Loyola Marymount University.

This, then, is a well-traveled book, with debts to many gracious hosts. I want to thank all of my contributors for their patience as I wandered from one mailbox to another, and I especially wish to thank Ann Lowry and the staff at the University of Illinois Press for their support and their efforts on my behalf. It was Anna Everett who first pointed out to me the probable effects to be expected from combining the words "race" and "poetry" in one title. I will always be grateful to her for her advice, criticism, and generous helpings of sympathy. As always, my many students at San Jose State University, the University of California at Los Angeles, and Loyola Marymount University have been the real inspiration for my work.

A number of the following chapters have appeared or will appear elsewhere, often in barely recognizable relationship to the present text. I wish to acknowledge the varied prior editors and editors to come for permitting the nearly impermissible and for smiling on our improvements. Portions of chapter 1 appear in chapters 7 and 8 of Felipe Smith's fine new book from the University of Georgia Press, *American Body Politics* (© 1998 by the University of Georgia Press), but other portions do not. Inquiring minds will want to read both. An earlier rendering of chapter 4 appeared in *Modernism/Modernity* (3.3 [1996]: 1–23). An earlier version of chapter 5 was found in quite good company in *Obsidian II* (2.3 [1987]: 69–87). Chapters 7 and 9 were first glimpsed in Ed Foster's journal *Talisman* (11 [1993]: 167–82 and 5 [1990]: 86–99, respectively), though on those occasions one was considerably longer, and one was a bit shorter.

A personal word of thanks goes to Louise Bennett for granting us permission to quote at length from "Bans O' Killing," whose only author and copyright holder she is.

I find myself in the somewhat unusual position of thanking New Directions Press/New Directions Publishing Corporation for granting permission "on a 'fair-use' basis," as they put it, to quote from materials they have published. Further acknowledgments are as follows:

Collected Poems: Volume I, 1909–1939. © 1938 by New Directions Publishing Company. © 1982, 1986 by William Eric Williams and Paul H. Williams.

In the American Grain. © 1925 by James Laughlin. © 1933 by William Carlos Williams.

From *Letters of Wallace Stevens* by Wallace Stevens; ed. Holly Stevens. © 1966 by Holly Stevens. Reprinted by permission of Alfred A. Knopf, Inc.

From *Opus Posthumous* by Wallace Stevens; ed. Samuel French Morse. © 1957 by Elsie Stevens and Holly Stevens. Reprinted by permission of Alfred A. Knopf, Inc.

From *Collected Poems* by Wallace Stevens. © 1954 by Wallace Stevens. Reprinted by permission of Alfred A. Knopf, Inc.

Thanks to Roger L. Conover for permission to quote from the works of Mina Loy.

Quotations from the works of Marianne Moore are used with the permission of Marianne Craig Moore, Literary Executor for the Marianne Moore Estate.

Poetry from Jay Wright is quoted with the permission of the author.

Reading Race in American Poetry

In the Place of an Introduction: Eating Jim Crow

Aldon Lynn Nielsen

HELL any positivist can tell you "does not exist." There is no such place. But I feel there is an area of act that is hell. . . . A place of naming.
—Amiri Baraka, "Names and Bodies"

THEN I SAW THE CONGO, CREEPING THROUGH THE BLACK, CUTTING THROUGH THE FOREST WITH A GOLDEN TRACK.
Then along that riverbank
A thousand miles
Tattooed cannibals danced in files.
—Vachel Lindsay, "The Congo"

I envy the Congo Man;
I wish that I could go and shake he hand.
—The Mighty Sparrow, "Congo Man"

The reader must have remarked our propensity of putting scraps of poetry at the head of our chapters, or of interweaving them with the text. It answers as a sort of chorus or refrain, and, when skillfully handled, has as fine an effect as the fiddle at a feast, or the brass band on the eve of an engagement. It nerves the reader for greater effort, and inspires the reader with resolution to follow him in his most profound ratiocinations and airiest speculations.
—George Fitzhugh, *Cannibals All!; or, Slaves without Masters*

Few readers today will recognize the origin of this last epigraph, an 1857 book whose subtitle, *Slaves without Masters*, and whose title, *Cannibals All!*, are both drawn from the much better-known Thomas Carlyle and his text "The Present Time." The author of *Cannibals All!*, George Fitzhugh, makes his remarks on his tendency to overwhelm the reader with poetic citations at the opening of a chapter titled "Warning to the North," a chapter in which Fitzhugh's propensity for the close reading of verse is linked to his metaphoric extensions of the discourse of savagery. *Cannibals All!* conjoins Fitzhugh's taste for the literary and his taste for anthropophagy to his racialist casuistry. Like those of his contemporaries who would not abide the presence of black people at their social functions but who entertained themselves by blacking up, Fitzhugh delights in the fact that his own racist polemic will appear in a sort of blackface. His publishers, Morris and Wynne, he reports, have promised him that his volumes "shall be as black as Erebus without, and white as 'driven snow' within" (252). This odd combination of published discourse, minstrelsy, and cannibalism is in fact an American tradition, echoed in the individual talent of that Missouri-bred poet T. S. Eliot, whose "Fragment of an Agon" opens with Sweeney telling Doris he will carry her off to a cannibal isle, to which Doris replies all too excitedly, "You'll be the cannibal!" Sweeney responds, warming to the prospect, "You'll be the missionary!" (79), perhaps adding a disturbing new connotation to the sexual cliché of the missionary position.

We could, in the manner of Carlyle, pursue this thematics into the present time. In December 1993, Democratic Senator Ernest F. Hollings of South Carolina reported his own form of cultural studies. "Everybody likes to go to Geneva," said the senator, speaking of international trade talks recently concluded in that city. "I used to do it for the Law of the Sea conferences and you'd find these potentates from down in Africa, you know, rather than eating each other, they'd just come up and get a good square meal in Geneva" ("Hollings Remark" A38). Senator Hollings scripts himself into a signifying chain stretching back from the present time through Eliot and Vachel Lindsay, through Fitzhugh, to Christopher Columbus. If the senator ever attended a screening of the popular film *The Dead Poets Society*, he would have seen a reenactment of this ritualized discourse as the band of young men featured in that film dance out of their meeting-cave and through the woods, savagely chanting the chorus to Lindsay's "The Congo," a poem first premiered in public at the Springfield, Illinois, Lincoln Day Banquet, a somewhat perverse mode of memorial to the Great Emancipator. Were Hollings to attend a performance of T. S. Eliot's verse play *The Cocktail Party*, he would witness an exchange in which it is explained that the natives of Eliot's mythic "Kinkanja," instead of eating monkeys, "are eating Christians" (375). The act of cannibalism is something, presumably, that none of these white men ever witnessed in person. Yet so pervasive and so naturalized are images of African savagery in Western mass discourse that few white people have ever challenged their assertion. It was, after all, the *Chicago Defender,* not the *Chicago Tribune,* which revealed that the film *Jacko,* advertised as filmed in Africa and featuring a cannibal, was a hoax. The *Defender* quoted the film's "cannibal," a Harlem janitor who complained that the film's producers had not paid him. As Anna Everett has pointed out in her recent research into the history of African-American film criticism, while the janitor had never been to Africa, he had been taught by the film's director to growl in what might be recognizable to American audiences as an Africanesque manner (389n.34). The persistence of such phenomena may explain in part why Senator Hollings was so taken aback by the outcry that the publication of his remarks brought about. In my own university courses, I have been deeply troubled by the unquestioning readiness of some students, even those already well-versed in the concept of the unreliable narrator, to accept at face value the claims made by the narrator of Joseph Conrad's *Heart of Darkness* that some of Marlow's companions on his Congo voyage are cannibals. This narrator, like Senator Hollings, has never seen anyone eaten, and yet he finds nothing surprising in the naming of these tormented Africans as cannibals. Many students express surprise when I ask them how they know that the men Marlow sees *are* cannibals and what difference the answer to that question might make in their interpretations of the text. Eliot appears to have had no substantive knowledge of Africa, but the public record in England during Eliot's lifetime affords numerous sources for the poet's Africanist tropes of savagery. At one point, the *Evening Standard* reported that a representative of the Stanleyville rebels in the Congo region threatened to "devour" European hostages (it was a similar report that inspired the Mighty Sparrow to compose his calypso "Congo Man"). The *Standard* emphasized that this savage suggestion was made by an African who had been to Harvard, and who had hosted "some lively parties" when previously posted in London (qtd. in James 17–18).

The very word "cannibal" may have had its origins in just such a secondhand manner. The *Oxford English Dictionary* reports that Christopher Columbus first represented the word as *"Canibales,"* a name spoken to him by the inhabitants of the island now known as Cuba. By 1555, the proper noun had gained currency as an English noun and had become associated with the eating of human flesh. Already, accusations of cannibalism had become a central part of the English mythos of Africa, accusations that very few scholars had begun to question as early as 1680 (Turner 18). The lack of firsthand evidence of African cannibalism, though, had little discernible effect on English traders and colonizers, who feared possible direct experience of the practice. Such inconsistencies did not much matter to the survival of the belief among whites, however. As Patricia Turner observes: "Over the course of two centuries, it seems, European explorers uniformly assumed that although the particular African tribal group with whom they were trading did not intend to eat them, there were other, less friendly African peoples eager to add white meat to their cuisine" (20). The Mighty Sparrow sings, "I never ate a white meat yet," but his song seldom reaches the ears of white readers, who are far more likely to be attuned to Eliot's *Cocktail Party*.

So widespread was acceptance of the factuality of African cannibalism that even white poets who opposed the barbarities of the slave trade still left that assumption unchallenged. In 1737, for example, an anonymous poem appeared in the *Tunbridge Miscellany*, attacking the hypocrisy of slave traders who were self-professed Christians.

> Kind are the Cannibals, compar'd with you,
> For we must give to every one his Due;
> They are by Hunger prompted to destroy;
> You murder with a Countenance of Joy;
> They kill for sake of Food, and nothing more,
> You feed your Cruelty with Christian Gore (Anon 15–16)

From the beginning of the Atlantic slave trade, through its eventual abolition, and well into the present century, Anglo-American literature recorded and transmitted a discursive formation that posited the "Basic Savagery," as Vachel Lindsay terms it in "The Congo" (47), of African persons and that codes Africanist savagery in self-authenticating narratives of pervasive cannibalism. Africanist discourse so thoroughly formed the terms of American thinking about Africans, was so much a naturalized part of Western culture, became so deeply embedded in the ideologies of poets and critics alike, that it has continued to operate within the critical reception of American poetry into the recent past. When Robert Duncan submitted his 1942 composition "An African Elegy" to the *Southern Review* in 1944, it was accepted. This poem has subsequently become something of a legend among readers of Duncan due to the later refusal to print the poem by the journal's editor, John Crowe Ransom. Duncan's elegy, like portions of George Fitzhugh's *Cannibals All!*, is built around a dramatic extension of the tropes of African barbarism, in which Africa comes to serve once more as the heart of the poet's own darkness. The poem's second section begins:

> Negroes, negroes, all those princes,
> holding cups of rhinoceros bone, make
> magic with my blood. Where beautiful Marijuana

towers taller than the eucalyptus, turns
within the lips of night and falls,
falls downward, where as giant kings we gathered
and devoured her burning hands and feet. (34)

It was not Duncan's description of Negroes as "princes / holding to their mouths like Death / the cups of rhino bone" (34) that disturbed Ransom sufficiently to cancel the *Southern Review*'s acceptance of the poem. As yet, no query regarding this tired imagery, so reminiscent of Lindsay, has surfaced in Ransom's writings. Nor was it the hallucinatory reference to the consuming of illicit substances that caused Ransom concern. According to Andrew Schelling, Ransom determined that "An African Elegy" would not appear in the journal after reading Duncan's essay "The Homosexual in Society" (Schelling 173). Where Ransom's intrinsic mode of critique had, evidently, found little or nothing to remark in the racialized tropes of Duncan's poem, the extrinsic appearance of Duncan's social criticism had rendered the poem unpublishable. Duncan was, of course, hardly alone among the poets of the San Francisco and Berkeley Renaissance in his turning to Africanist imagery for his metaphysics of divine savagery. Just a few years later, Jack Spicer wrote in his *Imaginary Elegies* that "God feeds on God. God's goodness is / a black and blinding cannibal with sunny teeth" (106). These lines have attracted no more critical attention than have Duncan's, yet they give a distinctively ideological flavor to the often-quoted final imperative of Spicer's poem: "Poet, / Be like God" (107). It is as if the subject of race had been swallowed up by the lethean waters of recent critical history—or at least white literary history—with its seemingly godlike assumption of scholarly omniscience and objectivity.

What had not been swallowed up, however, was the critical currency of cannibalism as a trope for primitivism, exoticism, Africanness, and poetry. As recently as 1964, in a seemingly unlikely context, Kenneth Rexroth was heard to advance a metaphoric cannibalism as a critical category in defense of the poetry of the young LeRoi Jones, the same LeRoi Jones who, having renamed himself Amiri Baraka, would be denounced by Rexroth as "a professional Race Man of the most irresponsible sort" just a few years later (qtd. in Harris, "Introduction" xxvi). In August 1964, a conference sponsored by the University of California Extension on "The Negro Writer in the United States" was held at Asilomar, California. Black critics, including J. Saunders Redding and Arna Bontemps, spoke at the conference in the company of white critics of black writing, such as Robert Bone and Nat Hentoff. One day of the conference, both Gwendolyn Brooks and LeRoi Jones read their poems. In the course of the discussion session that followed, a number of the critics in attendance attempted to direct the audience toward a consideration of the aesthetic differences between Brooks and Jones, though the poets themselves were not terribly interested in the exercise. The obvious import of the comparisons the white critics were making was that Brooks was a writer of light, imitative verse, perhaps in the "mockingbird" tradition, and that Jones, aligned with the Beats and the Black Mountain School, was beyond the pale of what white critics would consider poetry. Brooks responded by letting the audience know that she held Jones and his work in very high regard, and Jones characterized the debate as something more appropriate to a "Poetry 101" course. Robert Bone and Jules Chametsky, both white critics, returned tenaciously to their determinedly New Critical assessments of the poets. In his own panel session, Bone had, according to Adam David Miller, indulged in an angry outburst, telling his audience: "You Negroes should grow up and learn to take criticism" (10). The arguments of Bone and Chametsky at the panel with Jones and Brooks evidence a similar level of patronizing superiority. As Miller observed after the conference, "Faced with a body of literate Negroes possessing some knowledge, who are not anxious to please, whites are nonplussed" (11).

By the time Kenneth Rexroth intervened in this dispute, it was evident to all that his patience with academic criticism was at its limits. Nonetheless, the particular mode of expression chosen by Rexroth must have surprised even some of the "nonplussed" whites in the audience. Taking to the microphone, Rexroth began his remarks with a startling simile: "This is like Ornette Coleman is cooking missionaries" (Baraka, *Poetry with Jones* n.p.). What Rexroth wanted to address was his belief that there was inevitably a lag time between the appearance of innovative art forms and the readiness of critics and "laymen" to understand and approve them. For Rexroth, this is a simple fact of artistic life that all writers given to formal experimentation must deal with. Picking up on the formal distinctions that some of the white poets had drawn between the earlier works of Brooks and Jones's new poetry—rooted in Olson's projective verse and the jazz-inflected poetics of black literary arts—Rexroth compared the reception that met Ornette Coleman's startling new modes of music to the reception that Jones's poems from *The Dead Lecturer* and *Black Magic* had just met at the conference. "Ornette Coleman is just as disciplined an artist as Mozart, let alone Fats Waller," Rexroth averred, but he then once more returned to his controlling simile of savagery: "He may sound like jungle drums and Watusis in the night killing Pygmies to people who don't know anything about music" (Baraka, *Poetry with Jones* n.p.). What Rexroth seemingly wishes to convey is that those who hear Coleman's music as savage and primitive, like those unable to comprehend Jones's poetic forms, simply do not know their music. Yet in making this analogy, he takes for granted the communicability of his critical categories: jungle drums, Watusis killing Pygmies, and Coleman at a pot cooking missionary critics. Never for a moment recognizing the extent to which these categories indicate his own complicity in the very forms of incomprehension he is denouncing, Rexroth ends by advising: "The only thing to do is read lots of LeRoi Jones, as you have read lots of Gwendolyn Brooks, and then maybe you'll dig it" (Baraka, *Poetry with Jones* n.p.). Having made his critical distinctions within the most racist tropes of savagery, Rexroth could then in a few years deride Jones/Baraka as a "Race Man of the most irresponsible sort" (qtd. in Harris xxvi) with little fear that he would be held responsible by white readers for his own professions of race. Among the many benefits of white privilege in American culture is the power to make race appear and disappear at will. As literary criticism has been able to make race and the role it plays in poetry disappear from the reading of Robert Duncan and Jack Spicer, Rexroth is able to invoke race and cannibalism in his role as critic of black poetry only to rule out of order those black poets who, in response to just such criticism as his, turn from the demands for orthodoxy from missionary critics and seek an art formed out of the aesthetics of their own lives as black people in America. Decades later, Baraka, perhaps recalling episodes such as this one, included in his collection *Heathens* a poem that describes how "Heathen Technology & Media":

> Seek to modernize
>   cannibalism
>   & make it
>   acceptable to
> the food. (*Transbluesency* 215)

There was still less critical circumspection about race, and virtually no desire to make it disappear, in earlier periods of American literary culture. In his 1900 volume *The Negro a Beast,* Charles Carroll argued from scriptural evidence that Africans, and African Americans, were a species apart, beasts; but, as Carroll's subtitle explains, the African was "created with articulate speech, and hands, that he may be of service to his master—the White Man." Not content to rely on Scripture, Carroll turns to science for evidence to support his argument. In a chapter that might not be out of place in Richard Herrnstein and Charles Murray's *The Bell Curve,* Carroll asserts the inherent intellectual inferiority of Africans, correlating this incapacity with gross brain weight, even arguing that the Negro brain is darker in color (and thus deficient in ability) than that of the superior white (48). This is only one of many reasons Carroll advances to explain the "fact" that the achievements of the Negro, including the literary, are invariably inferior, an observation echoing Thomas Jefferson's *Notes on the State of Virginia*. Not content to "prove" the inhumanity of the African, Carroll also attributes Christ's crucifixion to "atheism, negroism and idolatry" (252). In *The Negro Is a Man*, W. S. Armistead's 1903 refutation of Carroll's book, Armistead turns to questions of diet in contesting Carroll's argument that the Negro is in fact an ape. (That the Negro is an ape, in Carroll's recounting of the deluge, explains why a Negro was on board Noah's Ark [233]). Armistead points out that apes are not flesh-eaters, and that both Negroes and whites do eat flesh (30)—though, presumably, not one another's.

Presumably, too, apes do not consume metrical verses, but the consuming powers of poetry were of particular, and particularly strange, interest to George Fitzhugh's rhetorical strategies in *Cannibals All!* Like many other antebellum authors, Fitzhugh derided the abolitionists at every opportunity. He writes in "Warning to the North": "they are vastly fond of young cannibals, and employ much of their time in sewing and knitting and getting up subscriptions, to send shirts and trousers to the little fellows away over in Africa" (252). But Fitzhugh, who begins this chapter with an ironist's response to the worry that his poetic epigraphs might consume his prose argument, now fears that the abolitionists might abduct his literary productions. The defender of slavery, a system of oppression whose first act is abduction, now raises his concern that the abolitionists might abduct the child of his mind, the book, which he now satirically presents as a "Little Cannibal." In his commentaries on Karl Kraus, Walter Benjamin remarks: "The satirist is the figure in whom the cannibal was received into civilization. His recollection of his origin is not without filial piety, so that the proposal to eat people has become an essential constituent of his imagination" (260–61). Fitzhugh simultaneously warns his northern readers that his writings, "born with teeth" (252), may bite, and worries that, because "the Abolitionists are so devoted to the uncouth, dirty, naked little cannibals of Africa, haven't we good reason to fear that they will run away with and adopt ours, when they come forth neatly dressed in black muslin and all shining with gold from the master hands of Morris and Wynne?" (252). In an addendum to *Cannibals All!*, Fitzhugh reproduces a letter he had mailed to William Lloyd Garrison's *Liberator*, following it with the prediction that his own literary cannibals will be greeted "with applause, instead of hisses" (261). Garrison had printed Fitzhugh's letter, thus taking up one, at least, of Fitzhugh's cannibals. Compounding these ironies, in the period immediately following the Civil War,

George Fitzhugh was appointed an agent of the Freedman's Bureau, and thus the literary cannibal was indeed received into Reconstruction—and reconstructed—civilization.

There has always been another corresponding passage through this discourse. The *Oxford English Dictionary*, having mapped the twisting progress of the word "cannibal" from Columbus's misapprehensions, through its ominous appearance in the first act of Shakespeare's *Othello*, and into the nineteenth century, arrives at Africa and Livingstone's belated report, in his 1865 *Zambezi*: "Nearly all blacks believe the whites to be cannibals." (Here, too, we must note the intersections between the discourse of poetics and the discourse of anthropophagy. The *Oxford English Dictionary* also notes a telling appearance of the term in Macaulay ten years prior to Livingstone's note: "The street poets portioned out all his joints with cannibal ferocity.") Cross-cultural charges of cannibalism are easily located throughout human history, but, as Patricia Turner has pointed out, the rumors reported by Livingstone clearly have a different epistemological status from those found in the poetry of Lindsay and Eliot. While millions of whites read and repeated narratives of African cannibalism, weaving them into their fiction, their poems, their politics, and their humor, Africans, from the end of the fifteenth century on, witnessed the mass disappearance of their brethren into the seemingly insatiable appetites of the whites. Whites were, as Turner puts it, "large-scale consumers of African peoples"; and while Africans "born into New World slavery recognized that their white masters and mistresses had no intention of actually eating them . . . the metaphor of human consumption remained strong in the discourse" (25). In England, Thomas Clarkson began his abolition work by investigating the events that transpired on board the ironically named slave ship *Brothers*, which returned to its home port bearing the bodies of thirty-two dead mariners and the mutilated remains of a black man (Baum 3). And, as Joan Baum reminds us in her study of slavery and the English Romantic poets, British writers learned from sailors that the Middle Passage might on rare occasions lead to "cannibalism as a way of managing dwindling supplies" (4). The American-born Captain Theophilus Conneau joined his slave-trading colleagues in publishing tales of African cannibalism; but, perhaps evincing incipient nationalist biases, he also accused European traders of encouraging the practice, describing his disgust at meeting, in the course of his 1828 voyage to the river Pongo, an "anthropophagian Frenchman" who served him a stew with a skull in it (167–68). The widespread belief among Africans that whites might eat them appears often in the literature of the African diaspora and quickly became a powerful trope for the systemic cruelties of slaveholding societies. Among black writers of prose and verse alike, the metaphor of cannibalism was powerfully connotative of the hypocrisy of the whites. René Depestre, in his "Epiphanies of the Voodoo Gods," addresses an exorcism against the white American South: "This water will do battle with your hysterias, your manias, your moral frailty, your white superstitions, and all the supposedly incurable cannibalism which in each of you Southern men and women cries out its old dissatisfaction in the desert. I bestow on your vices an acid made to their measure: the water of the ocean we once crossed to discover in our turn the splendors of America!" (113). Such moments recur often among contemporary North American poets, many of whom have been influenced by earlier poets of negritude such as Depestre. In his 1984 collection *Lucid Interval as Integral Music,* Ed Roberson concludes one poem with imagery that unites the postemancipation trope of white cannibalism with disciplinary orderings of the literary that have evident genealogical links to Fitzhugh's proslavery discourse. "Photograph: The House of the Poet" ends with this image:

    white tree worshippers of paper
their cannibalist sacrifices
flipping through them   offered that order
be maintained white   where his ink darkened those
    sheets[.] (62)

A somewhat different gestural mode occurs in poems that redeploy the white mythology of cannibalism in a form of communal ritual irony. Aimé Césaire's *Notebook of a Return to the Native Land* rejects the Enlightenment's claims to rational order, those same sacral logics that denied Africans inclusion in the category of the human, and embraces ironically the very signs of savagery.

Because we hate you
and your reason, we claim kinship
with dementia praecox with the flaming madness
of persistent cannibalism (49)

Still another kindred moment is located in the texts of the North American surrealist and Beat poet Bob Kaufman. Kaufman's poetry, though as yet undiscovered by Stanley Fish, offers particularly strong instances of the self-consuming artifact. Clearly exercising the filial piety that Benjamin cites as a distinguishing feature of the satiric cannibal author, Kaufman's poem joins the irrationalism of the Beats' rebellion against post–World War II conformity to Césaire's legacy of counterrationalist and counterracist poetics. In

"Like Father, Like Sun," Kaufman opposes the practice of poetry to the practice of the slave trade. Written in memory of "Africa's stolen babes" and against "the liars who stole the soul," Kaufman describes an anti-European orphic mode: "The poem comes / Across centuries of holy lies, and weeping heaven's eyes, / Africa's black handkerchief, washed clean by her children's [honor]" (36). Surrounded by those "liars" who do not notice that "their hearts no longer beat, they cannot die, they are in hell now" (36), Kaufman chooses, in his poem "The Traveling Circus," breakfast at the "home of free association," with:

> . . . The world's champion padlock salesman, who
> wore impeccable seersuckers, & whose only
> oversight is cannibalism, & who is someday going
> to eat himself and get busted if he stays in the
> flesh game. (26)

There still remains, though, a deeper layer of ironies to be traced in America's Africanist discourses of anthropophagy. Perhaps it comes most forcefully into view in one of our most canonical texts, Nathaniel Hawthorne's *The House of the Seven Gables*, a novel in which race and original sin mingle in disturbingly premonitory ways. With the visit of the first customer to Miss Hepzibah Pyncheon's cent-shop, we encounter a figure that continues to haunt American literature, perhaps most memorably toward the end of Ralph Ellison's *Invisible Man*. Hawthorne's narrative details the petty wares Hepzibah has put up for sale, and one takes on a peculiar prominence: "Jim Crow . . . executing his world-renowned dance in gingerbread" (36). It is this figure that attracts Hepzibah's first customer into her shop, a shabbily clad boy on his way to school, book and slate clutched under his arm. It is the Jim Crow in the window that fires the young scholar's desire, and Hepzibah Pyncheon, completing a savage metaphorical economy, gives the figure to the boy without charge, feeding him with motherly greeting: "You are welcome to Jim Crow!" (50). As though this were not a sufficient scene of instruction and racial interpellation already, Hawthorne describes the ensuing moment in the same language that George Fitzhugh was to use in *Cannibals All!* just a few years later. "No sooner had he reached the sidewalk," Hawthorne relates, "(little cannibal that he was!) than Jim Crow's head was in his mouth" (50). This must be one of the most overdetermined moments in American writing. Though the young customer is on his way to school, his slate not yet inscribed with the day's lesson, the boy has already taken up a position within a dynamic signifying chain of race and hunger. Jim Crow is here quite literally a commodity fetish, already desired by the child, when Hepzibah Pyncheon forgoes her first profit and welcomes the cent-shop's first visitor to her Jim Crow. The boy takes to his assigned role greedily, eating away at the gingerbread head, decerebrating the dancing figure. This is strange sustenance for a young republic, peculiar merchandise for a free market. That first customer, having purchased a second Jim Crow, thus confirming the insatiable depth of his and America's appetite for the black body, leaves, and his brief transaction with Hepzibah has enacted a transformation of her class position. Hepzibah feels herself irremediably soiled by her newly close commerce with the world of trade, and Hawthorne underscores the allegorical value of this primal scene for the American state. "The little schoolboy," the narrator remarks, "aided by the impish figure of the negro dancer, had wrought an irreparable ruin" (51). In Hawthorne's telling, this transaction is one in which "the structure of ancient aristocracy had been demolished" (51), but the scene also delineates another social order, a racial hierarchy transmitted by symbol as much as by slave ship.

What is especially destabilizing about this scene, of course, is that it offers readers the representation of a social order feeding on its own representations. The same schoolboys who eagerly eat icons of black bodies will be taught in their schools—and will read in their national literature—that Africans are eaters of human flesh. The endlessly repeating charge that Africans are cannibals is accompanied by repeated white ingestion of the Jim Crow image, paralleling the West's ingestion of millions of African bodies. The irony located in New England cuisine by Hawthorne is reproduced throughout the West. In Germany, one popular pastry is known as *Mohrenkopf,* or "head of a Moor." Sieglinde Lemke views this fact as "an ironic confirmation of the fact that the European conquest itself was barbaric: making the colonized into savages was meant to conceal the cannibalistic nature of European colonization itself" (150). In the Spanish-speaking Americas, one of the most commonly consumed dishes again suggests a racially stratified anthropophagy. In one of the poems of Nathaniel Mackey's *School of Udhra,* the poet alludes to this fact, describing diners in a café "eating moros y critisanos, meaning / that mix, black beans and rice" (68). In her 1975 collection of poems titled *Barefoot Necklace,* Elouise Loftin seizes on a similar act of racist troping, by which Brazil nuts have been metaphorically linked to black bodies. She asks readers, "can i stuff your ear with nigga / toe nuts and eat what you hear" (25), a question that profoundly echoes Hawthorne's strange scene in *The House of the Seven Gables.* Loftin wonders what form of sustenance white consumers find in their images of blackness, and her poem indites a synesthetic racial madness. Lorenzo Thomas, in his poem "Hiccups," which follows the negritude poet Leon Damas in comically regurgitating the West's symbols of Africanness, reproduces a startling product label for "NEGRO HEAD Shrimp" (66).

This simultaneous ascription of cannibalism to those African others considered savage by whites, and the evident pleasure so many of those same whites have taken in representing themselves as eating African body parts, is found in our literature from its beginning to the present time. On one side, the self-authenticating discourse of black cannibalism is readily seen as a mask for the white savagery of the slave trade, in the same way that the continued discourse of African-American inferiority finds expression in such terms as "permanent black underclass" and in such literary commodities as the recently published autobiography titled *Monster*. At the same time, though, the discourse of cannibalism signals a deep and abiding dread of difference, what Guianese poet and novelist Wilson Harris once described as "fear of life ... fear of the substance of life, fear of the substance of the folk, a cannibal blind fear in oneself" (52). Finally, however, the completion of this signifying chain in symbolic ingestion of blackness by white mouths suggests a further complication of these tropes. As he traces "The Dialectics of Cannibalism in Modern Caribbean Narratives," Eugenio Matibag argues that "a metaphor of incorporation and/or differentiation, of subjective self-divisions and mergings with respect to an other, cannibalism ... de-defines and re-defines the divisory line between self and other, with the consequence of transforming what was considered an antimony into a dialectical opposition to be canceled and subsumed onto a higher level of transindividual unity" (35). What begins as a means of distancing the other, by positing the most radical difference, ends as a means of symbolic incorporation of radical difference, and this describes a poetics of indigestion in American literary history. In the same way that the supposed cannibalism of the African became a rationale for bringing millions of Africans into the dark heart of American culture, a critical practice that commences, as in Thomas Jefferson's expulsion of Phillis Wheatley from his canon, by denying the very possibility of poetry to African Americans concludes by secretively and shamefully swallowing up blackness as a vital component of American verse.

Much as George Fitzhugh expressed ironic concern that his poetic epigraphs might engulf his argument, some twentieth-century American poets seemed to fear too open a confrontation with the racial contours of their own language. Robinson Jeffers, writing to Louis Adamic in 1939, said: "I am sure you will use discretion in discussing the negro and Jewish elements. These are special cases, likely to steal the show unless carefully handled" (278). What is one to make, in the end, of the apparently endless desire of white poets, performers, and politicians to mime Africanness, to speak in the voice of blackness, the voice of the cannibal of their dreams? Michael North points out that "the grotesque exaggeration of blackface makeup had always been meant at least in part to emphasize the fact that the wearer was *not* black" (7). Is that same effect available to black people? Did the blackface cork that Bert Williams was forced to wear onstage so that he would *appear* before whites as what he was, a black man, in the end emphasize his nonblackness? White Americans, as they digested the culture of black Americans, have often held themselves forth as African delineators superior to the original model; indeed, they have often presented themselves as preserving a blackness that was on the point of disappearing. Were African Americans, then, never more white than when speaking or writing in a presumptively black dialect? When white American poets such as Gertrude Stein, Vachel Lindsay, T. S. Eliot, e. e. cummings, William Carlos Williams, and H.D. take the blackness that they have constructed back into themselves, like the product of the paint factory in Ralph Ellison's *Invisible Man,* they become still whiter.

In Eliot's "Fragment of an Agon," Sweeney's playful hints at cannibalism follow an already accomplished act of literary cannibalism, just as Eliot's *Cocktail Party,* with its suggestions of African cannibalism, follows Europe's already accomplished englutting of Africa. Michael North has shown that Eliot's "Fragment" is built around a half-digested fragment of a black lyric (88–89), for the song that is performed as a minstrel piece, complete with actors taking the parts of Tambo and Bones, is appropriated from a 1902 lyric by James Weldon Johnson. This central act of minstrel and compositional "passing" in Eliot's poem is rendered still more ironic by a further contextual element. Eliot has adapted his song from the author of *The Autobiography of an Ex-Colored Man,* the text of a fictive black man who has stolen into the bowels of white high society. The narrator of Johnson's novel, passing for white, entertains his rich, white friends by playing black music on the piano. The white characters of Eliot's "Sweeney Agonistes" entertain themselves by passing for black, and Eliot passes his rendering of Johnson's lyric as a free-floating signifier of blackness without authorship. The text of cannibalism proves to be a cannibalized text. Whites, who so often evidenced fear of being swallowed up by blackness (the nineteenth century expressed this as the dread of "amalgamation"), gave proof of their whiteness by representing themselves in the guise of blackness and by singing black lyrics.

In this sense, at least, both George Fitzhugh and Robinson Jeffers were right. The text of blackness steals the show, but only because it was written by white showmen. The outward representation of blackness by whites is a surface sign of their prior incorporation of blackness, but that very incorporation of the

African has the very much intended effect of increasing the social distance between races.

Claude Rawson has remarked that "the common factor in the long history of cannibal imputations is the combination of denial of it in ourselves and attribution of it to 'others' whom we wish to defame, conquer, appropriate or 'civilize'" (3). This much is acknowledged on all sides of the debates over the historical existence of cannibalism. From William Arens, who questions the grounds of nearly all accounts of cannibalism, through the studies of Hans Askenasy and Peggy Sanday that cast serious doubt on Arens's own conclusions, to the still more nuanced work of Michael Taussig's consideration of the colonial mirror of production, all agree on the cultural work that is effected by the imputation of cannibalism in the distinguishing of the "civilized" from its "uncivilized" shadow other. What we learn from our poetry and from our novels, however, is the paradigmatic irony as mapped by Hawthorne: the trope of cannibal horror is often spoken in the very course of a cannibal meal. This was true in the nineteenth century, when, as Leonard Cassuto observes, cannibalism served as "a source of national fear and fascination and one of the most potent American symbols of un-civilization" (186). It has remained true through the modernism of Eliot and the postmodernity of Duncan and Spicer. Cannibalism sustains itself as a lie that will never quite go down, that remains lodged in our throats, forming our speeches to one another.

In 1924, Allen Tate argued that "the complete assimilation of American culture will equip the Negro with the 'refinement' and 'taste' requisite to writing in a tradition utterly alien to his temperament" (22). Tate here speaks as the voice of American culture addressing a critique to those alien and unassimilated bodies who, in his view, have yet to develop proper taste. This must be seen as a tasteless critique in the context of an American culture that has taken into itself African bodies but has refused to accept the African body within the body of the nation. The body of American literary culture continues this unsavory tradition, until recently refusing to admit as literature the black writing that it has taken into itself, while all the while rewriting blackness in its lyric "refinement." In *Invisible Man*, Ralph Ellison seizes on this as a potentially revolutionary motion. The advice that the protagonist receives from his grandfather, advice that he is still pondering from within his brilliantly lit loophole of retreat in the bowels of an American city, is one response black writing makes to the cannibal stanzas of Lindsay and Eliot: "let 'em swoller you till they vomit or bust wide open" (16). What Michael North has described as a "pattern of rebellion through racial ventriloquism," a pattern uniting the modernisms of D. W. Griffith and Vachel Lindsay, of Al Jolson and T. S. Eliot, of Shirley Temple and Gertrude Stein, might also be seen as preliminary signs of an imminent busting open, a series of hiccups, a pattern of convulsive explosions, a poetics of indigestion.

///

> [T]he paradox is incontrovertible that the rise, growth and perfection of modern democracy has been the soil out of which has grown the expression of a more brutal antagonism waged in the interest of racial prejudice.
> —William Stanley Braithwaite, 1906

Seven years before publishing this remark in the Boston *Globe,* W. S. Braithwaite had submitted a volume of his poetry to L. C. Page and Company, publishers. In his letter accompanying the manuscript, Braithwaite wrote, "Do not be surprised therefore should I inform you that I am an American Negro, a Bostonian by birth" (237). Braithwaite's poems, *Lyrics of Life and Love,* were eventually published in Boston, where, more than a century before, Phillis Wheatley, "Negro Servant to Mr. John Wheatley, of Boston, in New England," had surprised an earlier generation of readers; but L. C. Page and Company had not recovered sufficiently from their own surprise to print Braithwaite, and it was Turner and Company whose name appeared on the title page of the poet's first collection of lyrics.

"But why should this be a problem?" (Michaels 134) In one variation or another, that question reappears throughout Walter Benn Michaels's 1995 study *Our America: Nativism, Modernism, and Pluralism.* Indeed, it should never have been a problem. The race of an author should not now be a problem. There should be no need for any such book as the volume that I here, at last, introduce. But in 2000, as in 1906, when Braithwaite published "A Grave Wrong to the Negro" in the theater of Boston's *Globe,* race remains both a problem and an opportunity. It remains the case that race, a consummate biological fiction, is a social fact affecting the lives and works of literary artists in our America. In fact, the question that Walter Benn Michaels continually poses to his readers is the most rhetorical of gestures at the end of the century that W. E. B. Du Bois predicted would be dominated by the problem of the color bar. What Michaels has done in his book is to substitute a moral question for an ontological question. As Linda Martín Alcoff argues in "Philosophy and Racial Identity":

> It is because the arguments against racial identity have merit that the paradox is a paradox and not simply an error. But in the face of these anti-race arguments, we need a better position than one which merely relies on the withering away of racial categorization. And we need one that can do two things the anti-essential-

ist positions cannot do: (1) take into account the full force of race as a lived experience, understanding this not as mere epiphenomenon but as constitutive of reality; and (2) acknowledge and account for the epistemological and theoretical importance racial perspective has had on, for example, the undermining of modernist teleologies (e.g. Du Bois's use of slavery to undermine U.S. supremacist claims, and the Frankfurt School's critique of Western rationality from the perspective of the Holocaust). These facts suggest that we need to understand racial identity as having both metaphysical and epistemological implications. (9)

Michaels, too, argues against the antiessentialist position on race, but his rhetorical question leaves us constantly with the answer that race should not make any difference, an answer that, while undeniably true, does not get us very far in our understanding of the metaphysical and epistemological implications of the social facts of race in the United States.

Reading poetry will not solve either the problems posed by Michaels or those so eloquently outlined by Alcoff; but in readings of American poetry, we may often find modernist teleologies undermined, we may discover much about the lived experience of race, we may find how America's ever-shifting categories of race have been constitutive of our reality, and we certainly will see that race has affected not only the thematics of American poetry throughout its history but also the approach to poetic forms adopted by American poets.

The reading of American poetry has itself been constituted by race. Race was a problem in the publication histories of Phillis Wheatley and William Stanley Braithwaite, and it continues to be a problem in their reception and republication today. In an essay surveying recent work in the study of race and literature, Shelley Fisher Fishkin notes: "A study published in January 1990 found that college courses with such titles as 'The Modern Novel' or 'Modern Poetry' continued to be dominated by 'works almost exclusively by elite white men.' Nonetheless, calling attention to the 'whiteness' of the curriculum was still considered bizarre and provocative behavior" (429). But race has affected even the literary works of white men that have been admitted to the curriculum, in ways that often remain unacknowledged.

On 12 June 1915, William Stanley Braithwaite published in the Boston *Transcript* an essay titled "Imagism: Another View." Writing in defense of free verse, Braithwaite also countered imagism's antagonists by pointing out the simple truth that "*vers libre* does not constitute the whole purpose of the imagist poets" (29), a sentence that today's champions of the new formalism might do well to contemplate. Yet, it is difficult to find mention of Braithwaite, or of any other black poets and critics, in literary histories discussing imagism. It was Ezra Pound who "injected race into the issue," to use a now-current term by which discussions of race are stopped in their tracks, when he wrote to the Boston

Transcript in response to another of Braithwaite's essays to complain about their "negro reviewer" (62), a fact that renders all the more ludicrous his subsequent defense to Harriet Monroe: "I didn't know it was the coon I was answering" (67). Race played a significant part in forming the reception of Braithwaite's literary work in his lifetime, and it appears to have something to do with his exclusion from much of the literary history in our own time. Most studies of modernity leave Braithwaite out of the picture entirely. Those that do include his criticism in their surveys, such as Michaels's *Our America* and Angelyn Mitchell's anthology of African-American literary criticism, *Within the Circle*, look only at Braithwaite's comments on black writers. Why should this problem be? In *The Dialect of Modernism: Race, Language and Twentieth Century Literature*, Michael North finds that "despite its promises of a transnational America and a multiethnic American modernism, the avant-garde proved ill prepared to include within its conception of the new American writing any examples that actually stretched the old categories of race and ethnicity" (150). On this much North and Michaels agree. But this has been a century in which the old categories of race and ethnicity were stretched, in which the epistemological ground of race continued to shift beneath our feet, even as the unmetered feet of the poetic avant garde were so often mired in the tar baby of America's racialist discourse.

The work collected in *Reading Race in American Poetry: "An Area of Act"* is intended as a tentative remapping of territories for further exploration. Though Americans have been reading race since Columbus transcribed the word he thought he heard on the lips of the locals as "Canibales," it has taken literary criticism a long time to come around to the hermeneutics of race in American writing. Though we have been a culture obsessed with race—as is evident to any reader of our literature—we have been slow to examine the rhetorics of that obsession. Considerable works have appeared over the years that take as their subject the representations of African Americans in American literature, and an ever-growing body of criticism has taken African-American poetry as its study. The late Sterling Brown offered important early models for both forms of critique in his studies *The Negro in American Fiction* and *Negro Poetry and Drama*. Still, there have as yet been few critical examinations of the modes in which race manifests itself in the reading and writing of American poetry. My own *Reading Race: White American Poets and the Racial Discourse in the Twentieth Century* appeared as recently as 1988 and was intended (so much for the intentional fallacy) to instigate a wider discussion of the subject. Michael North's *The Dialect of Modernism: Race, Language, and Twentieth-Century Literature*, a book that devotes much of its attention to poetry, did not appear until 1994. Three years later, it was joined by Susan Gubar's *Racechanges: White Skin, Black Face in American Culture*, a book that raises provocative questions about race and poetry but is seriously marred by significant errors (Claudette Colbert did not play the "passing" character in *Imitation of Life*; *Our Nig* is not "the first published novel by an African American" [24, 223]). Far more worrisome, though, is Gubar's failure to distinguish adequately between the multitude of black vernacular stylings and their representations in the poetics of dialect verse, a failure that leaves her arguments about the black poets of the Harlem Renaissance and her discussion of such later white poets as John Berryman strangely muddled. Critics now too numerous to mention have made significant contributions to our attempts to understand the workings of race in American thought through the study of prose literature; but, curiously, at a time when critical interest in both race and poetry as separate studies seems to have grown rapidly, American criticism remains in the early stages of its work on reading race in American verse. Yet another of the paradoxes offered to us by race is the fact that while books about rap recordings abound in this age of cultural studies, they have not yet been accompanied by studies of the culture represented in the most interesting of recent unaccompanied lyrics. Important new contributions to the study of race and poetics continue to be made public, including Lorna J. Smedman's "'Cousin to Cooning': Relation, Difference, and Racialized Language in Stein's Nonrepresentational Texts," Maria Damon's work on Bob Kaufman in her book *The Dark End of the Street*, and unpublished works-in-progress by Steve Evans and Ben Friedlander examining the works of Frank O'Hara. Still, the only recent volume entirely devoted to the subject of race and poetry included in Shelley Fisher Fishkin's most useful roundup "Interrogating 'Whiteness,' Complicating 'Blackness': Remapping American Culture" is the somewhat prematurely cited *An Area of Act*. Alcoff argues that "the meaning of race will shift as one moves through the terrain and interplay of different discourses" (8), and the discursive area of poetics and the history of poetry may have a great deal to add to what we are learning from our studies of prose fiction.

Race is a notoriously unstable category and has never been confined to questions of black and white in the United States (indeed, Americans have had some uncertainties even in defining these seemingly bedrock terms). Race in the very recent past divided Euro-American ethnic groups that now view themselves, and one another, as white people. Questions of race will acquire different particularities as we examine the writings by and about American Indians, Asian Americans, Mexican Americans, and the groups that will no doubt be constructed as racial in some future America. *Reading Race in American Poetry: "An Area of Act"* does not attempt to address each of those particularities, but, as the subtitle should imply, this book is proposing areas for additional critical acts. Like Shelley Fishkin, "I would not want my decision to frame this essay in 'black' and 'white' terms to be interpreted as a denial of the importance of these other groups and traditions in our efforts to reformulate and reconfigure our cultural narratives; I am simply choosing to focus, at this time, on one particular aspect of a complex set of issues" (457). Similarly, the choice to concentrate on the twentieth century in *Reading Race in American Poetry* is a strategic and economic choice. It should be evident to readers that our discussions here of twentieth-century poetries rest on readings of earlier periods. As Columbus carried a new word from the New World, a word that terrorized both colonizers and colonized even as it marked the murder of the people, the Caribs, whose name gave rise to the word, some of the interpretive acts in the following essays may travel into other areas of critical race studies.

Reading Race in American Poetry does not represent a school of thought on race—or on poetry, for that matter. The essays by contemporary poets and critics gathered here include modes of discourse analysis, literary history, genre studies, and such intertextual analyses as the monumental study by Nathaniel Mackey (excerpted from here, due to space constraints) that analyzes the role played by an African narrative in the poetics of a white poet, Robert Duncan. Some essays, such as Maria Mootry's and my own, look at the pressures of race on the use and reception of particular poetic forms in American culture. Future scholars may well wonder at the apparent lack of current critical curiosity about such phenomena as the widespread adoption of the haiku form by African-American poets, and Mootry's essay points toward the extensive work that remains to be done in historicizing the many ways in which black poets come to revise our readings of the sonnet. Others, such as Charles Bernstein's, examine poets' conceptions of American language against the background of race and dialect. Bernstein's view of a historical movement from dialect poetry to a "dialectical poetry" makes a crucial contribution to the arguments advanced by Michael North and others, for Bernstein is at pains to note that there is a real difference between the claim of an affiliation with a definable group's speaking practice and the *actual* speaking and writing practices of any such group. Similarly, where many critics have been all too quick to lay claim to a counterhegemonic value in the adoption by white poets of hegemonic representations of black speech, Rachel Blau DuPlessis describes a poetics by which whiteness is reconstructed as a monoracial "dialogue." Lorenzo Thomas's essay, by reinserting the figure of William S. Braithwaite into the debates swirling around modernism in the early part of the century, shows us once again how different history can look from the stories we have told ourselves so far. Where DuPlessis and Thomas provide us with important reconfigurings of literary history, Carole Doreski reads the reconfiguring *of* history *by* an African-American literary artist. Felipe Smith's opening essay is a virtuoso meditation on the tropes of race as they enter the twentieth century, and Kathryne

Lindberg performs a questioning excursion through the work of Bob Kaufman, one of America's least acknowledged but most provocative black poets of the second half of our century.

There are many other ways in which race signifies among the lines of American poems, other sites where race erupts within the formal feeling of New World prosody. *Reading Race in American Poetry: "An Area of Act"* may appear to some an invitation to a journey through the hell of America's racial consciousness, but it is offered as an opportunity, an area, there may still remain reason to hope, of equal opportunity.

Works Cited

Alcoff, Linda Martín. "Philosophy and Racial Identity." *Radical Philosophy* 75 (1996): 5–14.

Anonymous. *The Bath, Bristol, Tunbridge, and Epsom Miscellany.* London: T. Dormer, 1735.

Arens, William. *The Man-Eating Myth: Anthropology and Anthropophagy.* Oxford: Oxford University Press, 1979.

Armistead, W. S. *The Negro Is a Man: A Reply to Professor Charles Carroll's Book "The Negro Is a Beast."* Tifton, Ga.: Armistead and Vickers, 1903.

Askenasy, Hans. *Cannibalism from Sacrifice to Survival.* Amherst, N.Y.: Prometheus Books, 1994.

Baraka, Amiri. "Names and Bodies." In *The Floating Bear: A Newsletter: Numbers 1–37.* Ed. Amiri Baraka and Diane Di Prima. La Jolla, Calif.: Laurence McGilvery, 1973. 272.

———. *Poetry with Jones* (including discussions with Gwendolyn Brooks, Robert Bone, Jules Chametsky, Kenneth Rexroth, and others). 1964. Pacifica Radio Archive BB 1910.02.

———. *Transbluesency: Selected Poems, 1961–1995.* Ed. Paul Vangelisti. New York: Marsilio Press, 1995.

Baum, Joan. *Mind-Forg'd Manacles: Slavery and the English Romantic Poets.* North Haven, Conn.: Archon Books, 1994.

Benjamin, Walter. *Reflections: Essays, Aphorisms, Autobiographical Writings.* Ed. Peter Demetz. Trans. Edmund Jephcott. New York: Harcourt Brace Jovanovich, 1978.

Braithwaite, William Stanley. *The William Stanley Braithwaite Reader.* Ed. Philip Butcher. Ann Arbor: University of Michigan Press, 1972.

Brown, Sterling. *Negro Poetry and Drama, and the Negro in American Fiction.* New York: Simon and Schuster, 1969.

Carroll, Charles. *The Negro a Beast.* 1900. Rpt., Miami, Fla.: Mnemosyne Publishing, 1969.

Cassuto, Leonard. *The Inhuman Race: The Racial Grotesque in American Literature.* New York: Columbia University Press, 1997.

Césaire, Aimé. *The Collected Poetry.* Trans. Clayton Eshelman and Annette Smith. Berkeley: University of California Press, 1983.

Conneau, Theophilus. *A Slaver's Log Book; or, 20 Years' Residence in Africa.* Englewood Cliffs, N.J.: Prentice-Hall, 1976.

Damon, Maria. *The Dark End of the Street: Margins in American Vanguard Poetry.* Minneapolis: University of Minnesota Press, 1993.

Depestre, René. "Epiphanies of the Voodoo Gods: A Voodoo Mystery Poem." In *The Negritude Poets: An Anthology of Translations from the French.* Ed. Ellen Conroy Kennedy. New York: Viking, 1975. 112–13.

Duncan, Robert. *The Years as Catches.* Berkeley, Calif.: Oyez, 1966.

Eliot, T. S. *The Complete Poems and Plays, 1909–1950.* New York: Harcourt, Brace and World, 1971.

Ellison, Ralph. *Invisible Man.* New York: Random House, 1952.

Everett, Anna. *Returning the Gaze.* Durham, N.C.: Duke University Press, forthcoming. (Quoting from the typescript.)

Fishkin, Shelley Fisher. "Interrogating 'Whiteness,' Complicating 'Blackness': Remapping American Culture." *American Quarterly* 47.3 (1995): 428–66.

Fitzhugh, George. *Cannibals All!; or, Slaves without Masters.* 1857. Ed. C. Vann Woodward. Cambridge, Mass.: Harvard University Press, 1960.

Gubar, Susan. *Racechanges: White Skin, Black Face in American Culture.* Oxford: Oxford University Press, 1997.

Harris, William J. "Introduction." In *The LeRoi Jones/Amiri Baraka Reader.* Ed. William J. Harris. New York: Thunder's Mouth Press, 1991. xvii–xxx.

Harris, Wilson. *Palace of the Peacock.* In *The Guyana Quartet.* London: Faber and Faber, 1985. 15–117.

Hawthorne, Nathaniel. *The House of the Seven Gables.* 1851. Rpt., New York: Penguin Books, 1986.

"Hollings Remark on African Leaders, Cannibals Assailed." *Los Angeles Times.* 16 December 1993. A38.

James, C. L. R. *Nkrumah and the Ghana Revolution.* London: Allison and Busby, 1977.

Jeffers, Robinson. *The Selected Letters of Robinson Jeffers, 1897–1962.* Ed. Ann Ridgeway. Baltimore, Md.: Johns Hopkins University Press, 1968.

Kaufman, Bob. *The Ancient Rain: Poems, 1956–1978.* New York: New Directions, 1981.

Lemke, Sieglinde. "White on White." *Transition* 60 (1993): 145–54.

Lindsay, Vachel. *Selected Poems of Vachel Lindsay.* Ed. Mark Harris. New York: Macmillan, 1963.

Loftin, Elouise. *Barefoot Necklace.* Brooklyn, N.Y.: Jamima House Press, 1975.

Mackey, Nathaniel. *School of Udhra.* San Francisco: City Lights, 1993.

Matibag, Eugenio D. "Self-Consuming Fictions: The Dialectics of Cannibalism and Modern Caribbean Narratives." *Postmodern Culture* 1.3 (May 1991): n.p. (online journal).

Michaels, Walter Benn. *Our America: Nativism, Modernism, and Pluralism.* Durham, N.C.: Duke University Press, 1995.

Mighty Sparrow. *Trinidad Heat Wave.* 1965. Scepter Records (S)M10003.

Miller, Adam David. "The Negro Writer in the United States." *Graduate Student Journal* (University of California at Berkeley) 1965:3–12.

Mitchell, Angelyn, ed. *Within the Circle: An Anthology of African-American Literary Criticism from the Harlem Renaissance to the Present.* Durham, N.C.: Duke University Press, 1994.

North, Michael. *The Dialect of Modernism: Race, Language, and Twentieth-Century Literature.* New York: Oxford University Press, 1994.

Pound, Ezra. *Selected Letters, 1907–1941.* Ed. D. D. Paige. New York: New Directions, 1950.

Rawson, Claude. "The Horror, the Holy Horror: Revulsion, Accusation and the Eucharist in the History of Cannibalism." *Times Literary Supplement.* 31 October 1997. 3–5.

Roberson, Ed. *Lucid Interval as Integral Music.* Pittsburgh: Harmattan Press, 1984.

Sanday, Peggy Reeves. *Divine Hunger: Cannibalism as a Cultural System.* Cambridge: Cambridge University Press, 1986.

Schelling, Andrew. "The Tale the Hand Itself Reads." *Sulfur* 34 (1994): 172–75.

Smedman, Lorna J. "'Cousin to Cooning': Relation, Difference, and Racialized Language in Stein's Nonrepresentational Texts." *Modern Fiction Studies* 42.3 (1996): 569–88.

Spicer, Jack. "From *Imaginary Elegies.*" In *Postmodern American Poetry.* Ed. Paul Hoover. New York: W. W. Norton, 1994. 104–7.

Tate, Allen. *The Poetry Reviews of Allen Tate, 1924–1944.* Ed. Ashley Brown and Frances Neel Cheney. Baton Rouge: Louisiana State University Press, 1983.

Taussig, Michael. *Shamanism, Colonialism, and the Wild Man: A Study in Terror and Healing.* Chicago: University of Chicago Press, 1986.

Thomas, Lorenzo. *Chances Are Few.* Berkeley, Calif.: Blue Wind Press, 1979.

Turner, Patricia A. *I Heard It through the Grapevine: Rumor in African-American Culture.* Berkeley: University of California Press, 1993.

1

Prospects of AMERICA: Nation as Woman in the Poetry of Du Bois, Johnson, and McKay

Felipe Smith

> You're my Moby Dick,
> White Witch,
> Symbol of the rope and hanging tree
> —Eldridge Cleaver, "To a White Girl"

> What has been estranging has been AMERICA . . . [the] immanent idea of boundless, classless, raceless possibility in America.
> —Houston Baker Jr., "Discovering America"

Eldridge Cleaver included his poem "To a White Girl" in the opening essay of *Soul on Ice* (1968), "On Becoming," which defined his criminal career as a rapist with a revolutionary agenda. More than a simple expression of his aesthetic preferences, Cleaver's targeting of white women for sexual assault (after an apprenticeship spent "practicing" on black women) reflected his literal reading of white women's bodies as allegorical figures for white America. Appearing in the years after LeRoi Jones's controversial drama of interracial desire, *Dutchman* (1964), Cleaver's poem built on literary representations of America as a seductive, fatal white woman that had been established in the early twentieth-century poetry and prose of W. E. B. Du Bois, James Weldon Johnson, and Claude McKay. This essay will look at the evolution of the figure that Johnson was the first to call the "white witch" as well as the oppositional figure of immanent black nationhood, the "black madonna," in black American poetry. Specifically, I will show that these archetypes developed in response to the inescapable question of national belonging for black Americans—the dilemma of living in America from its colonial origins only to have full and unconditional acceptance as Americans perpetually contested and deferred. While the essay will trace the evolution of a tradition in African-American poetry to illustrate the prevalence of this typological rhetoric during the emergence of early twentieth-century black literature, I will freely refer to other writings by these authors.

Cleaver's backward glance at the tradition of the white witch was not merely and unproblematically a literary allusion. Rape as insurrection had a twisted seductiveness that Cleaver himself eventually denounced in *Soul on Ice,* though not before investing it with a certain perverse machismo (Brownmiller 248–51). His confused protest called attention to and drew significance from the omnipresence of the white female as a fixture of the American "good life" and the prolonged exclusion of black Americans from the freedoms, privileges, and opportunities that purportedly made the American Dream available to all citizens. The "wolf whistle" lynching of Emmett Till that inspired Cleaver's career as rapist underscores the utility of women's bodies in the American definition of race and national belonging. With freedom or bondage hinging on "the condition of the mother," according to the seminal slave statutes of the seventeenth century (Cassity 22), the bodies of black and white women were metaphoric spaces of confinement and of freedom, respectively, for the black male aspirant to AMERICA—Houston Baker Jr.'s term for the perpetually anticipated fulfillment of America's "egalitarian promise" of freedom and opportunity (Baker 65). The exclusion of blacks from the American colonial body politic in the seventeenth century ultimately evolved into the elaborate nineteenth- and twentieth-century rituals and taboos that sheltered "white Christian womanhood" from any form of "social equality" that might even remotely lead to black male/white female sexual relations, a prohibition sufficiently enduring to cost Till his life for whistling at a white woman in Mississippi in 1955. In the early decades of this century, the threat to lynch any black male who was suspected to have had or even to have desired access to a white female grew out of a determination to keep blacks outside all biological, social, and political bodies in America; this practice was instituted on behalf of the "white race," making sure that America would never become AMERICA.

Having defined access to a white woman's body as a requisite of national inclusion, whites understood that symbolizing America in female form implicitly advertised the white female body as a source of national identity. Though it was James Weldon Johnson who formally named the embodied female image of America "The White Witch" in a 1915 poem of the same title, it was W. E. B. Du Bois who had established the white seductress as an emblem of white America in his early poems. Du Bois himself was adapting Ida B. Wells-Barnett's allegorical figure, the "white Delilah"—a white woman whose amorous embrace proved fatal to the black Samson unlucky enough to be discovered in her presence. Under public pressure, according to Wells-Barnett, the white Delilah accused her lover of rape; in some instances, the mere discovery of his involvement with her was treated as a capital offense against the white race. With or without the woman's collusion, the white populace routinely lynched the African-American Samson as a warning to other blacks of the danger of attempting to gain access to white race privileges through a white woman's body (Wells-Barnett 1, 6). Cleaver's white witch as "symbol of the rope and hanging tree" looks backward toward this southern tradition of the fatal white female.

Wells-Barnett used the biblical story of Samson and Delilah to render the archetypal fatal white woman, no doubt, because of the tale's homiletic value in shaping the emerging concept of a special racial destiny for America's ex-slave population. Implicit in her phrase "black Samson" is an appeal for endogamy as a proper expression of racial-national pride in an era of increasing efforts by whites to sever all claims to citizenship rights won by black Americans during Reconstruction. Historically, such questions of interracial desire and treason against the race typically focused on black women, many of whom, during and after slavery, had uncertain control over their sexual and reproductive destinies. When Cleaver, in his final essay in *Soul on Ice* ("To All Black Women, from All Black Men"), abruptly, and not at all convincingly, addresses the black woman as "Queen," it is a pronounced reversal of earlier denunciations of the black woman as a sexually treacherous, emasculating "Amazon." "Every black woman secretly hates black men," announces Cleaver's mouthpiece, Lazarus. "Secretly, they all love white men" (148). Extending queenly status to black women whom he has previously reviled represents a belated effort to secure their allegiance for the project of building a black nation within a nation with separate social, cultural, and political institutions. In the era of Daniel Patrick Moynihan's declaration that a deviant, matriarchal structure in black households psychologically emasculated black males (*The Negro Family*), Cleaver's appropriation of black womanhood as an object of nationalist desire sought to transform the black queen from a potential competitor to a nonthreatening icon of black patriarchal aspirations.

Cleaver's elevation of black womanhood into nationalist symbol was also anticipated and influenced by the images of sacred "African Motherhood" that Du Bois had developed in the early years of this century, primarily through his poetry. The black madonna evolved from Du Bois's conflation of millenarian prophecies of "Ethiopia . . . stretch[ing] out her hands to God" (Psalms 68:31), popular among black Americans, with his own ideal of rehabilitated black womanhood as the center of a functional, productive black domestic order. For a black nation to flourish, Du Bois felt that it must first "guard the purity of black women" and "reduce the vast army of black prostitutes that is marching to hell." In "The Conservation of Races," he described this redemption of black womanhood as the key to racial integrity, arguing that African Americans "*must* be inspired with the Divine faith of our black mothers, that out of the blood and dust of battle will march a victorious host, a mighty nation, a peculiar people" (25). Du Bois interpreted the history of civilization in terms of women's roles, their primary obligation being homemaking: "[Motherhood] is a duty. The perpetuation of the race, the transmission of culture, the ultimate triumph of right depend primarily upon the physical motherhood of the nation" ("The Work of Negro Women" 139–40). More than "physical motherhood," Du Bois insisted that black women be "spiritual" builders as well: "There is no use trying to rear a race or nation on the physical foundation of mothers too weak or wanton to bring forth healthy children" (140, 142).

This domestic madonna soon merged in Du Bois's creative works with the feminized Ethiopia as the socially redeemed and spiritually redeeming mother of African peoples. In a 1905 allegorical prose piece, Du Bois approached the figure of embodied blackness with a restrained self-consciousness. Mother Earth questions her daughter Ethiopia about her comparative lack of achievement in comparison to her "tall sisters, pale and blue of eye" and her "strong brothers, shrewd and slippery haired," with whose technology, wealth, and "magic" Ethiopia cannot compete (Andrews 95). But two years later, in November 1907, Du Bois's poem "The Burden of Black Women" would reconsider the relation between Ethiopia and her siblings. Du Bois, by this time, had moved beyond scolding black women for holding back racial progress, increasingly choosing to present idealized images of black women compatible with their spiritual function as mothers of the nation. "The Burden of Black Women" consequently transformed Ethiopia from a mere "daughter" of Mother Earth into "Mother of God," an annunciation into primal agency and moral authority on behalf of the race. The poem opens with an invocation to the "Dark daughter of the lotus leaves" who is the "Wan spirit of a prisoned soul a-panting to be / free" to rise up and claim her heritage: "Crying: Awake, O ancient race! Wailing: O woman arise!" (*Creative Writings* 12).

The white world (specifically, "the Burden of white men"), though, threatens to prevent Ethiopia's awakening:

The White World's vermin and filth:
All the dirt of London,
All the scum of New York;
Valiant spoilers of women

And conquerors of unarmed men;
Shameless breeders of bastards
Drunk with the greed of gold.
Baiting their blood-stained hooks
With cant for the souls of the simple,
Bearing the White Man's Burden
Of Liquor and Lust and Lies! (*Creative Writings* 12–13)

Du Bois's response to Europe's boast of biological superiority as the basis of its world dominion was twofold. First, he noted that blackness was "ancient ere whiteness began." It was a point that Du Bois was to make with greater conviction in the coming years, that whites had benefited from earlier civilizations of dark peoples and then, while at the pinnacle of their world power, began to rewrite history to support the claim that civilization was synonymous with white skin, savagery with dark. "Who raised the fools to their glory / But black men of Egypt and Ind?" he asks. This reading of history asserts Ethiopia's irreplaceable role as the "mother"—not the daughter—of civilization. Du Bois adds the warning that all the despised peoples of the dark world—blacks, Chinese, Hebrews, and "mongrels of Rome and Greece"—had "raised the boasters" and, when they got tired of the boasting, would "drag them down again." This "shearing" of the "Devil's strength" would culminate in the "married maiden, Mother of God, / Bid[ding] the Black Christ be born!" (13).

Du Bois's second response was that a black civilization brought into existence by sacrificial black motherhood would necessarily be different in kind, if not degree, from the civilization raised by whites. Thus he sought to purge himself of those traits that he thought might inhibit the emergence of a black, world-historical civilization. For example, in December 1907, one month after publishing "The Burden of Black Women," a seemingly chastened Du Bois published a poem that reads almost like a warning to himself not to let his anger drive him to the three soul-destroying temptations he enumerates in *The Souls*—hate, despair, and doubt (152). The poem "Death" is a parable, a wedding of a dark warrior to Death, who is imagined as a white female: "the maid / Stands motionless—her pallid form / Swathed in the cold and clinging night" (*Creative Writings* 16). This poem is the prototype to James Weldon Johnson's "The White Witch," published more than seven years later in Du Bois's NAACP magazine, *The Crisis*. In "Death," Du Bois writes: "World and Warrior, Maid and Mist, / Met each other—met and kissed." The kiss, like the witch's withering touch or evil eye, proves deadly to the warrior, just as the hate, despair, and doubt that bedevil the poet of black national striving might push him, Du

Bois felt, toward a fatal embrace of the very spiritual deadness he wished to destroy. More than "the White Man's Burden" of "Liquor and Lust and Lies" (*Creative Writing* 12), the white witch would become the allegory of a tempting but corrupt white civilization that must be resisted to be transcended.

In the months of November and December 1907, then, one year after the horrifying Atlanta race riot that had put his immediate family in physical danger, Du Bois had mapped out the spiritual alternatives for black national allegiance through allegorical encounters between the race hero and these two female forms, the black mother of the dark world's epiphany and the pale white maiden of spiritual death. In a short piece from April 1907, Du Bois had offered a preliminary sketch of the madonna-witch dichotomy as the old black hag and the haughty white lady in his allegory "Wittekind," in which the women conduct a mock battle for the racial destiny of South Carolina. The white lady gloats over the arrival of 600 white servants and laborers aboard the ship *Wittekind,* expecting that they would tilt the balance in favor of white numerical superiority, until the black hag informs her that 18,000 black babies had been born in Carolina in the last six months (*Creative Writings* 63). Important to the allegorical intent is the name of the ship, suggesting the historical figure Hermann Witekind, who wrote a treatise on witchcraft in sixteenth-century Germany (Ginzburg 156–58). In pitting the black woman's generative powers against the transatlantic transport of Europeans, Du Bois perhaps for the first time articulated a vision of black national emergence as a battle between the organic magic of black motherhood and the technological witchcraft of white civilization.

In poems published in February and March 1908, Du Bois began to elaborate on and codify the discrete attributes of these feminized forces. In "The Song of America," he personifies America as the "Great I Will," leaving no doubt that the pallid maid of "Death" is the soul-image of white America, which signifies death for the black warrior:

> I doom, I live, I will,
> I take, I lie, I kill!
> I rend and rear
> In deserts drear—
> . . . .
> My Temples rise
> And split the Skies,
> My winged wheels do tell
> The woven wonders of my hand,
> The witch-work of my skill! (*Creative Writings* 18)

Long before Eldridge Cleaver would typify the black female as an emasculating "Amazon," America's apotheosis as the "Great I Will" in Du Bois's poetry revived and extended the old iconic tradition figuring America as a cannibal female, an "American Amazon" often depicted as carrying the severed head or limbs of her human victims in many of the earliest artistic renderings of the new continent. Hugh Honour's *New Golden Land* (1975) documents European perspectives on America, tracing the earliest imaginings of America as a naked female headhunter in the age of discovery to later allegorical renditions of the nation as a young, female social climber "cannibalizing" the European aristocracy in the late-Victorian period (Honour 84–89, 248–53), a figure associated with "the Bitch Goddess Success worshiped in the Gilded Age and beyond" (Banta 487). Du Bois could see that an inherent temptation in American culture for the race builder was the "can-do" spirit of American pragmatism, which, isolated from any sustaining purpose but self-aggrandizement, became spiritually corrupting. America's seductive myth of self-creation, coupled with its promises of freedom and equality, had been historically, Du Bois knew, spiritual flypaper for the black aspirant to AMERICA. Du Bois invoked the largely European tradition of a cannibal female America in figuring the "Great I Will" because the only way that white witch America could ever evolve into AMERICA would be if black citizens continued to resist her sky-splitting, temple-raising allure.

In his renditions of the alternative embodiment of black nationalism in the self-sacrificial black madonna, Du Bois relied just as heavily on Euro-American iconic traditions, though with a necessarily more revisionist posture. In "Ave! Maria!," published one month after "The Song of America," Du Bois envisioned the black madonna as the inspirational messenger of race commitment and collective agency. Anchored by the black woman's experience of sorrow in America, this icon is "Mother-maid" and "Mother of Miracles," offering a clearly different path of national development than white witch America's siren song of more, better, sooner. In "Ave! Maria!," Du Bois calls on the black race mother to "gather" in the "Daughter of Sin": "Gather them [sic] in!" (*Creative Writings* 19). In "The Prayer of the Bantu," he idealizes black womanhood as "Spirit of Wonder, / Daughter of Thunder" and "Adorable One" (*Creative Writings* 20). In the brief sketch "The Woman," she is the black woman pleading before the "Great White Throne" of the seemingly white God that she is not worthy to be His "Bride"; then God "swept the veiling of his face aside and lifted up the light of his countenance upon her and lo! it was black" (*Creative Writings* 78). In a 1913 pageant, "The People of People and Their Gifts to Men," she appears first as the "Veiled Woman," who, holding fire in her right hand and iron in her left, inaugurates humanity's slow climb into civilization (*Creative Writings* 1). At the end of the pageant, she reappears with the other black givers of gifts, now rechristened as "the All-Mother, formerly the Veiled Woman, now unveiled in her chariot with her dancing brood, and the bust of Lincoln at her side" (4).

In these allegories of the white witch and black madonna, Du Bois hinted at the dramatic potential inherent in the critical functions of the white female, black female, and black male bodies in the social maintenance of race difference and all that it entailed, organizing his own and others' creative works around a narrative core articulating all of the desires, resistance, and embedded ambivalence of the American race dilemma. Counterpointing the alienating spirit of American materialism to the soul-preserving agency of black motherhood, Du Bois designed a narrative frame wherein the black nation builder would be forced to choose allegiance with white American cultural values or with an evolving racial epic of African redemption. Du Bois overdetermined the "proper" choice by opposing a fickle, sometimes fatal, white bride to a nurturing black mother and conveyed moral urgency through the free adaptation of Christian symbolism to a secular variety of spiritual agency.

In his subsequent revision of the motif, James Weldon Johnson would opt for a more classical, pre-Christian mythological frame that, while less explicitly messianic, would retain and expand on the aesthetic and philosophical choices required of the black national striver. His 1915 poem "The White Witch" employs a speaker who warns his "brothers" that the only safety from the "white witch" is to flee: "For in her glance there is a snare, / And in her smile there is a blight" (*St. Peter* 34). In subsequent stanzas, Johnson reveals the following important characteristics of the witch: she does not look like the "ancient hag" she really is but appears deceptively "in all the glowing charms of youth" (34); behind her smile lurks the "shadow of the panther" and the "spirit of the vampire" (35); it is the "Antaean strength" of her victims that attracts her attention to "the great dynamic beat / Of primal passions," "the echo of a far-off day, / When man was closer to the earth" (35–36). The speaker identifies himself as a victim of the witch: he has been "bound" by "her yellow hair" (36), his strength drained from his soul as he lies helpless in the arms of the vampire woman.

The poem, written during the early stage of the massive migration of blacks northward during and after World War I, superimposes the form of the Du Boisian white witch on an evolving discourse of the failed promises of the northern black experience. Johnson's enumeration of the witch's "properties" becomes one of the signatory aspects of the motif, especially the great importance he attaches to color symbolism:

> Her lips are like carnations red,
> Her face like new-born lilies fair,
> Her eyes like ocean waters blue,
> She moves with subtle grace and air,
> And all about her head there floats
> The golden glory of her hair. (*St. Peter* 34)

His chromatic scheme suggests overlapping symbolic economies—the Aryan somatic ideal revealed as the red, white, and blue of the American flag, with the "golden glory" of the national wealth thrown in for good measure. As Michel Fabre's intensely semiotic reading of Ralph Ellison's Circean white witch in the "Prologue" to *Invisible Man* reveals, such codes of racial-nationalist desire inscribing her feminine form with the myths of freedom and opportunity make her vampirish seduction of the "brothers" a striking critique of American democracy and capitalism, even in their most benign manifestations (127).

Johnson's companion poem, "The Black Mammy," envisions the alternate interracial fantasy (white male/black female). Comparison of the two helps to explain the social context of the urban migration that ultimately transformed black Americans from rural Southerners to prisoners of the inner cities. Published in *The Crisis* five months after "The White Witch" appeared, the poem, according to Johnson's biographer Eugene Levy, was actually composed in 1900, although Levy's description of it seems different from the version of 1915 (70). As "foster-mother" to the whites, the "mammy" is economically locked into a position of dubious allegiance to her race:

> So often hast thou to thy bosom pressed
> The golden head, the face and brow of snow;
> So often has it 'gainst thy broad, dark breast
> Lain, set off like a quickened cameo. (*St. Peter* 40)

Here, the female form is more explicitly objectified as a site of competing male desires, using the mammy's age to mask the implicitly sexual tug-of-war. Unlike the white witch, the black mammy is a truly nurturing female, but the "bosom pressed [to] / The golden head" gives strength only to the "sons of the masters of the land," (Levy 40) to the detriment of her own black child.

As with Johnson's witch and her victim, the exploitation of the black body by a parasitical white figure defines interracial contact. Though the image of childhood innocence that includes her own body in the delightful cameo seduces the old mammy, the phrase "golden head" invokes the capitalist exploitation of black labor as the subtext of the tableau. While Johnson's earlier poem warned the black, male nation builder to beware becoming ensnared in the witch's golden hair, this lyric explicitly questions the ability of the black mother to understand the nature of the trap into which the white (male) child draws her. More than her lack of political astuteness, the poem raises doubts about the loyalty of the black female to her own domestic responsibilities: "Came ne'er the thought to thee, swift like a stab, / That [the golden head] some day might crush thy own black child?" (Levy 40).

The framing of the question reveals an identification between the adult observer and the deposed infant that the golden head supplants. At the same time, no black female perspective emerges from either poem: the mammy here is silent, not allowed to answer the rhetorical question that concludes the poem, while the witch poem unfolds as a conversation between "brothers." The mammy's absorption into American culture as a sign of domesticity thus masks her treachery against incipient black domesticity and, by extension, against the as yet unfounded black patriarchal interests. The colonization of her physical form, from a black male perspective, appears as a rejection with sexual overtones. Noting how often she has pressed her bosom to the golden head, the speaker insinuates that far from grudgingly submitting to the demands of her employment, the mammy envisions the golden head as the key to a fantasy of transcending her dark body through her mothering of a white child with the white employer/patriarch. The golden head displaces the absent black child not just out of economic necessity, then, but out of the mammy's self-erasure into a mere backdrop to "the face and brow of snow." On the other hand, no similar appeal to domestic responsibility interrogates the aesthetic preference of the "brothers" for the white witch.

Taken together, the poems reveal a pervasive distrust of the feminine—a black male deracination so profound that neither in the compromised domesticity of the South nor the impermanent sexual commerce of the North is there any hope of sanctuary. The white witch, siren of false hopes, blocks the advance of the black male into American national subjecthood, while the treacherous mother mortgages his refuge in the black world of the Jim Crow South to secure her own marginal position in the white world. Johnson's cosmos of black males' striving is a bleaker one than Du Bois's; absent a committed black madonna, it renders the African-American male as paralyzed between emasculating feminine ideations. After Johnson, the presentation of the feminine in black male texts (especially in prose and drama) will typically employ this misogynistic interracial construct.

Both Du Bois and Johnson contributed to the tradition of representing black Americans as slaves to the dream of American freedom in the North, a tradition that resonates from the slave era to the period of Jim Crow and beyond as a profound critique of American ceremonial and iconographic idealism and of the myth of northern liberal egalitarianism. In 1833, Maria W. Stewart portrayed black Americans as subjects of a captivity narrative of biblical dimensions: "America has become like the great city of Babylon.... She is indeed a seller of slaves and the souls of men; she has made the Africans drunk with the wine of her fornication; she has put them completely beneath her feet, and she means to keep them there" (Porter 134). Stewart's condemnation of a feminized America denies misleading sectional distinctions between the slave South and free North, anticipating Du Bois's composite America as the "Great I Will." If Du Bois continued Stewart's characterization of America as the corrupter of the "chosen" people, he also drew on other classical representations of demonic women.

In *The Souls of Black Folk* (1903), Du Bois appropriated the national symbolism of the American eagle to portray the black predicament: "if . . . we debauch the race thus caught in our talons, selfishly sucking their blood and brains in the future as in the past, what shall save us from national decadence?" (63). Du Bois curiously uses a self-inclusive "we," aligning himself with man-eating America; yet, his characteristic referent for America in *The Souls of the Black Folk* is "she." It might, under the circumstances, be provocative to envision Du Bois's "America" as more harpy than eagle, a suggestive figure that would look backward to Stewart's American Babylon. Key to this interpretation is Du Bois's use of "debauchery" and "decadence" to characterize interracial relations (as Stewart had previously figured such relations as "fornication").

James Weldon Johnson would later combine Stewart's Babylon and Du Bois's American harpy into an image of the northern metropolis as "enchantress." In his 1912 novel *The Autobiography of an Ex-Colored Man,* Johnson's depiction of New York City as "sit[ting] like a great witch at the gate of the country," disguising her hag-like deformity beneath the "folds of her wide garments" (65) anticipates the "white witch" of his 1915 poem—the "ancient hag" of "unnumbered centuries" who "appears / In form of youth and mood of mirth" (*St. Peter* 34). He telescopes the gendered national space, America, into a gendered urban space, New York City, and then into the gendered icon universally associated with the myth of America's nurturance of the immigrant dispossessed— the Statue of Liberty. Johnson cleverly renders "Liberty" as the symbol of the cruel irony of northern black migration, the outcome of which he foreshadows in the image of the white witch city "hiding her crooked hands and feet under the folds of her wide garment . . . crush[ing black immigrants] beneath her cruel feet" (*Autobiography* 65). Johnson's refiguring of Liberty recalls Maria Stewart's allegorical representation of America as the Whore of Babylon crushing Africans "completely beneath her feet. . . . her right hand supports the reins of government, and her left hand the wheel of power, and she is determined not to let go her grasp" (Porter 134). By making this cruel violation of black Americans the apotheosis of American Liberty, Johnson sets in motion a new series of metaphoric possibilities keyed to the more fluid interpersonal relations of the northern experience.

The blazon of the white witch in Johnson's poem, in her red, white, and blue, is only one element in Johnson's rich symbolism. Where Du Bois pictures a harpy-like America "sucking" the "blood and brains" of the black race, Johnson out-Du Boises Du Bois by making his witch a "spiritual" vampire who draws the strength from the very souls of black men. Du Bois was rendering a critique "of the training of black men," as the title of this essay in *The Souls of Black Folk* suggests, railing against an educational system that, under the influence of Booker T. Washington, would deprive black Americans of their "brains" in order to make them better carpenters and farmers. While Du Bois's polemic centers on America's political oppression of black Americans, Johnson extends his critique of the American "spirit of the vampire" to cultural and economic exploitation. Johnson, in effect, sounds one of the earliest literary warnings against cultural appropriation—the exploitation of black cultural productivity as homegrown American exotica. Though Johnson often expressed a naive faith in the liberating potential of the coming vogue of primitivism—which because of his experiences on the New York and European theatrical scenes he predicted would become an important social force—in "The White Witch" he reveals a structural ambivalence that would resonate through the decades of fluctuating African-American access to the American cultural center.

His white witch is the American consumer par excellence—the slummer, the bored habitué of Negro nightlife, the avant-garde stalker of novelty who would, within a decade, turn black Harlem into a peep show. Attracted by "strong young limbs" and "laughter loud and gay," the witch remembers "a far-off day, / When man was closer to the earth":

She feels the old Antaean strength
In you, the great dynamic beat
Of primal passions, and she sees
In you the last besieged retreat
Of love relentless, lusty, fierce,
Love pain-ecstatic, cruel sweet. (St. Peter 35–36)

The witch masks as Liberty to violate the greatest of the white world's social taboos, interracial sex. In a sense, the homogenizing effect of American culture is a by-product of her assault on the racial margin, for as she goes from victim to victim, she consumes the "primal passions" of the black disaffected, leaving each soul drained and pacified—forms empty of content. Her victims, therefore, do not speak from the grave but remain paralyzed, death-in-life, "twined [in] her arms, / And bound . . . with her yellow hair" (36).

The reference to Antaeus anchors Johnson's core narrative of black deracination. Like Antaeus, the black quester as primitive draws his strength directly from nature, in which, unlike the men of the industrialized North, the southern black has been firmly rooted. But the Earth Mother of the South whose nurturance he needs turns out in the companion poem "The Black Mammy" to have been colonized for the sustenance of the white patriarchy. Deprived of a nurturing southern soil to stand on as his own, the black Antaeus dies a slow, painful death in the North.

The blazon of the white witch in Johnson's poem becomes a staple of the motif for this reason: the "display" of the witch's "parts" is an element in the attempted territorial conquest of racially restricted American space, involving "simultaneously an act of unfolding, offering to the eye, and the more static sense of something to be gazed upon and seen":

> The economic motive of itemizing—the detailing of a woman's parts as an inventory of goods—makes explicit an aspect of the rhetorical tradition's own relation to natural plenitude, copia, wealth, or increase. . . .
> The "matter" of discourse, then, is to be made plentiful, by a shaper outside it who "opens" it to the gaze, but also to be kept firmly under control. The inventory or itemizing impulse of the blazon . . . would seem to be part of the motif of taking control of a woman's body by making it, precisely, the engaging "matter" of male discourse, a passive commodity in a homosocial discourse or male exchange in which the woman herself, traditionally absent, does not speak. (Parker 127, 131)

Du Bois's "Great I Will" speaks for herself, but Johnson narrates his tales of the white witch and black mammy entirely from a male perspective. In each instance, the underlying theme of black male victimization thwarts the proprietary impulse, arguing by negation the unfairness of a universe in which no woman can, finally, be owned by black men.

The tradition of the white witch demonstrates the paradox of living in an America determined to make the achievement of AMERICA impossible through an assault on black males' prerogatives. The white witch trope adopts the mode of the "prospect"—the gaze across the horizon at "gendered sign[s] of the territory to be conquered and occupied" (Parker 131, 140–41), yet it simultaneously announces America's resistance to such occupation. Calvin Hernton's observation that "any oppressed group, when obtaining power, tends to acquire the females of the group that has been the oppressor" assumes that black nation builders as "prospectors" of AMERICA read the white female form as an allegory of "Liberty" (79). But in a society that racializes genders and genders races, the gaze that colonizes is the witch's, not the black male watcher's. It is in this sense that Johnson's witch casts a "blight" on her prey through an evil eye that complements the sexual nature of her vampirism, punishing the black male who wanders into her visual field with a ligature that, if not unto death, certainly invests black males' spatial adventurism with imminent peril.

The tradition of the white witch consequently focuses on the social and spatial boundedness of America through images of an "enclosed" female white America that, once "penetrated" by the black male nation builder, becomes a space of confinement. Peter Stallybrass identifies three positions in the discourse of the "enclosed" female body, the third of which is that of the "class aspirant":

> Like members of the male elite, the class aspirant has an interest in preserving social closure, since without it there would be nothing to aspire *to*. But, at the same time, that closure must be sufficiently flexible to incorporate *him*. His conceptualization of woman will as a result be radically unstable: she will be perceived as oscillating between the enclosed body (the purity of the elite to which he aspires) and the open body (or else how could he attain her?), between being "too coy" and "too common." (Stallybrass 134)

Johnson's witch subverts the appropriating male gaze by beguiling her victims into the illusion that they have chosen her, even as she assails their "last besieged retreat" of "primal passions." Johnson's feminizing rhetoric of black primitivism thus recognizes that white witch America's refusal to grant national subjectivity to blacks requires a shift in perspective from the gaze of the male aspirant to that of the witch herself, making the black quester the commodified object of the discourse with which he is credited as speaker. Johnson's acknowledgment of the contextual masculinity of the white woman in an interracial relationship makes her the phallic woman, reducing the black male to an impotence and exploitation escapable only through flight. It is he who ends enclosed, itemized, colonized: "Around me she has twined her arms, / And bound me with her yellow hair." The black male's flight to freedom into the arms of the enchantress ends with the image of an enslavement more profound for its implicit emasculation.

Du Bois and Johnson undoubtedly influenced the imagery of entrapment and despair in the northern metropolis that permeates the poetry of Jamaican-born Claude McKay, an immigrant like Du Bois and Johnson in the American city famed for its "openness" to outsiders. In "The White House," the poem that occasioned McKay's vilification of Alain Locke, McKay's Marxist critique revisits Du Bois's "Great I Will" as a national space enclosed against black male aspiration. In this poem, the "door" shut against the "tightened face" of the "chafing savage" forces him to "keep [his] heart inviolate / Against the potent poison of your hate" (*Selected Poems* 78). McKay complained that Locke had changed the title of the poem to "White Houses" without consulting him, fearing that the original title "The White House" would be misconstrued as a criticism of the president, thereby jeopardizing McKay's ability as a resident alien to return to America from Europe. In his autobiography *A Long Way from Home*, McKay gives some insight into the whiteness of the enclosed spaces of his poetic landscape: "My title was symbolic," he writes, "not meaning specifically the private homes of white people, but more the vast modern edifice of American Industry from which Negroes were effectively barred as a group." Locke, said McKay, distorted the meaning of the poem, "making it appear as if the burning desire of the black malcontent was to enter white houses in general" (313–14). When McKay looked to Africa as a possible refuge, he found a still-colonized African body politic to be the plaything of the modern white nations. "The sciences were sucklings at thy breast," McKay exclaims in "Africa." Yet despite Africa's history as the mother of all civilization, it had since been "swallowed" by "darkness," and now has become "the harlot, . . . / Of all the mighty nations of the sun" (*Selected Poems* 40). Like Johnson before him, McKay's despair emerges as disbelief in the millenarian triumph of Du Bois's Mother Africa, a view that not even his later visit to Africa would materially alter (*Long Way* 295–305).

Looking no further than the possibility of a perpetual torture in America that perversely bestows a measure of redemption through conscientious resistance, McKay renders New York as a stark labyrinth where exclusion becomes a form of entrapment in the cruel talons of "Liberty." In "The City's Love," New York comes alive for him in a form clearly influenced by Johnson's white witch city:

> For one brief golden moment rare like wine,
> The gracious city swept across the line;
> Oblivious of the color of my skin,
> Forgetting that I was an alien guest,
> She bent to me, my hostile heart to win,
> Caught me in passion to her pillowy breast. (*Selected Poems* 66)

The city as feminized space shows the poet her tempting face, testing his "inviolate" heart by sweeping "across the line." Denied "masculine" prerogative in the maintenance and transgression of boundaries, however, the speaker is the one whose spatial integrity is at issue here, a circumstance magnified by his inability to hold the city's attention beyond "one flame hour."

However, such idylls are eventually disturbed by vampirish images that link McKay to Du Bois and Johnson before him, as in the moments of "loveliness" described in "The City's Love":

> Oh cold as death is all the loveliness,
> That breathes out of the strangeness of the scene,
> And sickening like a skeleton's caress,
> Of clammy clinging fingers long and lean. (*Selected Poems* 53)

McKay's adaptation of Johnson's witch, who twines her arms about her victim and binds him with her hair, is more fully realized in his sonnet "America":

> Although she feeds me bread of bitterness,
> And sinks into my throat her tiger's tooth,
> Stealing my breath of life, I will confess
> I love this cultured hell that tests my youth!
> Her vigor flows like tides into my blood,
> Giving me strength erect against her hate.
> Her bigness sweeps me like a flood. (*Selected Poems* 59)

McKay's earlier "Tiger" had similarly explored the sexual suggestiveness and sadomasochism of black/white contact, imagining the "white man [as] a tiger at" his throat, "muttering that his terrible striped coat / Is Freedom's" (*Selected Poems* 47). "America" employs the tiger image in a heterosexual encounter, following in the tradition of Johnson's witch. She is a phallic mother, simultaneously exploiting and nourishing the entrapped immigrant "stand[ing] within her walls with not a shred / Of terror, malice, not a word of jeer" (*Selected Poems* 59). The cruel paradox of life in a racist America is that the race hero stands "erect" only through resistance to America's resistance.

Similarly, McKay's "The White City" finds his victimization strangely invigorating:

> My being would be a skeleton, a shell,
> If this dark Passion that fills my every mood,
> And makes my heaven in the white world's hell,
> Did not forever feed me vital blood. (*Selected Poems* 74)

Only the hate engendered in the poet by the city's callous disregard keeps him alive, keeps him from being drained; and because that hatred is an ever-renewing source of energy, his death-in-life is eternal. McKay captures that simultaneous exclusion and enclosure in the image of the city veiled by a "mist." Thus, his failed "inventory" leads to a perversely gratifying hatred of that which he can see dimly through the veil of whiteness but never seemingly possess.

With McKay, exclusion from the myth of "Liberty" in New York necessitates a paradoxical, protective self-enclosure. The act of self-restraint becomes itself the imprisonment against which the poet's spirit rebels. McKay envisions the black American, then, as having internalized his own oppression sufficiently to love the possibility of AMERICA while hating the self that both disallows participation in that freedom and protectively numbs the spirit against such desire.

As Houston Baker has suggested, it has been this eternally deferred possibility of an egalitarian social order that has alienated black Americans, and McKay's poetry reveals clearly how entrapment in this myth of AMERICA is the form that social exclusion often takes. McKay thus became the forerunner of the poet Langston Hughes and the novelists Richard Wright, Ann Petry, Ralph Ellison, and James Baldwin, who would explore the contradictions of the urban ghetto's proximity but incomplete access to the wealth and power of America. Cleaver's embodiment of the black rapist stereotype stems from the fashionable 1960s belief that if America were ever to be "possessed" by the black male quester, it would have to be possession by violence. But the paradox of this literalization of the motif is that even rape as a gesture of frustration with the pursuit of AMERICA ends in a pathological tangle of love and hate—an entrapment that Cleaver's title, *Soul on Ice,* presents as a lingering paralysis in the cold embrace of white witch America.

Works Cited

Andrews, William L., ed. *Critical Essays on W. E. B. Du Bois.* Boston: G. K. Hall, 1985.

Baker, Houston A., Jr. *Blues, Ideology, and Afro-American Literature: A Vernacular Theory.* Chicago: University of Chicago Press, 1984.

Banta, Martha. *Imaging American Women: Ideas and Ideals in Cultural History.* New York: Columbia University Press, 1987.

Brownmiller, Susan. *Against Our Will: Men, Women, and Rape.* New York: Simon and Schuster, 1975.

Cassity, Michael J. *Legacy of Fear: American Race Relations to 1900.* Westport, Conn.: Greenwood Press, 1985.

Cleaver, Eldridge. *Soul on Ice.* New York: Dell, 1968.

Du Bois, W. E. B. "The Conservation of Races." In *W. E. B. Du Bois: A Reader.* Ed. David Levering Lewis. New York: Henry Holt, 1995. 20–27.

———. *Creative Writings by W. E. B. Du Bois: A Pageant, Poems, Short Stories, and Playlets*. In *The Complete Published Works of W. E. B. Du Bois*. Ed. Herbert Aptheker. White Plains, N.Y.: Kraus-Thomson, 1985.

———. *The Souls of Black Folk.* 1903. Rpt., New York: Bantam, 1989.

———. "The Work of Negro Women in Society." In *Writings by W. E. B. Du Bois in Periodicals Edited by Others*. Vol 1. Ed. Herbert Aptheker. Millwood, N.Y.: Kraus-Thomson, 1982. 139–44.

Fabre, Michel. "Looking at the Naked Blonde—Closely (or, Scrutinizing Ellison's Writing)." *Delta* 18 (April 1984): 119–31.

Ginzburg, Carlo. *Ecstasies: Deciphering the Witches' Sabbath*. Trans. Raymond Rosenthal. New York: Random House, 1991.

Hernton, Calvin C. *Sex and Racism in America*. New York: Grove Weidenfeld, 1965.

Honour, Hugh. *The New Golden Land: European Images of America from the Discoveries to the Present Time*. New York: Pantheon, 1975.

Johnson, James Weldon. *The Autobiography of an Ex-Colored Man*. 1912. Rpt., New York: Penguin, 1990.

———. *St. Peter Relates an Incident: Selected Poems by James Weldon Johnson*. New York: Viking, 1935.

Levy, Eugene. *James Weldon Johnson: Black Leader, Black Voice*. Chicago: University of Chicago Press, 1973.

McKay, Claude. *A Long Way from Home: An Autobiography*. London: Pluto Press, 1970.

———. *Selected Poems of Claude McKay*. New York: Bookman, 1953.

The Negro Family: The Case for National Action. Moynihan Report. U.S. Department of Labor, Office of Policy Planning and Research. Washington, D.C.: Government Printing Office, 1965.

Parker, Patricia. *Literary Fat Ladies: Rhetoric, Gender, Property*. London: Methuen, 1987.

Porter, Dorothy, ed. *Early Negro Writing, 1760–1837*. Boston: Beacon Press, 1971.

Stallybrass, Peter. "Patriarchal Territories: The Body Enclosed." In *Rewriting the Renaissance: The Discourse of Sexual Difference in Early Modern Europe*. Ed. Margaret Ferguson, Maureen Quilligan, and Nancy J. Vickers. Chicago: University of Chicago Press, 1986. 123–42.

Wells-Barnett, Ida B. *On Lynchings: "Southern Horrors," "A Red Record," "Mob Rule in New Orleans."* 1892, 1895, 1900. Rpt., Salem, N.H.: Ayer, 1991.

2

"Darken Your Speech":
Racialized Cultural Work of Modernist Poets

Rachel Blau DuPlessis

>Use dusky words and dusky images.
>Darken your speech.
>—Wallace Stevens, "Two Figures in Dense Violet Night"

>Are you afraid of Negro sculpture.
>I have my feelings.
>—Gertrude Stein, "Lifting Belly"

>Can you, after dark, become a darkie?
>—D. H. Lawrence, "After Dark"

Was Marianne Moore black? Ezra Pound's unexpected, eager question can symbolize the dynamic awareness of racial matters in Euro-American and African-American poets in early modernism.[1] The question appears as if an afterthought in the first letter from Pound to Moore in December 1918: "And are you a jet black Ethiopian Othello-hued, or was that line in one of your *Egoist* poems but part of your general elaboration and allegory and designed to differentiate your colour from that of the surrounding menageria?" (143; Scott 361)[2] To parody a question later central to American poetry: "are you a real black person, or did you make this up yourself?" If she were black, Pound would have to confront the cultural production and vocation of African Americans as coequals. If she was not, she could be seen as allegorizing the jungle as an incubator to her imagination in ways assimilable to the primitive trope in modernist writers. Pound's question therefore points up the two racialized modes for writers in early modernism that I shall engage with here. There is, for white writers, an aborted dialogue with African-American culture in which, after some acknowledging of the presence, and sometimes the speech, of one's fellows, Euro-American writers construct their whiteness by refusing to imagine dialogue and thus invent a black semisilence in which they could "darken their speech." A second mode (for both black and white writers) had to do with claiming ownership of Africa. Euro-American writers often, but not always, dislodged the products of blackness from Africa, recontextualized them ideologically, and exhibited them as part of their own treasury or as an aide to their cultural production. These modes (which can also intertwine, both involving appropriation) are central to the consolidation of whiteness and correspond in the American context to post-Plessy sets of laws and practices, blocking a biracial society of coequal citizens. In the European (and then American) context, these practices suggest the insistent practices of empire, still in their heyday, and, particularly, but in complex ways, the impact of museum exhibitions of African art and debates over "civilization."[3]

"Whiteness" is not a given, and a certain amount of critical comment has begun that, as Shelley Fisher Fishkin summarizes, "interrogates" whiteness by marking the unremarked in its dialectical formation (251). Whiteness also has historical variability in social and cultural practices. I am assuming that both general sociopolitical practices or tendencies and specific sociopolitical materials can be shown to be active, in a variety of ways, in the texts and textures of the writing of poets, although poetry, in contrast to the novel, has sometimes claimed exemption from such indications. Since my discussion often rests on close examination of textual materials, I call the mode of examination a social philology.

In February 1919, continuing their correspondence, Pound wrote Moore an important letter concerning (and intermingling) gender, sexuality, race, and poetic yearning. Pound said he is superior to those who are locked in single genders and their corollary traits—whether female chaos or male stupidity. For himself and others who seek a "third way," fixed gender binaries are limiting barriers that they have surpassed by a chiastic exchange of traits. Moore, he declares, is "a stabilized female"; Pound is "a male who has attained the chaotic fluidities" (Scott 363). Pound's tone was proudly positive about this positional androgyny. This is consistent with the *Egoist*/Dora Marsden notion that feminism is a battle won, especially since, by feminism, some meant a sense of antagonism and binary divisions between women and men.

But race—black and white—is a different story. Had Moore been a black writer, Pound postulates a different response: not fusions, or equal exchanges, but distance and even distaste, a far greater challenge than gender presented to him in 1919.

> I am glad you are red-headed and not
> woolled, dark, ethiopian.

It would have been a test case:
you dark, nubian ethiopian: could I
have risen to it; could I,
perceiving the intelligence from a distance,
have got over the Jim Crow law (qtd. in Scott 363)

Her fictively deployed blackness is acceptable; her actual blackness would have been more problematic for him, even at "three thousand miles distance."[4] He confessed that, had she been black, he could not have looked at her work "without squeams" (Scott 363). Crediting black intelligence and poetic vocation would have been a challenge given twenty-five years of laws (*Plessy v. Ferguson*, 1896) mandating segregation, legally disfranchising blacks, and supporting an array of white supremacist practices. Pound's letter is a mild, querulous examination of his prejudice; yet this examination was not totally private in implication in the U.S. context. Pound's political allusions testify to the importance of the Jim Crow aftermath of Reconstruction in the racial formation of white American modernists—as well as such African-American modernists as James Weldon Johnson and Langston Hughes, both of whom record, in their autobiographies, chilling encounters with racial hatreds, even up to the possibility of lynching. The era saw a crisis in the African-American and Euro-American communities, given the ways in which segregation was reaffirmed after *Plessy v. Ferguson;* the increase of political terrorism (lynchings, antiblack riots, the activity of a resurgent Ku Klux Klan) against African Americans both before and after World War I; and the Great Migration (the northward, urban migration of rural Southern blacks, beginning 1916–1919). The first twenty years of the twentieth century in the United States saw a terrific upsurge in "the level of white hostility" to blacks (Quarles 143), a time "which produced the greatest proliferation of anti-Negro literature"—scholarship, tracts, novels, essayistic studies, films (Newby xi). There was significant and lurid white commentary playing on the supposition of Negro inferiority, on fears of racial mixing, impurity, and mongrelization, and on whiteness as a synonym for civilization: a "national racist literature of the 'Yellow Peril' school and the flourishing cult of Nordicism," as C. Vann Woodward says[5] (78). Euro-American resistance to a multiracial society of coequals was enacted virtually everywhere in law, custom, and polemic. There were, at the same time, significant African-American political and cultural movements of consolidation and response to the 1896 defeat: the founding of the National Association for the Advancement of Colored People (1909) and its periodical *The Crisis* (1910) and of the National Urban League (1911). Alternative interpretations of possibility for blacks were presented in the works of Washington ("The Atlanta

Exposition Address" of 1895 and *Up from Slavery* in 1901) and Du Bois (*The Souls of Black Folk,* 1903).

Pound reveals that his sense of Moore's poetical intelligence was involved with and even qualified by Jim Crow assumptions about the inferiority and congenital inequality of African Americans (rather than by the social and spiritual ferment and commentary occurring within the African-American community). That Jim Crow laws were active within even questioning white imaginations suggests, in the words of Toni Morrison, "the impact of notions of racial hierarchy, racial exclusion, and racial vulnerability and availability on nonblacks who held, resisted, explored, or altered those notions" ("Unspeakable" 11). To get over Jim Crow, Pound sings an epistolary ode of liberal racial ideology. Can he assert "the milk-whiteness of souls" when the skin encasing that soul is black? (Scott 363). This commonplace offers a Manichean binary, affirming a hierarchical code of color still privileging whiteness.

To further address his conundrum about race, Pound spoke of his mental negotiations with even "blacker" and "thicker" members of other races (Russian, Armenian—Pound's categories, showing how curious a concept race is) and his admiration for the beauty of darker (Bengali and Japanese) friends. He asserted his (ideological) "Mediterranean colouring"—presumably a tendency to identify with the stereotypically darker, warmer elements of culture (Scott 364). Still, he was uncertain: "Could I have stood Ethiopia," he asked. But finally, he bracketed the racial discussion with another political marker: "No. I had better leave you to Mr Kreymborg and Bill William [*sic*] / and leave off meddling in American matters." Thus is race particularized as an American issue, which released him as an expatriate from the obligation of concluding. The rest of the letter turns to sexuality intermixed with religion: "my lechery" and his being "so 'confounded polygamous'," offering further examples of his gendered strategies of welcoming Moore's comradeship and sexualizing himself invitingly (qtd. in Scott 364).

Pound's lengthy commentary on Moore as Moor marks one site of that resistance to and fascination with articulate black cultural workers and social presences that I will track in white poets as part of their specific version of the consolidation of whiteness that went on, apace, in a number of forms and forums during early modernism.[6] The exchange between Moore and Pound shows at least that the question of blackness, the presence of blacks (African or African American), the sociocultural issues and mythic clusters, the strains, desires, and fears about race were all an active part of the imaginary of white American poets, part of the "expressive heritage of a biracial culture" (Sundquist 9). It is also clear that Pound feels he must construct some subject positions for his whiteness in relation to her (potential) blackness and that he has no single stance available. The Euro-American poets to be discussed here did not identify either with overt white supremacist ideas or with black striving but held a more unstable position while resisting coequal citizenship with blacks.

African-American service in World War I (and the use, by the French, of Sudanese troops in that war) had many repercussions for Euro-American writers. "I do not like stories mixed in in a story. This is an instance the colored regiment" said Gertrude Stein, evincing distaste for "mixing" African Americans into war stories of heroism or service, where the word "mixing" encoded "mongrelization" fears (*Geography* 132). In contrast, a Wallace Stevens letter of 1918 shows tremendous pleasure at and identification with black troops leaving for World War I; he resists and consciously comments on the patronizing attitudes of most white observers: "They regard negroes as absurdities. They have no sympathy with them. I tried to take that point of view: to laugh at those absurd animals" (*Letters* 209). But he could not, feeling "thrilling emotion" at the public ceremony; and, in a family-of-man sentiment, he wrote: "it makes no difference whether the men are black or white" (qtd. in Levy 50). And yet, two years later, he remarks sourly of the sight of his hometown Reading, Pennsylvania: "It was much like returning from the wars and finding one's best beloved remarried to a coon" (*Letters* 219). This disparaging remark locates postwar white resistance to African-American claims to have enhanced standing as citizens based on successful war service.[7] Stevens makes a political remark about power, ownership, and position but transposes these issues to a lurid sexual arena. Thus, while it is possible to note some distinct shift in the postwar period, still these contradictory attitudes of acknowledgment and resistance, desire and disgust, fascination and fear are not so easily separated—even by major historical markers. Euro-American volatility on the subject of race seems a general finding and a baseline.[8]

Although these white poets will differ among themselves, most seem not to have been incited by knowledge of the Harlem Renaissance (many of my examples here are earlier) or of specific political debates in the community of black intellectuals and spiritual leaders. Wallace Stevens's letters make clear that cultural or political movements like the post-Reconstruction crisis or the Harlem Renaissance were not subjects for his comment; there are, for instance, no references to such contemporaneous black writers and thinkers as Hughes, Cullen, Brown, James Weldon (much less Fenton, Georgia Douglas, or Helene) Johnson, Du Bois, or Washington.[9] But Stevens, Pound, and William Carlos Williams are involved with significant racial recognitions, as were Mina Loy and Moore. The epigraphs to this essay indicate the variety of these recognitions. Desire and fear are limned in what Stein and Stevens say; these emotions are linked. And Lawrence asks if one can assume "darkie-ness" through a dramatic event (such as confronting one's dark self after dark): "run up against the standing flesh of you / with a shock, as against the blackness of a negro" (*Complete Poems* 428). Lawrence thus links flesh, the unconscious, and complex feelings of white desire and need whose token or symbol is so conveniently "a negro." Whiteness has, at times, the privilege of assuming the profile of blackness. Indeed, the three epigraphs from whites writing on blacks suggest that their own art is challenged, called out, inspired, or provoked by "duskiness." Blacks have often been used by whites as an image of the unconscious of whites—fecund, productive, creative, but, as it were, in a colonial relation, the raw material of blackness fueling poetic production in the metropole of whiteness.

The Construction of Whiteness in a Monoracial "Dialogue" and Fabricated Black Semisilence

Some of these feelings about blacks are resolved by Euro-American writers' constructing black silence or limited speech to "darken" their own speech with indications of African-American cultural materials.[10] What I mean by Stevens's phrase "darken your speech" is this cluster of aborted dialogue, the fabricated silence or near silence of blacks, and white use of African-American materials. It has not yet been fully seen how much, in his early work (1908–1935), Stevens was involved with racial materials. Working with the poems of the 1930s, his biographer Joan Richardson, argues enthusiastically that Stevens identifies as black, proposing that Stevens enters "the black man's skin" in a Whitmanesque inclusiveness and from the sense (unexamined) that blacks had advantages of anonymity and closeness to the natural world. For Richardson, Stevens's unarguable racial prejudices ("ambivalences") were due to "the circles in which he moved" (*Later Years* 117).[11] It is clearly worth examining Stevens's representation of blacks (for one thing, it begins much earlier than the 1930s) and analyzing the cultural work he performs for the construction of whiteness.

Stevens's temporary blackface of imaginative play-passing is assumed for the sake of mining a rich strand of what he takes to be American/Caribbean primitivism—the pleasures of rural and tropical, though not urban, folk.[12] The fondness and even sweetness of some of the use of blacks in Stevens's lyric poetry might be a version of what Richard Brodhead identifies in the late nineteenth and the early twentieth centuries. Brodhead remarks that, as immigration—especially of Slavs, Jews, and Italians—increased, blacks became "desirable objects of regionalist contemplation, . . . as if blacks became an honorary extension of 'our' family in face of this more foreign threat" ("Regionalism"

174). Something of this sort is visible in Stevens; the familial use is one element of his presentation of African Americans; but, for the most part, only male figures function in this manner.

As early as 1908, in a letter to his future wife, Stevens is playing out his fantasy of being Sambo in a vaudeville/minstrel vignette of lady and servant filled with flirtatious and scandalous possibilities of sexual desire (*Letters* 111).[13] Sambo makes an important appearance again, at the climax of "Sea Surface Full of Clouds" (1924), as a clownish conjurer—again involved with an umbrella and some saucers—who rides the richly rocking sea.[14] He is only one part of the rich pointillist colors and curio-cabinet of oddities that the poem presents. Sambo is a black buffoon from American folklore—merry, ingratiating, endearing, lovable, harmless in his grinning and dancing, offering a comic cornucopia of bounty without aggression (Boskin 4–16). In the poem, the tamed sexuality of Sambo, a kind of circus harem prince, "turquoise-turbaned," is placed into the joyous joking subtext of the coy artifices of sexuality, while the main text speaks of a cosmic reflective encounter between sea and sky "rolled as one" in a triumphant transcendence (*Collected Poems* 102). Sambo in both instances seems to be a way of stating sexual desire, using race to express that desire.

The poems treating black males as sexual tokens are pastoral, rural, or natural in setting; here Stevens may be said to assume a blackface. As soon as there is any urban hint, or when black female figures are at issue, another tone surfaces, and there is none of the identification that Richardson has found. "Contents of a Cab" (1919) is a work of mocking puppetry. The "contents" is an African-American woman whose pretensions to refinement and elegance are dismantled by the poem, which brings her into a jungle setting, appropriate to her and sexually tempting to the speaker: "Victoria Clementina, negress, / Took seven white dogs / To ride in a cab" (*Opus* 20–21). The dogs are an indication of excessive and uncontrollable sexuality, as decadent depictions of women and dogs presented by Bram Dijkstra in *Idols of Perversity* make clear. The poem is a luxurious imagination of a black woman, so tempting as to be frightening, whose sexuality—whether of the urban setting she enters with the pretense (as the poet sees it) of elegance or of the imagined jungle where her "savage blooms" and gorgeous breechcloth have full play—is barely contained in the poem. The poem ends peculiarly, with an address to "you"—a correspondent of the black woman. Is the "you" a female, chastely chastened, whose sexuality seems pale and repressed once the "negress" rolls into town? Is it a man whose sexuality can never be the equal of the savage woman he projects? Richardson reads the poem as a work about the role of the imagination for Stevens: "here was a metaphoric illustration of the kind of completion indulging poetry allowed" (498). The "completion" is a sexual fantasy displaced of acts and desires deeply sinful and forbidden, the fuel of his poetry in general being desire. This is clearly so, but the social and racial contexts pointed to (urban migration and urbane blacks, changing sexual attitudes, the fantasy status of black women, the twenty-five antiblack race riots in the urban North in 1919, which is the poem's date) should not be discounted; "the imagination" is constructed by, and acts through, a social scrim of specific circumstances—and, thereby, through racial and gender ideologies.

Similarly, "The Virgin Carrying a Lantern" (1923) is a comic poem about sexuality wherein the very word "negress" (not to speak of the figure behind the word) is part of the punchline, the butt of a joke (*Collected Poems* 71). It is comparable in crudeness to Eliot's King Bolo poems or Pound's "Yiddischer Charleston Band." The "negress," in her lowercase form, is like Eliot's "big black kween": a sexual predator. The black figure sees her total opposite and becomes sexually excited by the sight of the white virgin: "The pity that her [the virgin's] pious egress / Should fill the vigil of a negress / With heat so strong!" (*Collected Poems* 71). The enlightenment prop (a lantern), supposed to shed light, is instead the source of sexual heat. The manipulative, comic rhyme in this stanza is the centerpiece of the poem, creating it as a *jeu d'esprit* of white erotic anxiety about the promiscuous powers of females and blacks: polysexuality, lesbianism, and fetishism intermingle with the sexual desire of a black beast for a white virgin—a rewriting of that virulently stereotyped rape (as in Dixon's *The Clansman*) that is seared into the American ideology of race. Here, it is only varied by Stevens by the gender of the predator and is thus produced as a mixture of comedy, mockery, and fantasy. These poems memorialize urban lusts involved with black female figures; the rural space is more generous: essentially, though not exclusively, populated with black male figures of a sexual and creative fecundity. For Stevens, the buoyant black muse figures are male; the females are dangerous. The imagined black male is an opening to fertile potency; the black female is unassimilable sexual license, and Stevens's poetic desire is marked with alarm. Both figures, however, fulfill what Toni Morrison sees as the cultural duties of the Africanist persona (*Playing*, 3–17), marking desires that can only be ventriloquized by the use of blacks.

Wallace Stevens created a tropical arena for his imagination, a Caribbean space, in which traveling "to Yucatan, Havana next, / And then to Carolina" offers a mainly sexual text undergirded by an unstated political subtext (*Collected Poems* 29). These places offer images of peaceful ("Stars at Tallapoosa"), desirous ("O Florida, Venereal Soil"), and aggressive sensuality ("Bantams in Pine-Woods")—of which the most striking in the combined anthropomorphic sexual force are the female/male primal-scene bananas appearing in "Floral Decorations for Bananas" (1922):

> Fibrous and dangling down,
> Oozing cantankerous gum
> Out of their purple maws,
> Darting out of their purple craws
> Their musky and tingling tongues. (Collected Poems 54)

Stevens's Caribbean space can also offer a creative indifference—the ground in which "foam and cloud are one"—and a site in which whiteness can be gathered. "Barque of phosphor / On the palmy beach" is instructed to "Fill your black hull / With white moonlight" (*Collected Poems* 23). The "fable" of Florida makes a place where a sense of whiteness can increase but also be enriched by blackness. The near tropics—Mexico, Cuba, Florida, the American South, and the Gulf of Mexico—are spaces in which one may be (sexually) possessed and obsessed because one (in an imperialist sense) possesses them. This by virtue of U.S. military incursions into Mexico and the Caribbean in the early part of this century and by virtue of the interior colony represented in the South.[15] Edward Said names the "structures of attitude and reference" created by the enormous and yet shadowy presence of imperialist and colonial relations in "major metropolitan cultural texts" such as these; one must also name the racial and gender ideologies represented (52, 53).

The general fecundity, exotic flora, and sometime female visitants are a spur to a magical kind of creativity: "As the immense dew of Florida / Brings forth hymn and hymn / From the beholder" (*Collected Poems* 95). Indeed, Stevens's Caribbean and Southern poems are comparable to Gauguin's symbolist and primitivist depictions of Oceania. The impact of this tropical site can carry over even to the North; in a poem entitled "Two at Norfolk," difficult passages of (white) life—death and sexuality—can be mediated by what Stevens calls "darkies" (*Collected Poems* 111). As a Euro-American son and daughter try to make love, the poet surrounds them with "the dark shadows of the funereal magnolias [which] / Are full of the songs of Jamanda and Carlotta" (*Collected Poems* 111). To make whiteness, one needs to invoke the willing assistance of blacks.

Within Stevens's general tropical topos, the black inhabitants of the American South are in a special category of address, occurring in twenty or more poems, or in sections of long poems in Stevens's early career—1915–35 (with the largest cluster from 1919–22). Stevens shows exhilaration and joy at black figures whose imagined activities open the sensual terrain of poetry for him as writer. He positions black figures as muses through whom and because of whom his poetic authority is felt. They have all the problematics of muses as well—they are vibrant, but silent; unsophisticated, yet unconsciously creative; desirable, but appropriated; givers, not owners.

The poems are uniformly celebrations of rural, innate joy and of the essential replenishing powers of black folks for what Walter Benn Michaels has, following Du Bois, cunningly named "the souls of white folks." For example, "Hymn from a Watermelon Pavilion" (1922) speaks directly to "You dweller in the dark cabin, / To whom the watermelon is always purple"[16] (*Collected Poems* 88). It argues that such a figure (the watermelon allusion produces him as African American) has no need for imagination, since reality gives and intensifies those desirable elements that others, more deprived, must sleep and only dream about. Three features enhance the fecund unconscious of the main character: a "best cock" with red feathers, a green "feme" (wife), and a cackling blackbird (fortuitously adding up to the colors of African nationalism). These figures are all so active in reality that the "dweller" is instructed: "Rise, since rising will not waken." He is already in a sexual dream, an Edenic landscape of pleasure and possibility; his rising is potent and stirring and does not break the spell (*Collected Poems* 88–89). This appreciative remark is part of a subtle colonizing move, arguing that the rural black man has no need of a dream life or an imagination, given that his reality is richer than the (white) speaker's dream. There is a phallic dynamism implied, bringing the dark dweller to a state of sexual bliss. The argument that poor and working-class figures have "plenty," especially a full sensual life, is very difficult to displace, as it here ascribes to blacks a bliss that seems at first glance like a benefit. However, it strips the figure so invested of any other emotion or human situation—intellection, grief, cunning, anger, narcissism, loss.[17]

A more tart assessment could be borrowed from Alain Locke. In his essay "The Negro in Art" (1940), Locke reviews the sweep of depictions of African Americans in American visual art, reporting that the plantation formula dominated the black subject: "Its widest currency ... was during the Reconstruction period, when, reenforcing a Southern school of fiction whose main objective was the glorification in retrospect of the slavery regime, it helped mould the typical popular American conception of the Negro. A plague of low-genre interest multiplied the superficial types of uncles, aunties and pickaninnies almost endlessly, echoing even today in the minstrel and the vaudeville stereotypes of a Negro half-clown, half-troubadour" (*Negro in Art* 139). To a sophisticated version of this "cotton-patch and cabin-quarters formula," Stevens has generally acceded; indeed, the discourses of "romantic racism" could be postulated as a contributing part of his cultural formation, as it would be for other American youths born around 1880 (Frederickson 97–129). Other poems of this Southern mythos of sensuality and bliss, if not this precise argument, are "The Load of Sugar Cane," with the rising of the kildeer "at the red turban / Of the boatman" (*Collected Poems* 12), and "O Florida, Venereal Soil" (1922), with the arrival in the night of a "donna, donna, dark" possibly to satisfy, or to further torment, "the lover" with "a pungent bloom against your shade" (*Collected Poems* 47–48). Or the address in "Two Figures in Dense Violet Light" (1923) to a difficult loved one, with instructions to improve sensuality: "Be the voice of night and Florida in my ear. / Use dusky words and dusky images. / Darken your speech" (*Collected Poems* 86). Rural blacks are depicted as creative, fertile, potent, acute, spontaneous, burstingly "natural."

In symbolic contrast to the Southern sensual and sexual bliss depicted by Stevens, one might put a stark imagist poem, Effie Lee Newsome's "Exodus" (1925), which eulogizes the South unreluctantly while alluding to the Great Migration:

> The dahoon berry weeps in blood,
> I know,
> Watched by the crow—
> I've seen both grow
> In those weird wastes of Dixie! (Honey 69)[18]

Or one might contrast Langston Hughes's penetrating couplet: "the lazy, laughing South / With blood on its mouth" (*Fine Clothes* 54). These poets, and other African-American writers, speak about the terroristic enforcement of segregation. And one might compare Gertrude Stein's meditation "Wherein the South Differs from the North" (1915–26), which, so far as one may surmise, is an attempt to undercut the assertion in the title, resisting both the rich romanticism of some and the political suspicions of others. Stein weaves an incantatory web of words between the regions by syntactic parallels so intense as to bridge their difference, especially as she pointedly excludes certain politically charged materials about race and the Civil War.

> North and south negroes.
> No one means that.
> South and north settles.
> No one means that (*Useful Knowledge* 20)

The piece is motivated to create a perverse, charming "in between," to fuse and bind two polarized regions by sheer linguistic spinnings and repetitions that say the same about both regions. About the South built as a representation, Stevens says, So good, so black that it is bliss; Newsome and Hughes say,

So bad for blacks that one must leave (and yet is haunted still); Stein says, South, North, same difference.

Stevens's plantation bliss of a rural Eden proposes the silent black figures as muses of sensuality and poetry, inducements to and enhancements of his writing. There is a second kind of appearance of black figures with whom the speaker bonds: folk poets and musicians. Despite their artistry, it is rare that Stevens makes them speak in the poems that represent them. In "Ploughing on Sunday" (1919), the speaker has become the joyous, effervescent "plough-boy"; his folk-bold lyric of poetic power is irrepressible. In the work, he demands to be celebrated for his access to pleasure and force as one rural worker to another:

> Remus, blow your horn!
> I'm ploughing on Sunday,
> Ploughing North America.
> Blow your horn! (*Collected Poems* 20)

As the one instructed to celebrate the Bunyanesque élan of the plough-boy, "Remus" is a name with virtually no connotation but black, a connotation drawn from the wise, wily "Uncle Remus" of Joel Chandler Harris. The speaker's exhortations to the black folk-world are effervescent but colonizing. For these poems of Stevens praise a folk feeling yet instruct blacks even as the (white) speaker participates with them and appropriates their sound.

Similarly, in "The Jack-Rabbit" (written before 1923) and "Some Friends from Pascagoula" (1935), Stevens proposes making poems as a folk poet and/or instructs others in the making of black folk-poetry as a (white) éminence gris. The two positions have in common an attempt to claim the sound of a black "maker," though not by the explicit dialectal imitation that Michael North has identified (9–11, 78–79). One might say that Stevens positions these black folk-figures as makers but situates himself always already as the speaker, showing how he both needs and does not need their intervention, in an ambiguous relation of yearning for a racially cross-fertilized culture and resistance to it. The poet ventriloquizes "darkened" poems as a self-conscious literary allusion to black folklore. In "Some Friends from Pascagoula," the speaker is listening to folksingers or fabulists whom he is also instructing:

> Tell me more of the eagle, Cotton,
> And you, black Sly,
> Tell me how he descended
> Out of the morning sky.
> . . . .

Here was a sovereign sight,
Fit for a kinky clan. (*Collected Poems* 126)

The "kinky clan" may be the source, but is not the arbiter of this material; the "sovereign sight" that evaluates suitability is owned elsewhere. "The Jack-Rabbit" contains the intensities of an Uncle Remus beast fable with its depiction of the threat to the caroling jack-rabbit by a buzzard, crocheted by a black grandmother:

The black man said,
"Look out, O caroller,
The entrails of the buzzard
Are rattling." (*Collected Poems* 50)

This is a unique instance of the imagined speech of a black character, and it is somewhat threatening. In comparable moments, Stevens instructs these inspiring characters how to speak, and in sympathetic imperatives asks for more of their speech, but does not cite them.[19] The ownership of speech is at issue.

The famous "blackbird" of Stevens is involved in the speech and poetic rhetoric of the "I," but its presence is shadowy, obscured, occluded:[20]

I know noble accents
and lucid, inescapable rhythms;
But I know, too,
That the blackbird is involved
In what I know. (*Collected Poems* 94)

No matter where one looks, what one imagines, or what speech or music is heard, the blackbird is always there. This mystical, mobile blackness has to be acknowledged—it has a power of which one is in awe; it shadows one's actions and possessions ("Once, a fear pierced him, / In that he mistook / The shadow of his equipage / For blackbirds" [*Collected Poems* 93]). And it is depicted, always, as making music, bearing witness, moving in its own direction, and waiting.[21] But the black element is more often kept silent and dispersed at the very moments in which its poetic potential is praised. Whiteness is consolidated by its expansive powers of taking, enjoying, admiring, and getting pleasure from blackness.

The interpenetration of the blackbird into all elements of the world and the rarity of black speech despite the strong presence of African-American figures in Stevens suggest that speech, interaction, and dialogue are precisely at issue. This is emphasized by a rare invention of what could be viewed as cross-racial dialogue, the epigrammatic couplets exchanged between "woolen massa" and "black man," ending with an arch stalemate, in the matching poems called "Nudity at the Capital" and "Nudity in the Colonies" (*Collected Poems* 145). "Woolen massa" suggests that the master has already been inflected with physical traits of blacks—a hair type. But the poems are only opaque snippets of dialogue about concealment and disclosure. Mainly, Stevens creates situations in which the white figures, instructing the speech of blacks, take both halves of the conversation.

The patterns of yearning identification leading to appropriation of black materials and of monologic speech in a situation inviting biracial dialogue are especially visible in two works that predate all the material discussed just previously; these poems may be said, therefore, to set out some motives for Stevens's racialized imagination. These works are also notable in that both make covert allusions to political materials that are visibly unassimilated by the poet. "The Silver Plough Boy" (1915) is a poem of inspirational blackness in which something evanescent but evocative occurs (*Opus* 6). By wearing the disguise of a sheet (stolen from the wash), a black youth (a "boy") has turned silver.[22] While silver, he is a lyric, creative, metamorphic sprite. But even before the transforming sheet, this "black figure . . . in a black field" had already been dancing. The silvery sheet only enhances the prior creativity of the black figure, making him even more fecund, with the "green blades" of the plough following his dance.

This artless poem trails a series of unresolved ambiguities and contexts, which may account for why it did not appear in Stevens's *Collected Poems*.[23] It opens with a racialized situation (a dark figure stealing something). And it makes the moment of silvery whiteness one whereby the "boy" can turn his work (ploughing) into a dance. The use of the term "boy" for a black male figure magnetizes the title beyond the pastoral. Then the pronoun "it" rather than "he" is attached to the ploughboy throughout the poem; thus, either he is gender neutral in a negative sense, his maleness voided, or he is gender neutral in a positive sense. For once taken to represent a further (whitened? silvered?) art or imagination, the impish figure can transcend gender—and, possibly, race. Yet the poem makes this figure wear the sheet of the Ku Klux Klan's night riders. This suggestion is absolutely not in tune with the poem's tone of epiphanic lightness. And yet, given its date, it is an irrepressible "contrapuntal" reading, to use Edward Said's word, for the poem was written in the year D. W. Griffith's *The Birth of a Nation* was released. This film was fiercely debated and richly appreciated (as "the truth") from its premiere in January 1915. In the film's construction of white mythology, the Klan is depicted triumphantly as rescuing white womanhood, civilization, the South, and the nation from the political excesses of Reconstruction (including a "black beast," a black militia, and equal justice for all). The year 1915 is also marked by the revival of the Klan, which was in part propelled by the film (Wade 119–39). Stevens uses poetry to mellow the racial materials he suggests—the night riders that are evoked, though in a reverse fashion, through the disguise of an epicene black youth. Stevens makes poetry construct a fantasy counter to that offered by contemporary history.

This pattern of detracking political allusions is even more visible in Stevens's first play. Between 1916 and 1918, Stevens wrote three works of poetic theater. For the first, "Three Travelers Watch a Sunrise" (1916), he was honored by *Poetry* with a prize that marked a public coming of age into his vocation as a writer. The cast of this play includes three Chinese (in European garb to begin with), two "negroes," and a white woman with a given name (*Opus* 127–43). These characters are hierarchically arranged. The Chinese are philosopher kings. They speak a mannered, oblique poetry and investigate the relationship between imagination and reality. They are divided in their opinions of what they are. One already lives in a world of metaphor or translation: he who seeks a spring is given a porcelain water bottle. Another rejects the beauty and knowledge that comes from meditative or aristocratic seclusion. Part of the puzzle of the play is that these players seem to propose, in a paradox about representation, that they are painted on the porcelain jug they hold. At the same time, they sing a ballad whose terms are about to come true in reality (that is, on the stage, not only inside the ballad) when the woman, named Anna, appears at the end, explaining the presence of a hanged man—her morose, rejected lover. These four characters speak and sing.

The "negroes" only serve; they are completely silent or gestural.[24] This fact is so striking and so suspicious that the poet himself comments on it in a contemporaneous letter to Harriet Monroe: "You will note that the negroes now have no speeches. I cannot well make them both servants. The negro who appears first has been searching for the [dead] man" (*Letters* 195). Despite his qualms, Stevens has done exactly as he says he will not: neither black character speaks; both continue to be cast as silent servants. And the dead man—otherwise an apparent non sequitur—is linked to this situation of black silence. Some racial anxiety about African-American agency and autonomous presence, some inability to reckon with what such characters might be imagined to say, perhaps vetoed Stevens's announced goals. The contradiction between his intention and practice bespeaks a certain kind of (white) problematic: he declares in the letter that he wants black speech but ends with a play in which he cannot create it, a drama that cuts out the black characters as speaking participants in a work in which they are invented and proposed as agents. Stevens knows, at least sometimes, the political or social fact of the active presence of blacks in the world (persons not to be patronized, as his letter of 1918 begins to understand), but he produces a cultural artifact that reduces blacks to silence and service, a racial ground in relation to the articulate, aristocratic Chinese.[25]

It is eerie to conceptualize this play being performed, because what one Negro character does—aside from walking back and forth onstage, moving lanterns, baskets, jugs, melons, clothing, bushes, and stringed instruments for the Chinese—is to find and fearfully examine a hanged body: "*When the curtain rises, the stage is dark. The limb of a tree creaks. A negro carrying a lantern passes along the road. The sound is repeated. The negro comes through the bushes, raises his lantern and looks through the trees. Discerning a dark object among the branches, he shrinks back, crosses stage, and goes out through the woods to the left*" (*Opus* 127). The anxiety and terror of lynching seem, for the bulk of the play, to be encoded in this body and in the fear that body causes. And therefore it seems like a dark, damaging secret, physically visible on the stage yet emotionally and politically hidden as a subject of the play: "unspeakable things unspoken," in Toni Morrison's resonant phrase ("Unspeakable" 1).[26] The apparatus, including the tree, is quite similar to materials in many African-American poems, such as the three-line stanza of Countee Cullen's "Colors" in *Copper Sun* (1927); the color is "black": "The play is done, the crowds depart; and see / That twisted tortured thing hung from a tree, / Swart victim of a newer Calvary" (*My Soul's* 145). Further, lynching was a fraught issue during that period, with such horrific examples as the Waco, Texas, torture and burning of an African American in 1916 (a summary report by the NAACP appeared in *The Crisis*, July 1916).[27] Stevens is able to suggest lynching, but he absolutely cannot elaborate it. Thus, by a long detour through the romantic plot, this surmise implicating a lynching turns out to be untrue—the hanging man was Italian and a suicide. While hegemonic art has never had any trouble dealing with unrequited love, suicide, and personal grief, as Eric Sundquist remarks, the Italian as type figured in anti-immigrationist thought as a kind of "colored" and degraded figure; in a sensational case in 1891, eleven Italians were lynched in New Orleans (Sundquist 260–61). So lynching is both there and not there, a strange counterpoint to the mannered philosophy of the Chinese and the familiar romance plot involving the female character. This "contrapuntal" reading (to once again evoke Said's method in *Culture and Imperialism*) expands attention to sociopolitical allusions within works, offering an analysis of the historical events to which they tangentially allude. It is also a reading that treats certain materials as encoded clues to political anxieties within a nonpolitical poetic texture.

With a down-home blackface diction, e. e. cummings announces in his 1935 "ump-A-tum" jazz poem:

theys sO alive
(who is
?niggers)" and "niggers
is
all
born
so
Alive). (305)

This is a fact (tautology?) that cummings clearly appreciates and envies. The insistence on the more-than-alive living, the preternaturally vibrant African American, when read contrapuntally, seems a perverse and motivated blindness to how many times (almost 4,000) up through this century, with increases in the 1930s after a statistical decline, lynching imposed torture and death on blacks—a practice making them, one might say, "sO dead." Other claims for blacks' preternatural, extra-alive vibrancy may have some motivation in white guilt for their vulnerability. The capital "O" of cummings's "sO" encodes this: there is a buried "zero" in it.

In any event, in Stevens, the Chinese are seated with their backs to the "dark object, hanging to the limb of the tree" (*Opus* 137). And while they will eventually discover it, the finding does not deal with the sociopolitical allusion inhering in this image, which, unresolved, thereby casts a free-floating ideological shadow across the play. When the sun shines on the earth (or the porcelain bottle, its mannered analogue), it will also shine on the trees:

And find a new thing
           [*indicating the body*]
Painted on this porcelain,
           [*indicating the trees*]
But not on this.
           [*indicating the bottle*] (*Opus* 142)

It is plausible, if not fully sanctioned, to read this as follows: such a body can be "painted" on reality, but art has a harder time dealing with it. Therefore, one cannot help but allegorize the allegory and see this play as an attempt to mute the scandalous reality of white political terrorism by constructing an elaborate cosmetic machinery for its containment. Stevens's defensiveness about these supremacist manifestations of whiteness precedes his more expansive consolidation of a whiteness that admires blacks and takes liberally from them to "darken" the speech of whites.

William Carlos Williams is a poet whose use of black figures seems, on the face of it, to contrast with Stevens's romanticization. In early poems, Williams (part Hispanic in his family origins) identifies himself as "dark"—the impacted power of a certain racialized self-image beyond whiteness inspires him. For instance, he remembers the cover of *Kora in Hell*: the "ovum surrounded by a horde of spermatozoa" has accepted "a dark one" (*Autobiography* 158). His "Apology" proposes that he writes specifically from the terrible beauty of "our nonentities"—"colored women / day workers" (*Collected Poems* 70). From the beginning, the blacks in his poems seem to be cited as "realistic" and neutrally present, just an "old negro" or "colored cooks" or "blackboy" inhabiting the poem as they inhabit life or the city (*Collected Poems* 132, 146, 292). This is a modernist resistance to the discourses of exclusion and nativism that were common in the 1890s and into the early decades of the twentieth century.

The sexualized image of the black male or female is hardly absent in Williams, but sometimes it is managed with a certain wry wit and realistic circumstantiality, as in "Sick African" (*Collected Poems* 59) or "To a Friend" (*Collected Poems* 158). The justification here is to depict things as they "actually" happened in poems that one might call occasional in genre. "Sick African" (1923) is a poem in which the fundamental ridiculousness and independence of sex drives are chuckled at; however, when looked at closely, the black man is indeed seen to be the very repository and exemplum of male license, his inflammation of the testicles "contracted" while his partner, Grace, was in her ninth month of pregnancy—and thus, presumably, not contracted in sexual relations with her. The poem stages and articulates a lot of familiar assumptions about sex, race, and gender in its eleven lines. In the most egalitarian—and also, for Williams, hopeful usage—the sexy working-class youths hot with springtime are both "white and colored"; his desire is to have antipuritanical sexualities blossom everywhere (*Collected Poems* 221).

The cultural myths functioning in these poems have been diluted, watered down precisely by realism as a mechanism; it is relatively rare to see the pure strain of primitive or romantic "savagery" evoked. However, as in Stevens, it occurs whenever gender (female) crosses with race (colored).

> But you
> are rich
> in savagery

Arab

Indian

dark woman (*Collected Poems* 236)

These, the notorious final lines of *Spring and All* (1923), are invoked with the cultural duty of enriching the pallidness of whiteness. "Arab" being a relative rarity in the American ethnic context, one wonders whether that odd word is not a displacement for "Negro." Williams often articulates the way some mestiza, brown, or black female presence would fertilize his poetry; the enormous powerful force of the black woman, Beautiful Thing, in book 3 of *Paterson* grows from these earlier dark women of his interested desire (DuPlessis, *Pink Guitar* 62–65).

In The American Grain (1925) contains the political unconscious of these mainly diluted mythoi. The four-page bricolaged rant "Advent of the Slave" is closest in style to the associative prose poems of *Kora in Hell*. The subject of the title is dismissed with the pious argument that the manner of Africans coming to the United States (enslavement, then the Middle Passage) does not matter. This argument makes a hopeful, astonishingly naive, egalitarian playing field for all "immigrants" that is belied immediately by Williams's essentializing the quality that blacks brought—a kind of "oriental grace" or "beauty." The word "oriental" occurs twice; as in Stein, it is a way to avoid giving Africanness any positive valence. In contrast, Africa is here described as "their own elephant-, snake-, and gorilla-filled jungles" (*American Grain* 208). Williams argues that this beauty allowed blacks to elaborate a performative style in song and dance, somewhat sexy, somewhat sumptuous, as if woven out of "nothing," out of "the soul of their own darkness," an interested play with Du Bois's title (*American Grain* 209, 208). To tell us this, Williams drops into an imitative blackface dialect totally consistent with Michael North's thesis of racial masquerades being generative to white modernism. This aesthetic admiration is interrupted by, and coexistent with, another racial argument: that African Americans themselves are "nothing," "saying *nothing,* dancing *nothing,* 'NOBODY', it is a quality" (*American Grain* 209). This is especially so, Williams writes: "When they try to make their race an issue—it is nothing" (*American Grain* 209). Two master tropes of race are richly present in this work. In Aldon Lynn Nielsen's terms, they are the romantic racism of African Americans considered as primitive libidinal forces and the existential racism of a race "beset by nothingness" and considered a void—but also, as is clear, a political challenge being erased by this void (*Reading Race* 8–22; *Writing* 188). These two broadcasts are then combined on this racial radio with a portrait of a black woman, filled with atavistic jungle metaphors: she leads a "tigerish life"; she has "long gorilla arms"; she was "bellowing like a buffalo" (*American Grain* 209).Female gender (and class) inflects race with a more lurid and titillating story, extending romantic racism with animal sexuality and expanding nothingness into a fecund void in which desires can be projected.

Given these materials, the proposal of cross-race dialogue seems fantastic; yet that is exactly what occurs next. Williams remembers a specific black man he knows (called "M——"; his name is unmarked), praising his linguistic inventiveness; "I wish I might write a book of his improvisations in slang. I wish I might write a play in collaboration with him" (*American Grain* 211). The wish for black-white artistic collaboration is a striking proposal of biracial dialogue and equal interchange. And a play is, of all genres, the most dialogic; the wish for "collaboration" proposes an interaction of coequals. Yet the dialogue for which this sentence hopes has already been compromised, for what precedes it is the wish to appropriate black talk in a white-authored book. The ownership of M——'s spoken improvisations has slid over to Williams: "a book" that "I . . . write." "Darken your speech" appears here as self-instruction: Williams's two sentences, abutted and juxtaposed, are a vivid example of the wistful, wishful appropriation of African-American cultural materials as raw materials and resources, marked with a voided dialogue.

Owning Africa

The second racialized nexus in the construction of whiteness involved the question of how Africa is owned—possessed, acknowledged, and owned up to. "Africa" suggested first a continent representing blacks and then what African sculpture and masks are taken to mean as they are cited and collaged into modern visual art, poetry, and novels. Picasso's *Demoiselles d'Avignon* (1907) is the major case of such a use; it shows five women, two with African masks, one with a dark face but whiter body. In Hal Foster's terms, the work overlayers two scenes—a visit to a brothel and a visit to the Musée d'Ethnographie, showing how women and the primitive, racial, and sexual materials compound each other (181). It was a major work of mastery, confrontation, and awe, illustrative of modern racialized motifs. Similarly, Man Ray's photograph *Noire et Blanche* (1926) links the face of a sleeping white woman and an elegant African mask, perhaps to represent the mysterious unconscious forces in both femininity and African materials (DuPlessis, "RE: Man Ray" 1990). Hannah Höch's collages from the 1920s also link female figures and African ethnographic photos in a synthetic grotesque certainly more critical of the feminine than Man Ray;

but, with her sutures, she suggests the same idea of Africa: it has allowed Europeans to see their desires and drives mirrored by and in African art.[28]

This use of cited African art appears in D. H. Lawrence at significant junctures. The (part-Jewish) artist Loerke in *Women in Love* (1920), whose presence forces a conclusion to the passionate stalemate of Gudrun and Gerald, is described as if he were an African sculpture animated: "his head round as a chestnut, with the brown-velvet flaps [of a cap] loose and wild over his ears, and a wisp of elf-like, thin black hair blowing above his full, elf-like dark eyes, the shiny, transparent brown skin crinkling up into odd grimaces on his small-featured face, he looked an odd little boy-man, a bat"[29] (494). The child, the daimon, the Jew, the African all cluster and compound themselves into an ambiguous provocation to the characters to acknowledge desire. Later manifestations, however, were not as mobile as this, but they have been invested with stasis. In Lawrence's *Lady Chatterley's Lover,* the Irish "bounder" Michaelis, Constance's lover before Mellors, is compared, in an extended passage, to a "carved ivory Negro mask." The terms pooled in this comparison are "immobility," "timelessness," "acquiescence," and "race destiny" (22), meaning a passive loss of individual will; not incidentally, it links the Irish with blacks. Colonialism creates passivity and stasis—or so the colonizer insists. In a sour 1927 review of Carl Van Vechten's *Nigger Heaven,* Walter White's *Flight,* and works by Dos Passos and Hemingway, Lawrence protests Van Vechten's important resistance to primitivizing his middle-class hero and heroine, a resistance that Van Vechten did not extend to the other black characters in his book. Lawrence deeply desires the illusion he also criticizes: "Reading negro books [White's], or books about negroes written from the negro standpoint [Van Vechten's], it is absolutely impossible to discover that the nigger is any blacker inside than we are.... It is rather disappointing. One likes to cherish illusions about the race soul, the eternal negroid soul, black and glistening and touched with awfulness and mystery" (*Literary Criticism* 423). His posturing irony still demands the smoke and mirrors of "awfulness and mystery"; he both punctures primitivism as a concept and demands it.

What is taken as the "primitive" character of such art creates an intervention into European psyches or expresses their fundamental bases. African sculpture is cited, with the apparent assumption of its innately confrontational qualities, to challenge a variety of ossified notions of beauty, harmony, and sentimental sexual or political innocence by its expression of timeless forces of the id. Africa "owns" these forces; Europe must recognize them. Whiteness is constructed in the frisson of "being afraid" of these forces, which it has deep inside itself. If carried to the logical extreme, all whites are blacks inside—an idea that was at once tempting and frightening but, both ways, still essentialist. In any event, the citation of Africa provoked a debate about civilization as a concept, with corollary notions of evolution (as opposed to stasis) and culture.

Marius de Zayas organized two exhibits of African art in 1914 and 1916 for which he produced a monograph, *African Negro Art, Its Influence on Modern Art* (1916), revealing a notable split in white attitudes: the proposition in the subtitle is treated in one paragraph at the end of forty pages.[30] The bulk of the analysis wanders among the propositions of scientific racism. Disparaging and final brain studies, the notion of superior and inferior races, the "fact" that Africans are like children, the sense that one has captured the first evolution of the human race in Africans are all outlined with no reservations.[31] This lively racist sketch (blacks are human but not as "evolved" as whites) lacks only one element. One can hardly tell why any modern Euro-American artist would choose to be motivated by African art, why one sees such art quoted everywhere.

De Zayas then remarks that Euro-American artists' kind of abstraction brings us closer to "our" feelings, as per Lawrence's admiring query and Stein's close-mouthed resistance (cited earlier as epigraphs). The more evolved naturalistic representations of Western art offer only "the reality of the outer world" (41). The price of white superiority and of evolutionary perfection is a modern loss of an inner world for which the "very primitive state" (39) offers solace and replacement. Some groundswell of need, below scientific rationalist worlds and inspired by black access to feeling, some voluntaristic devolution from a position of superiority—these are the strained explanations for African influence. It is clear that historical time creates pains that the postulation of timeless primitivism will solace.

Another notable analysis of the meaning of African art occurs in Stein's essay "Picasso" (1938). Stein names 1907 as "the negro period" in Picasso's art, but she resists its importance, attributing to him an essentially Spanish vision. She comments, damningly, that "African art [was] like the other influences which at one time or another diverted Picasso from the way of painting which was his" (*Picasso* 38, 47). Such art was not only a diversion but an unworthy one, caught in cultural stasis and immobility, as the universalizing singular insists: "The african is not primitive, he has a very ancient but a very narrow culture and there it remains" (*Autobiography* 257); this parallels de Zayas's conviction that "there is no evolution in Negro art" (36). Stein expends serious effort to explain away African sculpture both in itself and in its impact on Picasso. She thus sidesteps a very popular word and concept—the primitive—but in a scandalous manner, insisting that African art is civilized because its traditions were in fact created by Arabs.[32] This perverse point is a version of the nervy and nervous disparaging in which Stein engaged: as she said in *The Autobiography of Alice B. Toklas,* "negroes were not suffering from persecution they were suffering from nothingness" (257).[33]

Similarly, in *Vision and Design,* Roger Fry reprints his 1920 review of a show of "negro sculpture." After a stunning introduction about cultural relativism, showing Greco-Roman assumptions of superiority being "blown away," and after appreciative formalist praise of certain works, Fry recuperates superiority by the remark that "it is curious that a people who produced such great artists did not produce also a culture in our sense of the word" (103). The "negro" exhibits a "want of a conscious critical sense and the intellectual powers of comparison and classification" (103). A set of related oppositions has been put into play in these explanations—timelessness/evolution and primitive/civilization (or culture). Whiteness is made by claiming it is inside time—which is figured as historical, moving, ongoing—and by positioning Africa as timeless, static or nonevolved, and thus—a very charged word—primitive, part of a psychic space before real time and before intellect.[34] To put mind and Africa together, to reframe the issue of civilization, would offer important critiques of these notions.

Primitivism summarizes a contradictory set of assumptions and attitudes inflecting modernist practice; it is impossible to consider these fully here, but one might review some findings. Primitivism as an "ensemble of tropes" (in Marianna Torgovnick's words) makes a complex of evocations about a "Them" that is childlike, violent, mysterious, dark, irrational, lower, docile and yet resistant, taboo in their lust and yet natural in sexual matters (Torgovnick 8). In some modern works, positive primitivist tropes provide a simply irresistible mythology about these convenient Others. For whatever distressed Euro-American culture, blacks of all kinds (whether Africans, African Americans, persons, sculptures, rural sharecroppers, urban jazz musicians, and so forth) seemed to have the cure. This is precisely the mark of romanticism—hoping for salvation or creative massage at the hands of people designed to solace and service (Cooley 13–17). This interested encomium for (apparently) simple peoples, peasants, closeness to the land and to nature, folk sweetness or special wisdom could pass into fear-laden pejorative tropes of tribal mystery, preternatural strength or perception, the thicker, resistant nature represented by "the jungle," unusual sexual prowess, lurking rites, and so on. Nathan Huggins punctures all this in his critical discussion of the white vision of Harlem as primitive, romantic, and vitalist. Harlem offered "a means of soft rebellion for those who rejected the Babbittry and sterility of their lives," a rebellion conveniently involving only "a taxi trip to the exotic" (Huggins 91, 89).

According to Robert Coles and Diane Isaacs, "cultivating primitivism" offered "a spiritual and cultural alternative to modern technological society" (3–

4), especially tempting in a society that had just undergone the nausea-provoking violence of the First World War (although the infusion of African art and its influence did begin earlier, as did the seeking for primitivist alternatives to Western worldviews). Coles and Isaacs argue that, although innocent, the search for new values that went under the name of primitivism "made the pursuit an entirely healthy endeavor" when it was distinguished from "exoticism or sensationalism" (3–4), something more easily said than done, for these strands fuse and twine in the discursive bundle, as Torgovnick shows. A more sophisticated antimodernization thesis is central to the argument of the art historian Gill Perry. He writes that the "so-called 'primitive' subjects and techniques" visible in the visual arts in the early twentieth century made a serious critique of modernization (Harrison et al. 3). Perry discusses the ways in which "primitive" has at one and the same time been used "positively and pejoratively" in European discourses (Harrison et al. 5–6). This is a very useful insight; furthermore, these double attitudes were not necessarily separated in texts, arguments, and oeuvres but played out dialectically in a perpetual oscillation. Descriptive terms that are idealizing, and sometimes admiring (though never really respectful), can at the same time be disparaging and dismissive. If so-called primitives are, for one example, "libidinous" or "sexually free," the valence of these terms can extend from admiration into prurient voyeurism, from jealousy to disgust.

One of the central uses of the primitive is to manage contemporary gender issues, as both Hal Foster and Torgovnick make plain. Foster has shown how the use of the primitive is a "psycho-aesthetic move by which otherness was used to ward away others (women, death, [racialized figures])" (182). Primitivism, he argues, is a "fetishistic discourse" in which tokens of Otherness are used to substitute for loss and to mark loss; the loss he tracks is of patriarchal and Western hegemony. Correspondingly, in her searching study of the "rhetoric of control" and the "rhetoric of desire" in the uses, seductions, and projections of the primitive, Marianna Torgovnick focuses most acutely on how the regeneration of masculinity is at stake (245). Primitivist materials as compensatory for some wound to the West is a constant from de Zayas to contemporary comment.

As compensation for an imagined injury or lack, primitivist ideas can be taken to express an unspoken guilt for imperialist claims to the land, the livelihood, and even the lives of a variety of Othered peoples. Modernist primitivism is, then, both symptom and putative cure for the wounds of imperialism and related versions of appropriated labor and land, such as the American sharecropping system. It is a complex of ideas that veils these political and economic relations. This is why primitivism always denies history, real time, autonomous agency, maturity, and intellect to its native denizens. As an ideology, it erases tribal peoples as functioning adults, political agents, and serious artists who operate in historical circumstances in favor of infantilizing visions that preserve for Western civilization a role as capstone, for Euro-Americans their role as the dominant, civilized, and ever-so-helpful "race" (Price 56–67).[35] Tumbled together with timeless stasis and nonevolved peoples are negative notions of societies without culture and lacking "cultural 'progress,'"—notions visible in Stein and Fry.

It is clear that primitivist thinking will resist the notion that any civilization, tribal or urban, is a complex webbing of forces and that all participants in any civilization possess intellect and mind—in Jerome Rothenberg's dialectical aphorism, "Primitive means complex" (*Pre-Faces* 69). Indeed, primitivist thinking is a way of ascribing to one's own culture the beneficent term "civilization" and resisting the ascription of civilization elsewhere than one's own place. "On your shoulders now rests the burden of civilisation" means the affirmation of Nordic/Aryan superiority, a greatness coterminous with pure whiteness (Dixon 441).[36] Thus "Africa" is a token or trophy of this debate; to consider "Africa" as an ensemble involving intellection and analysis is a directed response that links civilization with all races. Hardly a small question to begin with, the analysis of uses of the primitive and the ownership of Africa and things African must account for the racial position of the user and the position constructed in the work. This material is a site of discursive conflict and of questions of ownership between writers of different races, despite the similarities of the images they use.

In Mina Loy's poem "To You" (1915–17), the term "nigger" has pride of place and is further accelerated with the phrases "hybrid-negro," "mask of unborn ebony," and "aboriginal."[37]

> The city
> Wedged between impulse and unfolding
> Bridged
> By diurnal splintering
> Of egos
> Round
> The aerial news-kiosk
> Where you
> Statically
> Hob-nob
> With a nigger
> And a deaf mute
> of introspection (89)

This work—crisp, cubist, and challenging, like much of Loy—is addressed to an artist (painter or writer), and suggests that to own up to one's cultural ambitions, one must own a piece of Africa.[38] The setting is urban but also mental—a space of consciousness in which some problem is being played out by a set of related actors. The problem is blockage, the compromise of an ability to write. The gestalt image of this paralysis is a "diurnal splintering / Of egos" that has divided someone into three parts: "you," "a nigger," and "a deaf mute / of introspection." These personae have various origins and are variously called into play.

> Plopping finger
> In Stephen's ink
> Made you[r] hybrid-negro
>
> A couple of manuscriptural erasures
> And here we have your deaf mute
> Beseech him (Loy 89; correction in Januzzi n.p.)

This is the heart of the poem. The "you" seems torn between being a writerly black color, hybrid by having a [white] finger in black ink, and being muted, turned speechless by [her/his] erasures. There is a stalemate here between creation and inhibition or erasure; as each tactic is tried, these figures (black person, deaf/speechless person) are alternatively called up, made present. "Stephen's ink" is a very layered image—a British brand-name, an allusion to Loy's first husband (the painter Stephen Haweis), and a suggestion of Stephen Dedalus, hero of Joyce's *Portrait of the Artist as a Young Man*. But what is most striking is the way that this blackness is, no matter the allusion, an image of creative or artistic power: ability, agency, textuality in a male name or figure.

The yearning for speech and creative expression must therefore address the "deaf mute," since erasures are the paralyzing element. Therefore, as the poem continues "Beseech him [the mute]," it suggests that erasure cannot or will not be absolute. Hence, the speaker has moved to a higher or more intense level of the problem of creative expression; again, the figure of blackness is the powerhouse of artistic venture.

> Lit cavities in the face of the city
> Open their glassy embrace to receive you
> In your mask of unborn ebony
> And the silence of your harangue (Loy 89)

The "you" has become less split; where once there were three separate personae, now they are gathering into one; this one is not marked by gender but by race. The increasing power of "you" is told by the image of a mask of ebony. The mask (or the ebony) is unborn, because the creativity of the "you" is still potential, preverbal. Similarly, muteness has grown troubled and qualified in a paradoxical phrase that describes a "harangue" just under the surface of "silence." This paradoxical image recalls the analysis, above, of the white fabrication of black semisilence. But the urban surface opens to a black mask in a welcoming gesture of cultural syncretism. Artistic ambition is authenticated by a black mask over a white face. Possessing a token of the deep creativity of Africa inside urban space completes this space. This mode is part of primitivist discourse, in which white civilization is enhanced and completed by tokens of primal force helping its creative production.

As the "you" comes into its creative own, it walks a tightrope above the city. In this new situation:

> shadows are yours for the taking
> Where the mono-rabble
> Plays the one-stringed banjo
> On the noise of its ragged heart[.] (Loy 90)

This is also an unusual and difficult set of phrases, but it certainly suggests that blackness (urban "shadows") can be appropriated from a rabble playing an African-American instrument that, unlike most banjos, has been limited: its *one* string parallels the "*mono*-rabble." Presumably the "you" has the more complex skills to hear and register the deep "aboriginal" sounds of the heart inside the city; these skills occur by the cosmopolitan fusion of a subjectivity in which African materials are owned to contribute to the new modernism. Virtually every mention of African-derived materials or persons is positive, an indicator of creative agency and force, and is used to mark intense poetic desire; but this is consistent with the enhancement of civilization by "primitive" forces.

It is notable that in many works of visual art, fiction, and poetry, African arts (especially masks) are taken out of the venue in which they would probably have been seen (an ethnographic museum or collection or a gallery) and recontextualized as part of the quotidian life of white characters. When one considers that museums were increasingly expressing a statist or national agenda, the artistic use of Africa may have offered a mechanism for protest of this form of bourgeois ownership, but the ownership of Africa in artworks is recuperated by the same gesture; for so long as Africa meant stasis and id frozen in ebony, it was a talisman enhancing white civilization.

The alternative would be a discourse in which Africa and civilization were affirmed in one breath. This occurs, to some degree, in the poem of Marianne Moore to which Pound addressed himself. In this work, mind and Africa are more closely fused than they are in most other Euro-American cultural sites discussed here. "Black Earth" (1918) is an assertive apologia for poetic vocation:

Openly, yes,
. . . .
I do these
things which I do, which please
no one but myself. (*Observations* 45)[39]

Moore has buttressed her examination of how doing poetry makes her feel with the largest land-based mammal—"Black earth preceded by a tendril" (*Observations* 47). She presents her/self (the speaker) as an elephant—thick skinned, multitextured, on guard, but with a proprioceptive proboscis. There are other images of physical pride, as metaphors for poetic pride and promise, including the jaunty, charming "the blemishes stand up and shout when the object / / in view was a / renaissance" (*Observations* 45). Moore sees her "I" as a fecund and productive site (parallel to the jungle and filled with active, assertive jungle animals) touched by "the patina of circumstance" or "unpreventable experience" (45). Indeed, this poem assumes that the black skin and the grasping (masculine?) trunk of the elephant offer a "poise" or alertness that will answer more feminine or retiring self-images.[40]

In this poem, the "indestructibility of matter"—represented by this pondering/ponderous black elephant—is also compared (in the coral-like branching of its trunk) to a "cortex," thereby evoking an image of mind.[41] The elephant in the jungle is a cure for a mind-body split. This trope proposes a positive incubation of one's own terms for seeing, unimpeded by claims made by others, even if these bring (so-called) "light." The speaker declares:

This elephant skin
which I inhabit, fibred over like the shell of
the cocoanut, this piece of black glass through which no light

can filter[.] (*Observations* 45)

Opacity and resistance (figured as black) are an important force for Moore's affirmation of her unique vision. After the interesting insistence on autonomy, Moore states: "Black / but beautiful, my back / is full of the history of power."[42] This image of blackness is an assertion of moral strength triumphant, a kind of Christian narrative of trials overcome; it may be the way that enslavement is acknowledged by Moore (*Observations* 46). One sees why Pound asked about her race. Moore has asserted beauty and power in blackness, recasting the sensual *Song of Songs* into a poetic manifesto. She has also done so in a poem, like her others, whose rhetorical complexity (even opacity) is a challenge to the mind of the reader. This poem makes Africa consistent with mind; and thus, despite the jungle materials, it is not a primitivizing work.

IIII

African-American writers also face Africa and the primitive as a discursive cluster; they have the complicated tasks of articulating a vision of that place and answering and debating a vision of Africa that has hegemonic power. The primitive is sometimes figured in these works as an idyllic "firstness." So Africa is Eden, a place where brown and black skin is natural, unmarked, undespised, where the bearer will not have to beat on the "leaden door" of racism (to cite Georgia Douglas Johnson) (Hughes and Bontemps 76). Langston Hughes's "Dream Variation" (1926)—

To fling my arms wide
In some place of the sun,
To whirl and to dance
Till the white day is done (Hughes and Bontemps 183)

—is a yearning for the place where to be black and expressive and joyous is comfortable, with an undercurrent of two politicized ideas: to have a "place in the sun" as an unpatronized people and to allegorize the end of white hegemony and its damaging claim that whiteness and civilization are coterminous. Sometimes the trope of Africa asserts a reality behind a (primitivizing) mythos to contest Africa's appropriation while appreciating its impact: "I know now," says Hughes in 1927's "In Africa," that "tom-toms [really] do beat / In village squares under the mango trees" (Hughes and Bontemps 196). The poem mentions a series of foreign places (Paris, Antwerp, Venice—and Africa) that Hughes, with his attitude "from Missouri," has seen with his own eyes and can attest to. Africa is not just a myth.

Helene Johnson's "Magalu" and Countee Cullen's "Heritage"—which begins, "What is Africa to me"—put the poet-speakers into Africa to resist or criticize the denatured qualities of Euro-American civilization, including Christianity. Johnson, with idealizing simplicity, asks the African: "Would you sell the colors of your sunset and the fragrance / Of your flowers, and the passionate wonder of your forest / For a creed that will not let you dance?" (Hughes and Bontemps 263). Cullen's poem offers a rich argument about the urgent and compelling emotions that the visionary fantasy of Africa sets going in him. He tries to resist these emotions—and the "outlandish, heathen gods" of polytheistic religion—in favor of Christianity. But, with Marvellian resonance, he writes that he will

> ... always hear,
> Though I cram against my ear
> Both my thumbs, and keep them there
> Great drums throbbing through the air[.] (*My Soul's* 104–5)

He desires that his God be black, he feels an urgent dance rhythm, and, in the fierce last lines whose couplet rhyme is a measure of the control that the poem has elaborated, declares: "Not yet has my heart or head / In the least way realized / They and I are civilized" (*My Soul's* 108). Of course, fusing Marvellian diction with a statement about African glory makes the double claim of civilization (via elegant poetic allusion) and ownership of that evocative site. Given the debates that made whiteness and civilization coterminous, Cullen's use of the word "civilized" (not to speak of its rhyme "realized"—intellection at work) is layered with a multipointed irony—self-ironizing a denatured self and ironizing the claims that civilization should exclude the colored races.

African-American writers have a double position and can thus play with the binary primitive versus civilization or inhabit a fusion of primitive and civilization. The primitive can also be as talented and culturally rich as the civilized but, in trickster terms, play with its own apparent innocence of its cultural resources. This is proposed by Fenton Johnson's "The Banjo Player" (1914–16), which begins: "There is music in me, the music of a peasant people." The poem ends aswirl in disingenuous ironies: "Last night a woman called me a troubadour. / What is a troubadour?" (Hughes and Bontemps 86). It is also possible that white/light mentors, or the external pressure of hegemonic cultural ideology about "Africa," can compel black writers into primitivizing; Gwendolyn Bennett's poem "Advice" (1927) discusses this situation.

> You were a sophist,
> Pale and quite remote,
> As you bade me
> Write poems—
> Brown poems
> Of dark words
> And prehistoric rhythms . . .
> Your pallor stifled my poesy (Cullen, *Caroling* 156)

In general, "primitive" and "Africa" are interpreted somewhat differently in the two racial communities. In many poems by African Americans, Africa and a claim of primitive joy mean a kind of inner freedom, a self-expression untempered by white scrutiny and white judgment, or a flare of freedom and beauty representing an unenslaved past and bypassing racial prejudice and pain. Cullen's poem on a waiter ends:

> Sheer through his acquiescent mask
> Of bland gentility,
> The jungle flames like a copper cask
> Set where the sun strikes free[.] (*My Soul's* 85)

The eleven poems in the final section of Hughes's first book, *The Weary Blues* (1926), collected under the rubric "Our Land," turn and return to the repressive coldness of the white world that "tortures" a variety of black people; the several "primitive tom-toms" are a straining reminder of black authenticity and autonomy.

Furthermore, many poems by African Americans try to reclaim, or trope on, the complicated word "civilization." Civilization is a social and spiritual burden (and the jungle is a free space) because civilization has placed exorbitant, unforgiving demands on African Americans; it is a trope for enslavement, supremacist, or imperialist claims. Fenton Johnson explains the interest of "resting" in these terms: "I am tired of work; I am tired of building up somebody else's civilization" (Hughes and Bontemps 88). Insofar as drinking, dancing, and gambling can make up for the pain of growing up to "find that you are colored," as Johnson says, such activities may appear full of "primitive" license but may have other causes than the essential libido so frequently touted for its explanatory value. Claude McKay's sonnet "America" limns as a jungle predator the vigorous new country (to which he immigrated from Jamaica):

> Although she feeds me bread of bitterness,
> And sinks into my throat her tiger's tooth,
> Stealing my breath of life, I will confess
> I love this cultured hell that tests my youth! (Hughes and Bontemps 100)

In "Lament for Dark Peoples" (1926), Langston Hughes proposes the way "civilization" depends on circuses or zoos of Others:

> Now they've caged me
> In the circus of civilization.
> Now I herd with the many—
> Caged in the circus of civilization. (*Weary* 100)

Lillian Byrnes has a poem from 1929 in which she attempts, pushing against an intractable cliché, to make "the 'Great Blond Beast'" (that is, an uncivilized, lascivious predator) from a man of Nordic race, a move performed to counter or match the "black beast" of America's lurid racial melodrama (Honey 85). In his poem "Dust," Waring Cuney offers "Ozymandias"-like reflections about "the skill / With which you ["proud ones"—whites] play this game—Civilization"; pointedly, "The Coliseum tells a story / The Woolworth Building may repeat"—that is, of the downfall of this civilization (Cullen, *Caroling* 211). The critique by African-American writers of the notions, and location, of the "civilized" is one response to Euro-American ownership of Africa.

Thus, for many African-American poets, "primitivism" and the claim to know the real Africa mean representing a place and a time where whites cannot touch or bother one, where one can resist white culture. For many Euro-American poets, on the other hand, "primitive" seems to mean a site in which one can capture and touch the deepest spirit of blacks by owning talismanic bits of Africa (masks and tribal art) or owning up to the "black" core of libido in oneself. For African Americans, Africa is a preimperialist, preenslavement affirmation of a time and place "really" there; for Euro-Americans, Africa proposes a cure for (or vacation from) the pain, or even recognition, of their political and economic masteries.

Notes

1. A note on the use of "white" and "black": at a transitional time with regard to race, one wants in utopian fashion to resist these categories, but they have tremendous historical meaning, and such a study must use them, if under suspicion. That is, thinking of race as biological is ridiculous; knowing that it is a historical and material reality with myriad effects is central.

2. A first letter to Moore in 1918 shows Pound facing an accomplished woman writer provokingly unknown to him (Pound 141). In a disarming response to her work, he constructs a welcoming and yet controlling demeanor. He incorporates her in his networks of gossip and practice, carefully indicating that his queries are a mark of his interest and respect; he had done the same, he mentions, to Eliot and Yeats without impeding their friendships. Yet he also warns her about using a distinctive word ("pneumatic") that Eliot had used previously (in "Whispers of Immortality"). The remark is not atypical of what poets notice, sometimes with the same thin-skinned exaggeration, about each other's work. It can be a double-edged observation, implying ownership of words, order of access or originality, enforcement of community norms, and possible gender interests about preserving priority.

3. Note that the writers with whom I shall be concerned were virtually all transatlantic, operating culturally on both sides of the Atlantic, and, therefore, possibly susceptible to both those historical formations.

4. This passage is also notable for the use of (lowercase) African nationalities as synonyms for "Negro" or "colored"—ennobling choices, perhaps, given the vocabulary of other Euro-American poets. In Stevens's poetry and letters, "Negro," "negroe," "black," "coon," "darkies," "blackest of pickanines [sic]," "nigger," "Sambo," "dusky." Appearing in Williams's poetry and prose are: "dusky," "African," "negro," "colored," "black-man," "blackboy," "nigger," "wild nigger wench," "negress." In her poetry and a novel, Loy uses "nigger," "colored," "negro," "black," "negress."

5. Titles such as Robert Shufeldt, *The Negro: A Menace to American Civilization* (1907), Madison Grant, *The Passage of the Great Race* (1916), and Lothrop Stoddard, *The Rising Tide of Color against White World-Supremacy* (1920), should give the flavor of this polemic.

6. This pun on "Moor" is authorized by Moore herself, for in her early work Moore sometimes identifies as, or with, people of dark skin, as is seen in a discussion of "Black Earth," also known as "Melancthon," the poem to which Pound has referred. Moors appear in her poem "Sun!" (1916), a work of the transcendence of limits—of gender and race—by the appropriation of the traditional North African enemy of European hegemony as the sign for a poetics. The "Sun!" is imaged like an Arab prince, rich in exoticism and alterity and described by the use of Moore's own birthstone, the topaz. The "Sun!" fuses all binaries and "internecine fighters" in its "device / of Moorish gorgeousness." Moore apostrophizes the sun: "You are not male nor female, but a plan / Deep set within the heart of man"; this plan creates a space for visual and textual splendor (Arab design is based on calligraphy) that plays between genders and is pointedly given her own name: "Moorish gorgeousness" (*Contemporary Verse* 7). This name of a transcendent third way cuts above fixed gender but also assimilates itself to a non-European male figure as a sign of its fruitful and imaginative powers.

7. The political ironies were not lost on the African-American community. Consider Roscoe Jameson's "Negro Soldiers," published in *The Crisis* in 1917: "These truly are the Brave, / These men who cast aside / Old memories to walk the blood-stained pave / Of Sacrifice, joining the solemn tide / that moves away, to suffer and to die / For Freedom—when their own is yet denied!" (Locke, *New Negro* 39). The position on war service is consistent with the "Close Ranks" editorial of Du Bois in the July 1918 issue of *The Crisis*.

8. My word "volatility" parallels a finding of Marianne DeKoven; writing on Stein and Conrad, she says: "Racial otherness . . . functions chaotically in these texts" (DeKoven 68).

9. No black writers were noted in Stevens's letters, as Richardson's biography of Stevens records, until 1952. The one is a compromising allusion to Gwendolyn Brooks: "I know you don't like to hear people call a lady a coon, but who is it?" asked Stevens on noticing Brooks in a photograph of the former judges of the National Book Award (Richardson, *Later Years* 388). This calculated scene as reported in the biography also involves a banal Irish joke and discussion of the word "womb"—"I can't even pronounce the filthy thing"—resulting in a clean sweep of aggressively

offensive behavior by Stevens during the 1952 National Book Award committee on which he served.

10. To claim that they preempt African-American speech by their invention of it brings me close to Michael North's thesis. In *The Dialect of Modernism,* North proposes the "contradiction of racial cross-identification and racial hatred" (161) as a motivation for white appropriations of a black sound. I am attempting to show two strategies, separating the paradoxes to which North points, and to link them, at least in general, to locatable national interests and specific historical periods. We are both part of a project to interpret modernism in its social filiations.

11. This exculpation is not useful analytically, for it misunderstands how ideology inflects and creates subjectivity; Stevens's attitudes are neither casual nor compelled by external pressure.

12. For white to play black, the ethical and cultural issues of appropriation are enormous, although not necessarily noticed by the poets. To depict oneself as black might well be seen as a perverse expression of even more mastery, not more humility—or humanity. One might take this identification as attempting, in one's own poetic persona, to sweeten the guilt of rampant white supremacy, an important discourse in the early part of the twentieth century. Furthermore, the pain and social seriousness of black passing are well documented in African-American literature, not the least in poems by Countee Cullen and in novels by Nella Larsen and James Weldon Johnson. This chapter was completed before Susan Gubar's live study of play-passing, *Racechanges,* appeared in 1997.

13. Sambo was also a signature of choice for his letters to Elsie (Stevens, *Letters* 199). In discussing this material, Joan Richardson does not analyze the racial narrative at work (*Early Years* 308–11). This kind of fantasy could also have a class twist, as another imagined encounter between a servant and Elsie, detailed later, shows (Stevens, *Letters* 113).

14. Crediting Joan Richardson's interpretation of this poem as not only one of the great French symbolist poems in English (i.e., poésie pure, without referent) but also as commemorating the conception of Stevens's only daughter (with an absolute referent), the importance of the Sambo figure as joyous potency certainly demands comment.

15. Stevens traveled to Florida on business from 1916 on; his descriptions in letters of Palm Beach and Miami are admiring.

16. To gloss watermelon as a racialized image, one that must, in the poet's argument, be kept racialized, see a dreamily weird section of Carl Sandburg's "Potato Blossom Songs and Jigs" (1918): "Does a famous poet eat watermelon? / Excuse me, ask me something easy. / I have seen farmhands with their faces in fried catfish on a Monday morning. / And the Japanese, two-legged like us, / The Japanese bring slices of watermelon into pictures. / The black seeds make oval polka dots on the pink meat. // Why do I always think of niggers and buck-and-wing dancing whenever I see watermelon?" (96–97).

17. Marianne Moore noticed Stevens's African Americans in her review of *Harmonium,* "Well Moused, Lion" (1924). She sees the depictions in "Hymn from a Watermelon Pavilion" and in "Contents of a Cab" as realistic, offered with "accurate gusto" (*Prose* 93). This comment is an example of what Kenneth Warren argued:

"what emerges [in the early part of this century] is an inadvertent alliance between Northern realism and Southern romance in an assault on the political idealism of the New England tradition" (15). Because Moore was somewhat less invested in racial stereotypes than Stevens, and could criticize Vachel Lindsay fiercely, one gets a sense of what was "realistic" comment by whites in the 1920s, the Gershwin "plenty of nothin'" jauntiness ascribed to blacks.

18. Other Harlem Renaissance poems about the Great Migration would include the ironic "'Carry Me Back to Old Virginny'," by E. E. Levinger (Honey 71). By these comparisons, I do not mean to shame Stevens (by his majority and/or interpretations) nor Newsome (by her minority—in both senses of the word—and/or interpretations); I mean to suggest that representations of material made by well-known poets need to be qualified and contextualized by alternative or parallel representations by other practicing poets. This strategy depends on study of less-known texts and on setting texts in new dialogic relations.

19. Note Toni Morrison's exemplary analysis of a Hemingway work, in which she shows the syntactic and rhetorical contortions Hemingway produces to prevent his black, male character from being depicted as speaking (*Playing* 70–91).

20. The fact that this bird stands at the core of a "Chinese" poem compels me to note, only in passing, that African Americans are not the only race treated at length in Euro-American modernist poetries. The Chinese play a very important role as well—as works by Pound, Stevens, Lindsay, William Rose Benét, Djuna Barnes, Moore, Williams, Toomer, and others testify. Sometimes, as in the Stevens play *Three Travelers Watch a Sunrise*, the discussion occurs in relation to the three "races"—yellow and black as seen by white. The complicated love-hate relations of race are compounded by whites being able to play off stereotypes of *two* other races in relation to each other and to play both sides of the street in their sympathy and contempt for both. The epigram for this enterprise could be Pound's blackface jibe on his then-forthcoming book *Guide to Kulchur,* and his questioning of T. S. Eliot's potential response "when I brings in deh Chinas and blackmen in a bukk about Kulchur" (Pound, *Letters* 288).

21. In an analysis of this poem, Daniel R. Schwarz also pursues the blackbird's connotation of desire, sexuality, and the black phallus; this parallels certain of my findings (Schwarz 53).

22. The poem says a "black figure"; the rural site of the poem and its consistency with others of this type make me interpret this as a "black person" rather than the weaker "[white] person [who is] dark because he walks at night."

23. This poem was published in the first edition of *Harmonium* but excluded, along with "Exposition of the Contents of a Cab" and "Architecture," in the collection's 1930 edition.

24. To be exact: once, one whispers (words unwritten) to a Chinese person; another time, one "makes a sound to attract their attention." A third time, an African American picks up a discarded instrument and strums a sound. However, there is no voice: they appear only in stage directions (*Opus* 140, 128, 143). In contrast, Stevens has no difficulty imagining what the characters he designates as Chinese would say.

25. An account of a production in 1979 explains that the problem of the voiceless blacks was solved by treating "these visible stagehands as *mo*, prop men on the Chinese stage who dress in black to be 'invisible' but available." In the production, they dressed in monk's cowls, with faces invisible (Evans 30). This ingenious solution, well in keeping with the Orientalizing mode, still betrays the unassimilable aspect of the play, by protecting us from Stevens's silencing of "Negroes."

26. In the letter to Monroe (*Letters* 194), Stevens notes that Monroe and the prize donor both resisted the actual stage presence of the hanging body; he says he has revised some of the stage directions; but finally, as Holly Stevens notes, "the hanging body remained in the play as published" (*Letters* 194).

27. In 1919, the NAACP published *Thirty Years of Lynching in the United States, 1889–1918*, which showed that over 2,000 African Americans were lynched between 1885 and 1910 (Thorpe xxiii).

28. One must note the ending of Apollinaire's "Zone" (1914) with the proposition: "You've had enough of living in the Greek and Roman past." In the Christian one, the end nonetheless evinces ambivalence to the desirability of other pasts: "You walk toward Auteuil you want to go home on foot / To sleep among fetishes from Oceania and Guinea which put / Christ in another form with other inspirations / They are inferior Christs of dark aspirations" (Rothenberg and Joris 124).

29. See Torgovnick for an expanded discussion of the use of African art in this novel and of the primitive in Lawrence (Torgovnick 159–73).

30. Charles Sheeler took the photographs in the 1918 portfolio *African Negro Sculpture* (Tashjian 109).

31. "Art is an effect which has for cause the conditional state of the mental organs which produce it"; "an ethnological group can exist to-day whose brain is in a very primitive state and which, therefore, produce a very primitive art" (de Zayas 39). The brains of Africans "can be considered as being in the first state of the evolution of the brain of man" (40).

32. "After all one must never forget that African sculpture is not naive, not at all, it is an art that is very very conventional, based upon tradition and its tradition is a tradition derived from Arab culture. The Arabs created both civilisation and culture for the negroes and therefore African art which was naive and exotic for Matisse was for Picasso, a Spaniard, a thing that was natural, direct and civilised" (Stein *Picasso* 52). Presumably because of the Arab influence in Spain, that is. Stein's leap over Africa by assigning its culture to Arab influences totally decivilizes that continent.

33. Aldon Lynn Nielsen has foregrounded this remark as a key expression of a central Euro-American attitude, an existential and ontological erasure of Negro reality into a black hole of white fear (*Reading Race* 1–28).

34. Another structure is to show white as figure and black as ground to retain a binary relationship. Elinor Wylie's "Incantation" asserts, in quick dimeter, a Nordic superiority to match and triumph over blackness. White stands out, bodies forth, gives hope; black is magnetic suction into nullity or, even, a spoiler: "A white well / In a black cave; / A bright shell / In a dark wave. // A white rose / Black brambles hood; / Smooth

bright snows / In a dark wood" (39-40). Similarly working with this mine of a black-white binary, Wylie's sonnet "August," beginning "Why should this Negro insolently stride" (9), passes through the heat, copper, jungle, and "captive leopard" palette to regret that there are no white, cool, northern flowers "plucked . . . by [the] fair-haired" in his wheelbarrow, a question about a month (August)—but one with a racialized import. In Wylie's poems, then, white wants hegemony.

35. Consider an ironic passage in F. Scott Fitzgerald: "It's up to us who are the dominant race to watch out or these other races will have control of things. . . . This idea is that we're Nordics . . . and we've produced all the things that go to make civilization—oh, science and art and all that. Do you see?" (14). Tom Buchanan in *The Great Gatsby* (1925) is paraphrasing an imaginary book by "Goddard" that is based on an actual book, *The Rising Tide of Color against White World-Supremacy* (1920), by Lothrop Stoddard. My thanks to Cyraina Johnson-Rouillier for the Gatsby citation. Walter Benn Michaels also identifies the Stoddard materials (193-202).

36. "For white civilization is to-day coterminous with the white race. . . . If white civilization goes down, the white race is irretrievably ruined. It will be swamped by the triumphant colored races" (Stoddard 303).

37. Nor is Loy the only modern poet prominently to use the word "nigger"; my discussion of Stevens's "Like Decorations in a Nigger Cemetery" occurs in another chapter from my book on modern poetry.

38. This is a poem whose very context is in debate. It may be the introductory or dedicatory poem to Loy's 1917 long poem *Songs to Joannes* (themselves transformed to *Love Songs* [1923]). My use in this chapter will pass over this debate and treat the poem in isolation. See Marisa Januzzi's Ph.D. dissertation, "Mina Loy and the Matter of Modernist Poetics."

39. See Moore, *Observations*, 45-47. The poem was first published in *The Egoist* 4 (April 1918): 55-6; later titled "Melancthon," it was published in the 1935 *Selected Poems* and again in the 1951 *Collected Poems* but excluded from the 1967 *Complete Poems of Moore*. This work is also discussed by Cristanne Miller, an analysis that I had not read when I first prepared this chapter.

40. This poem is, like many of Moore's meditations, difficult, even obscure. I take the assertion "I see / and I hear, unlike the / wandlike body of which one hears so much, which was made / to see and not to see; to hear and not to hear" as a way of describing a new sensibility not compromised by fickle, feminine demands for politeness and for the conciliatory—and proud—a sensibility pleased by "the beautiful element of unreason" (in the final line) that one produces in poems.

41. That white should mean mind, that black should mean body is a pattern that goes coursing through any number of works. Bonnie Costello has been one discussant of Moore's poem. In *Marianne Moore: Imaginary Possessions,* she reads it within the context of poems emblematic of the poetic vocation as concerned with the complex ties between body and spirit; she reads blackness as either an "emblem of evil" or a positive "obscurity" (60). Cristanne Miller's discussion comes in a notable chapter on race in Moore's oeuvre that analyzes her social attitudes in her poems about racialized

subjects and about commitments—an attempt to reject racism. Miller also argues that works by Moore that create such a dialogue between body, soul, and experience in a black body override mind-body splits with attention to interdependencies of material and spiritual being (128–66).

42. Let me repeat Christopher L. Miller's manner of citing this famous line: "Negra sed [*sic*] formosa sum" (23).

Works Cited

Boskin, Joseph. *Sambo: The Rise and Demise of an American Jester.* New York: Oxford University Press, 1986.

Brodhead, Richard H. "Regionalism and the Upper Class." In Dimock and Gilmore, *Rethinking Class,* 150–74.

Coles, Robert A., and Diane Isaacs. "Primitivism as a Therapeutic Pursuit: Notes toward a Reassessment of Harlem Renaissance Literature." In Singh, Shiver, and Brodwin, *Harlem Renaissance,* 3–12.

Cooley, John. "White Writers and the Harlem Renaissance." In Singh, Shiver, and Brodwin, *Harlem Renaissance,* 13–22.

Costello, Bonnie. *Marianne Moore: Imaginary Possessions.* Cambridge, Mass.: Harvard University Press, 1981.

Cullen, Countee. *My Soul's High Song: The Collected Writings of Countee Cullen, Voice of the Harlem Renaissance.* Ed. Gerald Early. New York: Doubleday, 1989.

Cullen, Countee, ed. *Caroling Dusk: An Anthology of Verse by Negro Poets.* 1927. Rpt., New York: Harper and Row, 1968.

cummings, e. e. *Poems, 1923–1954.* New York: Harcourt, Brace and World, 1954.

DeKoven, Marianne. *Rich and Strange: Gender, History, Modernism.* Princeton, N.J.: Princeton University Press, 1991.

de Zayas, Marius. *African Negro Art: Its Influence on Modern Art.* New York: Modern Gallery, 1916.

Dijkstra, Bram. *Idols of Perversity: Fantasies of Feminine Evil in Fin-de-Siècle Culture.* New York: Oxford University Press, 1986.

Dimock, Wai Chee, and Michael T. Gilmore, eds. *Rethinking Class: Literary Studies and Social Formations.* New York: Columbia University Press, 1994.

Dixon, Thomas, Jr. *The Leopard's Spots: A Romance of the White Man's Burden, 1865–1900.* New York: Doubleday, Page, 1903.

Du Bois, W. E. B. *The Souls of Black Folk* (1903). In *Three Negro Classics.* Ed. John Hope Franklin. New York: Avon Books, 1965. 207–389.

DuPlessis, Rachel Blau. *The Pink Guitar: Writing as Feminist Practice.* New York: Routledge, 1990.

———. "RE: Man Ray." *Sulfur* 26 (1990): 204–12.

Evans, Robley. "Three Travelers Watch a Sunrise." *Wallace Stevens Journal* 4.1–2 (Spring 1982): 28–31.

Fishkin, Shelley Fisher. "Interrogating 'Whiteness,' Complicating 'Blackness': Remapping American Culture." In *Criticism and the Color Line: Desegregating American Literary Studies*. Ed. Henry Wonham. New Brunswick, N.J.: Rutgers University Press, 1996. 251–90.

Fitzgerald, F. Scott. *The Great Gatsby*. 1925. Rpt., Cambridge: Cambridge University Press, 1991.

Foster, Hal. "The 'Primitive' Unconscious of Modern Art; or, White Skin, Black Masks." In *Recodings: Art, Spectacle, Cultural Politics*. Seattle: Bay Press, 1985. 181–210.

Fredrickson, George M. *The Black Image in the White Mind: The Debate on Afro-American Character and Destiny, 1817–1914*. New York: Harper and Row, 1971.

Fry, Roger. *Vision and Design*. London: Chatto and Windus, 1920.

Gates, Henry Louis, Jr., ed. *"Race," Writing, and Difference*. Chicago: University of Chicago Press, 1986.

Gubar, Susan. *Racechanges: White Skin, Black Face in American Culture*. New York: Oxford University Press, 1997.

Harrison, Charles, Francis Frascina, and Gill Perry. *Primitivism, Cubism, Abstraction: The Early Twentieth Century*. New Haven, Conn.: Yale University Press, 1993.

Honey, Maureen, ed. *Shadowed Dreams: Women's Poetry of the Harlem Renaissance*. New Brunswick, N.J.: Rutgers University Press, 1989.

Huggins, Nathan Irvin. *Harlem Renaissance*. New York: Oxford University Press, 1971.

Hughes, Langston. *Fine Clothes to the Jew*. New York: Alfred A. Knopf, 1927.

———. *The Weary Blues*. New York: Alfred A. Knopf, 1926.

Hughes, Langston, and Arna Bontemps, eds. *The Poetry of the Negro, 1746–1970*. Rev. ed. Garden City, N.Y.: Doubleday, 1970.

Januzzi, Marisa. "Mina Loy and the Matter of Modernist Poetics." Ph.D. dissertation, Columbia University, 1995.

Lawrence, D. H. *The Complete Poems of D. H. Lawrence*. Ed. Vivian de Sola Pinto and F. Warren Roberts. New York: Viking, 1971.

———. *Lady Chatterley's Lover*. 1928. Ed. Ronald Friedland. New York: Bantam, 1983.

———. *Selected Literary Criticism*. Ed. Anthony Beal. New York: Viking, 1956.

———. *Women in Love*. 1920. Rpt., London: Martin Secker, 1930.

Levy, Anita. *Other Women: The Writing of Class, Race, and Gender, 1832–1898*. Princeton, N.J.: Princeton University Press, 1990.

Locke, Alain. *The Negro in Art: A Pictorial Record of the Negro Artist and of the Negro Theme in Art*. 1940. Rpt., New York: Hacker Art Books, 1968.

Locke, Alain, ed. *The New Negro: An Interpretation*. New York: Albert and Charles Boni, 1925.

Loy, Mina. *The Last Lunar Baedeker*. Ed. Roger L. Conover. Highlands, N.C.: Jargon Society, 1982.

Michaels, Walter Benn. "The Souls of White Folk." In Scarry, *Literature and the Body*, 185–209.

Miller, Christopher L. *Blank Darkness: Africanist Discourse in French.* Chicago: University of Chicago Press, 1985.

Miller, Cristanne. *Questions of Authority: The Example of Marianne Moore.* Cambridge, Mass.: Harvard University Press, 1995.

Moore, Marianne. *The Complete Prose of Marianne More.* Ed. Patricia C. Willis. New York: Viking, 1986.

———. *Observations.* New York: Dial Press, 1924.

———. "Sun!" *Contemporary Verse* 1.6 (1 January 1916): 6.

Morrison, Toni. *Playing in the Dark: Whiteness and the Literary Imagination.* Cambridge, Mass.: Harvard University Press, 1992.

———. "Unspeakable Things Unspoken: The Afro-American Presence in American Literature." *Michigan Quarterly Review* 28.1 (January 1989): 1–34.

Newby, I. A. *Jim Crow's Defense: Anti-Negro Thought in America, 1900–1930.* Baton Rouge: Louisiana State University Press, 1965.

Nielsen, Aldon Lynn. *Reading Race: White American Poets and the Racial Discourse in the Twentieth Century.* Athens: University of Georgia Press, 1988.

———. *Writing between the Lines: Race and Intertextuality.* Athens: University of Georgia Press, 1994.

North, Michael. *The Dialect of Modernism: Race, Language, and Twentieth-Century Literature.* New York: Oxford University Press, 1994.

Pound, Ezra. *The Letters of Ezra Pound, 1907–1941.* Ed. D. D. Paige. New York: Harcourt, Brace and World, 1950.

Price, Sally. *Primitive Art in Civilized Places.* Chicago: University of Chicago Press, 1989.

Quarles, Benjamin. *Black Mosaic: Essays in Afro-American History and Historiography.* Amherst: University of Massachusetts Press, 1988.

Richardson, Joan. *Wallace Stevens—A Biography: The Early Years, 1879–1923.* New York: William Morrow, 1986.

———. *Wallace Stevens—A Biography: The Later Years, 1923–1955.* New York: William Morrow, 1988.

Rothenberg, Jerome. *Pre-Faces and Other Writings.* New York: New Directions, 1981.

Rothenberg, Jerome, and Pierre Joris, eds. *Poems for the Millennium.* Vol. 1: *From Fin-de-Siècle to Negritude.* Berkeley: University of California Press, 1995.

Said, Edward. *Culture and Imperialism.* New York: Alfred A. Knopf, 1993.

Sandburg, Carl. *The Complete Poems of Carl Sandburg.* Rev. ed. New York: Harcourt Brace Jovanovich, 1970.

Scarry, Elaine, ed. *Literature and the Body: Essays on Populations and Persons.* Baltimore, Md.: Johns Hopkins University Press, 1988.

Schwarz, Daniel R. *Narrative and Representation in the Poetry of Wallace Stevens.* New York: St. Martin's Press, 1993.

Scott, Bonnie Kime, ed. *The Gender of Modernism: A Critical Anthology.* Bloomington: Indiana University Press, 1990.

Singh, Amritjit, William S. Shiver, and Stanley Brodwin, eds. *The Harlem Renaissance: Revaluations.* New York: Garland Publishing, 1989.

Stein, Gertrude. *The Autobiography of Alice B. Toklas.* 1933. Rpt., Harmondsworth, U.K.: Penguin, 1983.

———. *Geography and Plays.* Ed. Cyrena N. Pondrom. Madison: University of Wisconsin Press, 1993.

———. "Lifting Belly." In *The Yale Gertrude Stein.* Ed. Richard Kostelanetz. New Haven, Conn.: Yale University Press, 1980. 4–54.

———. *Picasso: The Complete Writings.* Ed. Edward Burns. Boston: Beacon Press, 1970.

———. *Useful Knowledge.* 1928. Rpt., Barrytown, N.Y.: Station Hill Press, 1988.

Stevens, Wallace. *The Collected Poems of Wallace Stevens.* New York: Alfred A. Knopf, 1957.

———. *Letters of Wallace Stevens.* Ed. Holly Stevens. New York: Alfred A. Knopf, 1966.

———. *Opus Posthumous.* Ed. Samuel French Morse. New York: Alfred A. Knopf, 1957.

Stoddard, Lothrop. *The Rising Tide of Color against White World-Supremacy.* New York: Charles Scribner's Sons, 1920.

Sundquist, Eric J. *To Wake the Nations: Race in the Making of American Literature.* Cambridge, Mass.: Belknap Press, 1993.

Tashjian, Dickran. *William Carlos Williams and the American Scene, 1920–1940.* New York: Whitney Museum, and Berkeley: University of California Press, 1978.

Thorpe, Earl E. "Introduction." In *the Negro in American History.* Vol. 2: *A Taste of Freedom, 1854–1927.* Chicago: Encyclopedia Britannica, 1969. ix–xxviii.

Torgovnick, Marianna. *Gone Primitive: Savage Intellects, Modern Lives.* Chicago: University of Chicago Press, 1990.

Van Vechten, Carl. *Nigger Heaven.* 1926. Rpt., Urbana: University of Illinois Press, 2000.

Wade, Wyn Craig. *The Fiery Cross: The Ku Klux Klan in America.* New York: Simon and Schuster, 1987.

Warren, Kenneth. *Black and White Strangers: Race and American Literary Realism.* Chicago: University of Chicago Press, 1993.

Washington, Booker T. *Up from Slavery* (1901). In *Three Negro Classics.* Ed. John Hope Franklin. New York: Avon Books, 1965. 23–205.

Williams, William Carlos. *The Autobiography of William Carlos Williams.* 1951. Rpt., New York: New Directions, 1967.

———. *The Collected Poems of William Carlos Williams.* Vol. 1: *1909–1939.* Ed. A. Walton Litz and Christopher MacGowan. New York: New Directions, 1986.

———. *In the American Grain.* 1925. Rpt., New York: New Directions, 1956.

Woodward, C. Vann. *The Strange Career of Jim Crow.* New York: Oxford University Press, 1957.

Wylie, Elinor. *Nets to Catch the Wind.* New York: Alfred A. Knopf, 1928.

3

W. S. Braithwaite vs. Harriet Monroe: The Heavyweight Poetry Championship, 1917

Lorenzo Thomas

> Tradition, however grand and old, ceases to be of use the
> moment its walls are strong enough to break a butterfly's wing,
> or keep a fairy immured.
> —Harriet Monroe, "Tradition"

> The Negro race must come to a consciousness of itself before it
> can produce great literature. The civilization of a people is
> reflected in its literature.
> —William H. Ferris, *The African Abroad*

Cultural inventories are usually excited manifestos or jeremiads. What is interesting and instructive is to compare such pronouncements from various decades. In that way, we can chart the movement of the glacier.

The United States has been enjoying a poetry renaissance of a sort. The "poetry slam," an event where drunken audiences hoot down sensitive poems about dying grandmothers or inevitable divorces and bestow $20 prizes on scatological doggerel, is sweeping the nation. It is an amusement that seems to have unsealed a gold mine for saloon keepers too sophisticated for "Hot Buns" contests; recently, it has been possible to find at least three such events every week at different venues—even in a city like Houston. Perhaps, for a new generation, the poetry slam is the equivalent of the beatnik coffeehouse scene; perhaps not.

If the Beat Generation of the 1950s appeared to abandon all bourgeois values, it is clear—at least from hindsight—that they took their poetry seriously. However, the present situation does not seem much like even earlier times. At the turn of the century, while some popular journalists bemoaned American poetry's "inadequacy . . . to sustain a large and vigorous modern national life," the poets themselves were plotting an artistic revolution that would change the voice of poetry and the terms of its popular reception. In Boston, the African-American poet and critic William Stanley Braithwaite (1873–1962) emerged as the nation's most visible advocate of the new poetry. Through his column in the Boston *Evening Transcript,* he was able to launch the careers of Robert Frost and other major figures. For Braithwaite, the critic's job was making modern literature accessible to readers. Though many of his mainstream readers were unaware of his race, Braithwaite also exerted an enormous influence, through the NAACP's journal *The Crisis* and other publications, on African-American literary developments that would culminate in the Harlem Renaissance. Some recent reevaluations of Braithwaite—in particular, excellent essays by Kenny J. Williams and Craig S. Abbott—have attempted to avoid the political biases of earlier commentators, but Jean Wagner's severe and egregiously inaccurate dismissal of Braithwaite in *Black Poets of the United States* (1973) continues to mislead scholars. Contrary to Wagner's often repeated claim, there is no evidence at all that Braithwaite indulged the slightest ambivalence concerning his racial identity. Nevertheless, W. S. Braithwaite has been undeservedly neglected by critics, and it is clear that understanding his unique accomplishments requires a clear-sighted investigation of the production of poetry in the half-century 1880–1930.

In 1991, Dana Gioia was bemoaning the current state of poetic affairs in the pages of *The Atlantic.* "Outside the classroom—where society demands that the two groups interact," wrote Gioia, "poets and the common reader are no longer on speaking terms" (100). Gioia longed for the popularity that poets apparently enjoyed in the nineteenth century, when Longfellow and his peers produced volumes that were best-sellers; and, apparently, Gioia was unaware of such vital interactions as the poetry slam. Yet even the depressing combination of those nightclub travesties and the closed-circuit boredom of academic creative writing poetry that worried Gioia cannot come close to the truly depressed state of the art at the beginning of this century. The period from 1890 to 1910—which historian Rayford Logan dubbed "the nadir of American race relations"— coincided with what anthologist Edmund Clarence Stedman called, in 1900, "the twilight interval" of American poetry. One is almost tempted to think that the enervated condition of the best that culture has to offer was somehow connected to the mean-spiritedness evident in other social expressions of the times.

The cultural ecology of the United States is in some ways very different at the end of the twentieth century than it was at the beginning. It was not until the late 1950s, for example, that radio stations began nonstop programming of both popular and classical recorded music—thereby creating a megaindustry with economic dimensions undreamed of in any previous era. Poetry, like music, was mostly a part-time occupation at the beginning of the century and—unlike today—the majority of published poets maintained careers as businessmen, lawyers, and journalists. Many were women who had the advantage of being married to supportive husbands (many of whom were also a considerable notch above "good providers"). Some poets, apparently not as many as today, were teachers or college professors. Similarly, the audience for poetry ranged from those who simply enjoyed the patriotic, humorous, or sentimental verses that newspapers used as column fillers to readers who delighted in the serious study of traditional and contemporary literature.

Nevertheless, the American "Poetry Renaissance" that began in 1912, followed by the Harlem Renaissance of the 1920s, definitely increased both the size and diversity of the audience and those readers' perceptions of the importance of the art. The socially engaged writing of the Depression era and the oddly "mediagenic" Beat Generation of the 1950s continued to keep poetry at least newsworthy.

It is possible, however, that the basic cultural context for poetry in the United States has remained fairly consistent for more than a century. Those who love poetry expect it to offer both instruction and delight; those who do not read it think that these benefits are precisely what it offers to those who do (whom they assume to be smarter than themselves). Similarly, poets seem to maintain a bizonal concept of their craft, always aware of its power and privacy. In the 1840s, John Greenleaf Whittier and Henry Wadsworth Longfellow used their verses to campaign for the abolition of slavery; they were as aware of literature's social and propagandistic function as the African-American writers of the Harlem Renaissance. From another angle, one can compare Longfellow's patriotic epics—composed in stanzaic forms adopted from the European tradition—to Walt Whitman's idiosyncratic experiments and a long list of later practitioners whose creative energies oscillate between attention to matters of technical form and the need to document the elusive presence of the eternal in the quotidian. But that, after all, is precisely what the art of poetry is about.

The early years of this century, however, present readers with a period in the history of American literature that is notable for its exciting complexity and a sense of volatile change that mirrors other developments in society. In 1912 Chicago, Harriet Monroe launched *Poetry: A Magazine of Verse,* and her journal became an influential force in the modernist movement. William Stanley Braithwaite's work at the Boston *Evening Transcript* and as editor of an annual *Anthology of Magazine Verse* brought him recognition as the major proponent of poetry in the nation's press. The possibly inevitable clash of these literary titans in 1917 foregrounds important issues of artistic innovation, literary politics, editorial influence, and the mechanisms of cultural change.

In 1910, as Columbia University professor Joel E. Spingarn was calling for a "New Criticism" that would "recognize in every work of art a spiritual creation governed by its own law," contemporary poets were also seeking ways of avoiding the old conceptions of literary genre that, according to Spingarn, classicists had made into "a fixed norm governed by inviolable laws" (28). Ezra Pound and his imagist coconspirators found a way out by looking to Provençal folk song and Japanese court poetry and exploring a radical reinterpretation of the Greek classics. Their activity was similar to that of the European painters who turned to Oceanic and African tribal sculpture for inspiration. The poets felt that what was at stake was much greater than a revolution of literary style. Their optimistic attitude was expressed succinctly by Wallace Stevens. "You know, Stevens confided to Orrick Johns, "we *can* change it all" (Johns, *Times* 226).

Things began to change on the American poetry scene with the publication in 1912 of *The Lyric Year: One Hundred Poems*, edited by Ferdinand Phinny Earle. The book was first announced as a poetry contest with $1,000 in prizes. As his fellow judges, Earle chose Edward J. Wheeler, president of the Poetry Society of America, and William Stanley Braithwaite (Earle iii–v; Rittenhouse, *My House* 250–51). Earle's anthology included estimable works—chosen from 2,000 entries—by 100 poets representing a wide range of occupations and located in all sections of the country, from New York and Chicago to Kentucky and Iowa; from big cities, small towns, and rural areas. The quality of the work is surprisingly high. Among the contributors whose names are still easily recognizable are William Rose Benét, Witter Bynner, Arthur Davison Ficke, Joyce Kilmer, Vachel Lindsay, Edwin Markham, Josephine Preston Peabody, Sara Teasdale, Ridgley Torrance, Louis Untermeyer, and John Hall Wheelock.

Having read 2,000 poems in making a selection he felt was "representative . . . of the work done today in America," Earle announced that the "twilight interval" was over. "Our twentieth century poetry is democratic, scientific, humane," he wrote. "Its independence reveals the liberating touch of Walt Whitman, sweet with robust optimism" (viii). Though he thought Edna St. Vincent Millay's entry was the best poem submitted, Earle was somewhat taken aback by the reaction accorded the winning poem of *The Lyric Year* competition.

Orrick Johns, a St. Louis journalist, visited New York in 1911 and was delighted to be welcomed into the circles of people such as the poet Sara Teasdale and the social activist Emma Goldman (Johns, *Times* 202). Against the background noise of the nation's growing nativist hostility toward immigrants, Johns's poem "Second Avenue" surveyed the tide of still-wretched humanity swirling through New York's Lower East Side ghetto and sounded a properly respectable note of intellectual sympathy:

> Are you, O motley multitude,
>   Descendants of the squandered dead,
> Who honored courage more than creeds
>   And fought for better things than bread? (132)

The dehumanization depicted in Edwin Markham's celebrated "The Man with the Hoe" (1896)—"Slave of the wheel of labor, what to him / Are Plato and the swing of Pleiades?" (496)—has become, Johns notes, an epidemic condition in this quarter of the nation's greatest city. All that a poet finds alluring, the natural beauties of earth and life, are denied these workers "who live from hour to hour" (135), trapped in a city that is "a temple and a shrine / For gods of iron and of gilt" (134). Worse yet, it was the people's own labor that had built their prison. The poem's conclusion offers tepid, pseudosocialist hopefulness: "You, having brothers in all lands, / Shall teach to all lands brotherhood" (136). This was enough to enable Johns to win *The Lyric Year* prize on points (Earle iii–v). As Jessie Belle Rittenhouse later recalled: "The social movement in poetry was then at its height; the catchword, the 'Time Spirit,' was in everybody's mouth. Poets were adjured to write of the thing immediately important in modern life. The twentieth century came in on a wave of social consciousness inspired by Whitman and crystallized by Markham in 'The Man with the Hoe'" (*My House* 250–51). This mood explained Johns's prize. "It is not strange," Rittenhouse concluded, "that a social poem should have received attention wholly out of proportion to its poetic merit" (*My House* 250–51).

It should be noted that the much better poem, nineteen-year-old Edna St. Vincent Millay's two-hundred-line "Renascence," did not ignore social comment or politically correct empathy.

> A man was starving in Capri;
> He moved his eyes and looked at me;
> I felt his gaze, I heard his moan
> And knew his hunger as my own (182)

If the theme of the poem was intended to be social comment, one could fault Millay for conjuring an imaginary scene where Orrick Johns had in fact meditated on the genuine plight of real people he observed in New York City. But Millay's bright, rhyming couplets rapidly detour into an extraordinary scenario of imagined death and burial—a spiritual initiation—that leads to an astonishingly wise and beautiful epiphany:

> The world stands out on either side
> No wider than the heart is wide;
> Above the world is stretched the sky,—
> No higher than the soul is high[.] (188)

Even though Rittenhouse, one of the founders of the Poetry Society of America and a willing friend to young poets, had personally encouraged Johns to submit his prize-winning poem to *The Lyric Year* competition, she found the preference for his work over Millay's deplorable (Rittenhouse, *My House* 251). Nor was she alone in her reaction. Johns himself later commented: "when the book arrived I realized that it was an unmerited award. The outstanding poem in that book was 'Renascence' by Edna St. Vincent Millay, immediately acknowledged by every authoritative critic as such. The award was as much an embarrassment to me as a triumph" (*Times* 203). Rittenhouse and others, however, also realized that the great response of poets to Earle's announcement and the subsequent newspaper coverage of the debate over the winning entry had not only brought contemporary poetry to wider public attention but also indicated that an eager new generation of American writers was taking the form quite seriously.

III

The great American Poetry Heavyweight Championship battle of 1917 shaped up because the participants were ready for it. William Stanley Braithwaite was no stranger to literary infighting and was quite adept at the understated newscolumn uppercut and the "bread and butter note" jab. Conrad Aiken—a would-be aristocrat from Savannah, Georgia, acted more as an instigator than referee, writing essays in the *New Republic*, *The Dial*, and *The Poetry Journal* in which he insisted on attacking the "New Poetry" movement and, much to their mutual annoyance, always bracketing Braithwaite and Harriet Monroe as targets for his critical abuse.

As a poet, Aiken did not mind recognition; but as a critic, he was unhappy with Braithwaite's annual anthology and *Poetry* magazine's cash prizes for the best poems published during the year. Aiken castigated "Mr. Braithwaite's annual parade and Miss Monroe's annual graduation exercises" ("Prizes" 99) and felt that, between the two of them, poetry was "too much rather than too little recognized in this country" (Williams, *Harriet Monroe* 178). In his view, no contemporary poetry was worthy of prizes or honors. "In all this," he wrote, "it is perhaps possible to detect a central fallacy—the belief that poetry can be made essentially popular, in this time and place. Mediocre poetry—yes.

... But the finer poetry, now as always, needs time for valuation" ("Prizes" 99). Like James Fenimore Cooper and Ezra Pound, Aiken was unhappy that America was not the Europe of an earlier, grander century.

For her part, Monroe was a formidable contender. The slight, middle-aged former schoolteacher's appearance was deceptive. Born in 1860, Monroe was the daughter of a prominent Chicago attorney and became a powerful woman in her own right. If anyone could be called a poetry activist, the term is certainly applicable to her. When Chicago's 1893 World's Columbian Exposition neglected to include poetry in its showcase of the nation's arts, Monroe convinced the officials to allow her to organize a Poetry Day. When the New York *World* reprinted her celebratory World's Fair ode without permission—a standard newspaper practice of the period—she initiated a copyright infringement lawsuit and won a $5,000 judgment two years later. In her view, the result was the vindication that the copyrights of poets were as important as those of other artists (Williams, *Harriet Monroe* 8).

After 1899, she was daring enough to make her living as a freelance journalist and art critic for several newspapers and magazines. Indeed, Monroe did everything with flair. Upon deciding to publish *Poetry: A Magazine of Verse*, she turned to civic leader H. C. Chatfield-Taylor for advice and built the magazine with an endowment from a group of subscribers that mirrored the Chicago Symphony's founding patrons (Williams, *Harriet Monroe* 8–17).

Monroe was also good at grudges and loved a fight. Not everyone, however, appreciated the amusement she apparently found in literary disputes. John G. Neihardt was among her early enthusiasts, but in 1913 his Minneapolis *Journal* column's harsh review of Pound's contributions to *Poetry* placed him on the receiving end of Monroe's wrath. Neihardt, best known today for his excellent oral history *Black Elk Speaks* (1932) rather than for his epic poems of the American West, backed away from the fight and from Monroe's friendship (Aly 64–65). The fuss did not, however, prevent Monroe from including Neihardt's poems in her coedited anthology *The New Poetry* (1917).

Risking a charge of assigning guilt by association, it also seems clear that Monroe found pleasure not only in Pound's poetry but also in his pugnacity. His ranting correspondence as her magazine's European Editor must have amused her. She herself was never inclined to shrink from a battle. Visiting New York City in 1917, Monroe compared the American city to her experience of France: "As for the poets, they seem as numerous as sparrows ... and almost as quarrelsome. This is not to deride but to declare! I have always admired the vigor and enthusiasm with which battles of the intellect are fought in Paris" (*Poet's Life* 404–5). In William Stanley Braithwaite, Monroe was to find a worthy opponent.

Monroe and Braithwaite had first faced off in 1912 when, independently, each announced the establishment of a journal devoted to contemporary poetry. Monroe assumed that Braithwaite's *Poetry Journal*, funded in part through the efforts of their mutual friend Amy Lowell, was an "impudent" attempt to compete with her own plan for *Poetry* (Williams, *Harriet Monroe* 26). As Braithwaite, decidedly unmellowed, remembered it forty years later, the dispute was not simply a matter of jealousy or the misunderstanding of motives. "This was the revolt of the West against the East under the leadership of Harriet Monroe," he wrote in his introduction to the *Anthology of Magazine Verse for 1958*: "They felt that the supremacy of the 'effete' East in poetic matters had to be challenged and overthrown because, to them, it no longer had the vitality nor the insight to express and celebrate American life and character" (xliii). The feud built in intensity over the next two years even though neither magazine was successful in market terms and Braithwaite's *Poetry Journal* struggled on for a few years under the editorship of Edmund R. Brown (Williams, *Harriet Monroe* 85).

In 1913, Braithwaite began editing his annual anthology of the best poetry appearing in magazines. Evident from the beginning was his intention to refute E. C. Stedman's low valuation of contemporary poetry. In his introduction to the anthology (which he published at his own expense), Braithwaite wrote: "Our poetry needs, more than anything else, encouragement to reveal its qualities. The poets are doing satisfying and vitally excellent work and it only remains for the American public to do its duty by showing a substantial appreciation" (xiii). Some readers argued, however, that the editor bestowed laurels too easily. In a review of Braithwaite's *Anthology of Magazine Verse for 1917* in *The Bookman*, his old friend Jessie Rittenhouse cautioned: "American poetry stands in much more danger of inflated praise than of balanced, judicious, even negative, criticism." Nevertheless, she noted, "Mr. Braithwaite has given to poetry a devoted, single-minded, unselfish service which all must appreciate, however they differ from his opinions" ("Contemporary Poetry" 679–80).

Conrad Aiken, of course, truculently dissented. In *Scepticisms: Notes on Contemporary Poetry* (1919), Aiken announced that he was not impressed with either Braithwaite's critical judiciousness or his generosity. "If in the presence of a piece of poetry the critic is content merely with the exclamatory," Aiken wrote, "he is not doing his work." Aiken was also displeased with the presence in Braithwaite's critical vocabulary of "such expressions as 'reverence for life,' 'quest for beauty,' and 'mystic illumination.'" To Aiken, this was evidence of the editor's "belief that poetry is a sort of supernaturalism" (*Scepticisms* 127–28). It would be a serious error, however, to think that Aiken's attack on Braithwaite involved issues related to modernist aesthetics or an endorsement of the rigorous (if self-serving) critical stances espoused by T. S. Eliot or Ezra Pound. Indeed, when Aiken took on the role of popularizer himself—as he did in editing *Modern American Poets,* published in London in 1922 and curiously including the very traditional and mediocre Anna Hempstead Branch among such modernists as Eliot, John Gould Fletcher, and Alfred Kreymborg—his own critical vocabulary included flimsy boilerplate: "American poetry, like any, must obey the principles of poetry; and they, whatever they may be, are presumably constant" (*Modern American* vii).

Despite his own rather conventional poetic style, as an editor, Braithwaite seemed quite receptive to newer, experimental poems. As the imagists and other young poets associated with what Monroe was calling the New Poetry Movement began to fill more of the pages of Braithwaite's anthology, the Braithwaite-Monroe feud boiled over into vicious acrimony in the spring of 1917. Monroe's quarrel with Braithwaite was not merely that he had ignored her favorite protégés in 1913 but that when he enthusiastically included some of them in later years, he meticulously avoided crediting Monroe's *Poetry* as the proving ground of their genius.

Braithwaite may have had reasons to resent Monroe's sniping, but many others were also annoyed by her proprietary stance. Jessie Rittenhouse, author of *The Younger American Poets* (1905), poetry critic for the *New York Times,* and the most energetic founder of the Poetry Society of America in 1910, was sometimes angered by Monroe's possessive attitude and particularly resented Monroe's claim to have "discovered" Vachel Lindsay in 1913. "He might have been a discovery to Miss Monroe," wrote Rittenhouse, "but he was no discovery to many others, since . . . he had been writing verse for seventeen years" (*My House* 300).

With Conrad Aiken's sallies as overture, Monroe attacked Braithwaite as "the Boston Dictator" in an intemperate *Poetry* editorial titled "Sir Oracle." "Last year," she wrote, "Mr. Braithwaite was almost a convert to 'radicalism.' This year his mind is at sea, wondering whether it should venture further out into the unknown, but on the whole steering shorewards, reverting to type" (212). Monroe made clear that her criticism of his editorial judgment was intended to be taken personally. "Mr. Braithwaite's tardy and reluctant recognition of our 'influence,'" she wrote, "is perfectly comprehensible. *Poetry* has from the first taken exception to his autocratic tone and criticized his somewhat provincial opinions" (212).

The issues that Braithwaite and Monroe clashed over were extremely personal and basically inconsequential; both of them were instrumental in advancing the careers of the same group of poets. Their dispute was primarily about ego and power, not aesthetics, but it also made poets choose sides, bringing out their true colors and worst behavior. There has never been any ambiguity about what poets think of editors and critics since, as Spingarn perceptively noted, "what each mainly seeks in his own case is not criticism, but uncritical praise" (9). Nevertheless, the role taken by the poets in the 1917 dustup was somewhat extraordinary.

Alice Corbin Henderson, coeditor of *Poetry*, had poems included in Braithwaite's *Anthology of Magazine Verse for 1916* but chose to stick with Monroe and began to organize poets to boycott future Braithwaite editions. Willard Wattles, editor of *Sunflowers: A Book of Kansas Poems* (1918), responded to her campaign with a satirical poem accusing those who appeared in Braithwaite's book of showing their naked bottoms:

> All the poets have been stripping,
> Quaintly into moonbeams slipping,
> Running out like wild Bacchantes
> Minus *lingerie* and panties. (52)

Carl Sandburg, whose recent work had been negatively reviewed by Braithwaite in the Boston *Evening Transcript*, offered to help spread the boycott, writing to Henderson: "A pathetic personage has been admitted to grow into a fungus mistaken for what it grows on. The popery and kaiserism of it, the snobbery, flunkyism and intrigue, I'm on to it" (124). The opportunistic Robert Frost, whose American popularity had been boosted by Braithwaite's articles in the *Evening Transcript*, did not have Sandburg's excuse. Nevertheless, like Ezra Pound, Frost was not reluctant to refer to Braithwaite as a "nigger" and, though never missing an opportunity to advance his own career, would hyperbolically complain to a correspondent that he resented "the climbing of every black reviewer's back stairs for preferment" (Thompson 542–43n.32).

Alice Corbin Henderson's own race card was viciously played in an April 1916 satire on contemporary poets that she mailed to Ezra Pound for critical comment. Regarding Braithwaite, Corbin wrote:

> It is very like Boston
> To accept as poetic arbiter
> . . . .
>   in a country where all men
> Are created *free and equal,*
> One so obviously handicapped
> By nature. (qtd. in Nadel 178)

The slur recalls a letter from Pound to Henderson on 16 January 1913 that described Braithwaite's race as an "affliction." Though Pound asked Henderson to destroy the slanderous page, it is now in the Harry Ransom Humanities Research Center at the University of Texas and has been reprinted in Ira B. Nadel's meticulously edited volume *The Letters of Ezra Pound to Alice Corbin Henderson* (1993). This letter and others suggest that while Pound was fluent with racist remarks, he may also have seen an opportunity to reinforce his alliance with *Poetry* by appearing to share their hatred of a man he had never met (Nadel 14–16; Nielsen 66–67).

The charges and countercharges went on for about three years (1915–1918) and eventually had a beneficial result for poets. As Braithwaite noted, perhaps with exaggerated gentility, in his *Anthology of Magazine Verse for 1958:* "The publicity given to poetry in the press, the appearance of other poetry magazines in different parts of the country, and the space given in general periodicals like *The New Republic* and *The Freeman*, made the public so conscious of the art that the renaissance took full stride" ("Introduction" xl). The African-American poet Fenton Johnson, editing *The Champion Magazine* in Chicago, had come to Braithwaite's defense on his editorial page; but, otherwise, the numbers seem to have been on Monroe's side. Braithwaite, however, emerged from the fracas as powerful and arrogantly genteel as ever, continuing to turn out annual anthologies for the next decade.

III

William Stanley Braithwaite was no victim of racism. The confrontation with Harriet Monroe in 1917 was really in the nature of a family squabble among the adherents and, in Braithwaite's case, perhaps unlikely supporters of the modernist movement in American poetry. If some of the printed comments and private correspondence took unsavory tones, it is merely more evidence of what Aldon Lynn Nielsen has identified in his fine work *Reading Race* (1988) as the ingrained antiblack attitudes of the period; attitudes that were reflected even in those we have been taught to think of as our most sensitive and advanced intellects. In the case of Sandburg, otherwise known to have been sympathetic to the African-American cause, the opportunity to retaliate for a bad review may be understandable, even if the vituperation of his response seems excessive. Our tendency may be to apply caution; it is possible to make too much of this. From Braithwaite's perspective, however, the racial implications of the affair might not have been so easily dismissed. It would, therefore, be useful to know what elements of character or pragmatic outlook shaped his responses.

"Braithwaite's view of poetry was pre-modern," contends Craig S. Abbott: "He was more poetry-lover than critic" (151). That is not quite the whole story. Despite his tendency toward a rhapsodic assumption of unquestioned and eternal verities, Braithwaite's critical commentaries suggest that he was not interested in poetry as a purely metaphorical discourse but as an effective and elegant means of preserving and transmitting the multivalent complexities of human existence and what Matthew Arnold called "the best that has been thought." In 1922, for example, Braithwaite became an enthusiastic supporter of Hughes Mearns's pioneering high school creative writing classes at New York's Lincoln School. In a properly Arnoldian mood, Braithwaite wrote that "even if [the students] do not become expressed poets later on, they will be possessed of that culture whose spirit is poetry" (Mearns 3; Myers 102–3). In Braithwaite's writings, it becomes clear that he does not believe that the culture transmitted in English-language poetry is *essential* or that one can avoid "the technical elements of the science of versification." In an article titled "Some Contemporary Poets of the Negro Race," published in *The Crisis* in 1919, Braithwaite identified the source of much bad poetry: "It is the hard and laborious task of mastering the subtle and fluctuating rhythms of verse that the average individual tries to escape which produces such a mass of mediocre work, often choking and wasting the substance of a passionate and imaginative poetic spirit" (55). This statement is not a specific criticism of African-American writers; it is advice from an accomplished poet to beginners of any racial background. In this context, Braithwaite's praise of "the glorious and perfect instrument of English poetic art" (51) refers to the *language* and the techniques developed over centuries that can be learned by anyone dedicated enough to do the work required.

Rather than being measured as an early integrationist, though, Braithwaite might best be understood as a person who actually lived—or at least worked—in a racially "integrated" milieu. This did not mean that he was ignorant of the harsher aspects of the racial status quo. Though his father died when he was only seven years old, Braithwaite felt that he was firmly anchored by his family heritage. He was as proud of the grandfather who had "the reputation of being the best Latin scholar" in Barbados as he was of his grandmother who "found her way to Boston from North Carolina with three young daughters" amid the chaos of 1865 (*Braithwaite Reader* 159, 162). Completing four years of school, Braithwaite went to work at age twelve, performing duties "reserved for a colored boy" in various firms. But young Braithwaite was smart, hardworking, ambitious, and—in no small degree—lucky (*Braithwaite Reader* 168).

Like Mark Twain and William Dean Howells, Braithwaite began his literary apprenticeship and advanced education in the print shop. He began writing poetry while learning to set type at the Boston publishing firm Ginn and Company. In the time-honored tradition of young poets, Braithwaite was not shy about writing to literary notables such as Howells and Edmund Clarence Stedman to ask for attention to his poems (*Braithwaite Reader* 238–42). In April 1899, he drafted a straightforward letter to publisher L. C. Page: "I am an American Negro, a Bostonian by birth, and received my M.A. from Nature's University of 'Seek, Observe and Utilize' and am now in my 20th year." Having revealed a sense of humor, the poet next tried a touch of modesty: "without advantage of even a highschool education and teeming with the faults inherent to youthful poetical genius, I beseech you to be indulgent of the minor imperfections that pervade my work" (*Braithwaite Reader* 237). Armed with impeccable manners and dignified carriage, Braithwaite seems to have had better luck presenting himself in person. Beginning around 1901, he busied himself as a contributor to William Monroe Trotter's Boston *Guardian* newspaper, the *Colored American Magazine* edited by Pauline E. Hopkins, and J. Max Barber's militant *Voice of the Negro* (*Braithwaite Reader* 11, 114; Johnson and Johnson 23). By 1903, he had met several of Boston's mainstream literati and compiled a collection of poems. With the help of poets Frederic Lawrence Knowles and Jessie Rittenhouse, he was introduced to literary doyenne Louise Chandler Moulton, whose astonishingly long-running weekly salon had been attended by Longfellow and John Greenleaf Whittier, and to Thomas Wentworth Higginson, the famed abolitionist who encouraged Emily Dickinson's poetic efforts. Encouragement and subscriptions for his volume *Lyrics of Life and Love* (1904) came from Boston luminaries such as Julia Ward Howe, Thomas Bailey Aldrich, Bliss Perry, and Edward Everett Hale. Braithwaite's reputation grew rapidly, and 1906 found him involved in editing several book projects and beginning an association with the Boston *Evening Transcript* that would result in one of the most influential book columns in the United States (*Braithwaite Reader* 182–86).

What should be understood is that Braithwaite belonged to that group of literary men who wrote for a living. Like Langston Hughes, or his early Boston associates Isaac Goldberg and Henry Thomas Schnittkind, Braithwaite was always seeking the next publishing contract—for editing a volume, writing prefaces or newspaper columns, or any other literary commission such as biographies. Only in 1935 at the age of fifty-seven did he succumb to the lure of a comfortable academic position (and its regular paycheck) by accepting an appointment at Atlanta University. Despite Braithwaite's lack of formal academic credentials, university president John Hope enthusiastically recommended his appointment as a professor of English. "I suppose," Hope wrote, "that there is no Negro living who is so steeped in English and American Literature and who has had such unusual opportunities for acquaintance with contemporary writers of prose and poetry. He has encouraged many young American authors of both races and by his friendly criticism has helped to make them writers of note" (Bacote 290). The transition to academia was not necessarily easy for the veteran freelancer; in 1940, for example, Braithwaite received a stern letter from university president Rufus Clement emphasizing the importance of attending faculty meetings.

In earlier days, Braithwaite not only wrote his literary surveys and book reviews for the Boston *Evening Transcript,* he also briefly held editorships at Boston magazines such as *The Stratford Magazine,* founded *The Poetry Journal,* and was on the editorial boards of African-American journals such as the short-lived *Citizen* (1915–16) and the National Association for the Advancement of Colored People's publication *The Crisis.* He also edited anthologies of British poetry aimed at a popular audience.

These projects are worth close examination because there is a quietly oppositional quality to some of Braithwaite's productions. *Victory!* (1919), an anthology of World War I poems, opens patriotically enough, with an introduction by Theodore Roosevelt and sonnets in praise of Allied heroes such as France's Marshal Ferdinand Foch. But the editor's real agenda soon became apparent in poems by Fenton Johnson, Louis Untermeyer, and others that address the war to focus pointedly on class struggle on the home front. Mary Carolyn Davies's "Fifth Avenue and Grand Street," for example, depicts two young women—one a socialite, the other a Lower East Side shopgirl—conversing as they roll bandages for the Red Cross. The poem ends: "We're sisters while the danger lasts, it's true; / But rich and poor's equality must cease / (For women especially), of course, in peace" (*Victory!* 27).

It is also significant that some of Braithwaite's associates on various editorial projects were men like Schnittkind (later a prolific author of popular nonfiction under the name Henry Thomas) and Goldberg, both of whom were involved with Jewish working-class education movements and socialist literary efforts such as Emmanuel Haldeman-Julius's Little Blue Books series. It is reasonable to suppose that Braithwaite shared similar enthusiasms. For his own part, he was never inactive in the black press and maintained close contacts with race leaders such as Benjamin Brawley, W. E. B. Du Bois, George W. Ellis, and Kelly Miller.

While he was editing *The Poetry Journal* and feuding with Harriet Monroe, Braithwaite also worked as editor of *The Stratford Journal.* In the fall of 1916, the first issue of this handsome bimonthly included an editorial written by

Schnittkind, Braithwaite's associate editor and a shareholder in the publication ("Statement" 86). Schnittkind clearly announced the editorial board's view of the important functional role of literature in society: "Who has not thrilled with the poetry, the tenseness, the homeliness, the living, throbbing *humanness* of the one-act plays of the Irish players? Who of us, on seeing these plays, has not exclaimed, 'Give us more and more of this, for this is the sort of stuff that life is made of.' Well, this is the sort of 'stuff' that we are going to publish in each issue of the *Stratford Journal*." The editors were not interested in merely exciting their readers with powerfully poetic exoticism: "After reading that sort of drama, our visions are Broadened, are they not? We no longer sneer at the benighted Russians, the hot-headed 'dagos,' the slimy 'Chinks'; but we feel a reverence for them, for in their eyes we recognize a gleam that reflects the soul of God" (Schnittkind 5–6). The editors did not, of course, intend any notion of religious brotherhood; rather, they saw that literature could be useful in promoting the sort of cultural pluralism that sociologist Horace Kallen was discussing in 1915 in a series of important articles in *The Nation*. The contents of *The Stratford Journal* certainly delivered on the editors' cosmopolitan promise, offering poems by the young Louise Bogan, translations of the Mexican poet Luis C. Urbina, stories by Knut Hamsun, and critical essays on American poetry and fiction. The editors also directed readers' attention to the works of the Bengali poet Rabindranath Tagore, Bertrand Russell, and Gilbert Cannan's novel *Mendel*, described as "a sympathetic study of a Jewish immigrant" ("Books" 86).

If Braithwaite's role in an enterprise such as *The Stratford Journal* has been previously unmentioned, neither has his role in the development of African-American literature been adequately assessed. In a sense, he was a forerunner of the Harlem Renaissance, yet he also was seen by some of the younger participants in that movement as one of their more antagonistic critics. Braithwaite shared Du Bois's distaste for some of the more sensationalized depictions of black life that were encouraged during the period. Some commentators, however, suspected that—unlike Du Bois—Braithwaite was not concerned primarily about strategies for presenting the race in a flattering light. Robert L. Poston, writing in Marcus Garvey's Universal Negro Improvement Association newspaper *The Negro World* in 1922, noted: "Braithwaite, because of his anthologies and his connection with a great white daily and because he does not in his poems indicate his racial extraction, is taken by many, who do not know him personally, to be a white man." Poston felt that such a mistake was understandable since "Braithwaite has become so Caucasianized in his writings, that he has lost his racial identity entirely, if he ever had any, and the white people claim him as their own" (70). Poston admitted, however, that Braithwaite was a good poet whose work had universal appeal.

William H. Ferris, literary editor of *The Negro World,* did not agree with Poston. Ferris had first met Braithwaite in 1896 and recognized in the ambitious teenager a "voracious reader, an ardent lover of poetry." By 1913, with Paul Laurence Dunbar dead and James Weldon Johnson struggling (with Braithwaite's help) to make the transition from popular songwriter to poet, Ferris had pronounced William Stanley Braithwaite "the poet laureate of the colored race" (*African Abroad* 870). In 1922, in the pages of *The Negro World,* Ferris cited Braithwaite as living proof that "the world of literature, art and music knows no color line" ("Negro Composers" 302). Such a statement did not compromise Ferris's Garveyite pan-African nationalism. Like Du Bois and Alain Locke, Ferris wished to demonstrate that the higher intellectual realm of culture might accomplish what seemed to be impossible in the meaner political arena. The example of Braithwaite's career—anomalous though it might have been—armed Ferris with evidence that he could use in his newspaper's ongoing assault on the irrationality of racism, evidence that proved the insupportability of white supremacist doctrines.

III

Scholarly assessments of African-American attitudes are frequently more self-serving than accurate. It is not that the African American, as Norman Mailer and others have quite arrogantly suggested, remains a projection of suppressed white desire; but that, as Claude McKay eloquently stated in his poem "In Bondage" (1921), black people in the United States have been merely "simple slaves of ruthless slaves" (122). From the Moynihan Report to the recent spate of affirmative action survival narratives on the best-seller list, the "mood of black America" that is offered for intellectual discussion usually supports an agenda that suits the political establishment's own desired self-image. For this reason, it is both important and difficult to understand the implications of Braithwaite's racial identification—or its ambiguity. Robert L. Poston's idea that Braithwaite simply identified with the caucasian status quo is insufficiently convincing and, in fact, incorrect. Others have suggested that, even though he did not come from a privileged background, Braithwaite's Boston milieu stifled the development of a militant race consciousness.

In nineteenth-century Boston, writes sociologist Oscar Handlin, "Negro awareness of race derived not from differences they desired to cherish, but rather from a single difference—color—which they desired to discard" (175–

76). Without speculating on Handlin's motives in crafting such a carefully phrased characterization, it is sufficient to say that his statement is misleading. The African-American community in Boston campaigned for the elimination of color as a handicap to advancement. Militant leadership was personified by William Monroe Trotter and his Boston *Guardian* newspaper. Trotter's adventures included a 1914 confrontation in President Woodrow Wilson's White House office over the issue of legalized segregation in government employment. In 1915, Trotter and the Boston community led the nation in protests against D. W. Griffith's vicious portrayal of African Americans in *The Birth of a Nation* (Weiss 133–37; Rogers 399–405; Fox 188–97).

Where Handlin discerns a lack of ethnic pride, a better understanding of the African-American mood during this period might be gleaned from considering J. Max Barber's May 1907 editorial in Atlanta's *Voice of the Negro* announcing that his journal "is devoted to the unraveling of the snarl of the Color Problem and is published to the end that justice may prevail in the land, that lawlessness and bigotry may be wiped out and that the fetish of color prejudice may pass away forever" (Johnson and Johnson 17). African-American race consciousness, based on the recognition that "the color line" should *not* be the boundary of opportunity, certainly did not arrive with the turn of the century; indeed, this type of race consciousness can be said to have formed the character of those born in the 1870s and the 1880s. Judith E. B. Harmon suggests, for example, that the talented, highly-educated James Weldon Johnson's "self-perception as a cosmopolite" was effectively a bold personal statement that "defied . . . the political restrictions" intended to limit his creative expression (1). A similar view may be accurate in the case of William Stanley Braithwaite and others of his generation.

It is important to understand that the intellectual color line was more complex than simple exclusion. Braithwaite's friend Benjamin Brawley, dean at Atlanta's Morehouse College and author of "The Negro Genius" (1915), *The Negro in Literature and Art in the United States* (1918), and other important works of the period, complained in a 1919 letter to Braithwaite that he was having trouble marketing a history of English drama that he felt would be suitable for adoption as a high-school text. Brawley felt that the manuscript was "the best thing I have ever done," but the response from publishers was "very good, but we are not in the text-book business. Send us more of the Negro stuff" (Brawley, Letter to WSB 4). Similarly, Paul Laurence Dunbar complained to James Weldon Johnson that publishers had forced him into the almost schizophrenic position of dividing his poetic energies between African-American dialect verse and attempts at a more "universal" expression in traditional forms.

Writers of the sensibility shared by Johnson, Brawley, and Braithwaite struggled to avoid Dunbar's dilemma.

Braithwaite's own poems are skillful and elegant, usually cast in the philosophical mood popular in late-nineteenth-century verse. His volume *The House of Falling Leaves* (1908) includes meditations on death and life, titles such as "A Little While before Farewell" (which can be compared to the effective—and predictable—musical "hooks" of today's pop songs), and well-turned lines intended to go directly into the reader's personal treasury of favorite quotations: "Failure is a crown of sorrows, / Success a crown of fears" (*House* 79). The reader will not find racial identification in Braithwaite's poetry. The nearest thing to it in *The House of Falling Leaves* is a poem titled "La Belle de Demerara," an answer to Oliver Wendell Holmes's wonderful "Dorothy Q." (1871):

> O Poet who sang of Dorothy Q.;
> I have a Great-Grandmother too,
> Born in a British colonial place,
> Sent to learn Parisian grace;
> Who won all hearts in her demesne
> By the Caribbean's warm blue sheen:
> And large is the debt I owe to her,
> La belle de Demerara. (*House* 88)

Some might mistake this for "caucasianized" values, but it seems more clearly to be Braithwaite's assertion of his own heritage, full of contradictions though it may be, and his willingness to present that heritage as the full functional equivalent of any Boston brahmin's. An invented African heritage may be purer and more politically useful, but Braithwaite is satisfied to celebrate his genuine roots. It would be an error, however, to conclude that Braithwaite was unconcerned about broader racial issues. He was; but he also felt that the proper subject matter of poetry was to be found elsewhere. "I am not one who believes," he wrote in 1919, "that a Negro writer of verse—or of fiction, for that matter—must think, feel, or write racially to be a great artist; nor can he be distinctively labeled by the material he uses." For Braithwaite as an artist, the quest for the universal should be the goal of artistic expression. "All great artists," he wrote, "are interracial and international in rendering in the medium of any particular art the fundamental passions and the primary instincts of humanity" ("Some Contemporary Poets" 276–77). This was the same principle that directed his editorial hand in his annual poetry anthologies and at *The Stratford Journal*, and it was this principle that he followed in composing his own poems.

Contemporary critical opinion of Braithwaite—what little there is—is not nearly as harsh as was J. Saunders Redding's 1939 assessment. "The world beyond the walled world of Negro life was not ready," said Redding, for African-American writers of "kinless verse" that—while excellent in technique—did not depict the expected African-American themes. Though he certainly abhorred racist stereotypes, Redding did not hold "color blind" attempts at universality in high esteem. Of Braithwaite, Redding concluded: "He is the most outstanding example of perverted energy that the period from 1903 to 1917 produced" (89).

Current views are more likely to resemble a recent comment from Michael Bérubé. According to Bérubé, Braithwaite—unlike Jean Toomer and Melvin B. Tolson, who "sought a negotiation of African-American cultural forms and Anglo-American modernist experimentation"—was merely old-fashioned enough to confidently assume that the word "universal" embraced all particularities (171, 186). Negative judgments aside, the critics are at least accurate about Braithwaite's staunch position as a universalist. In his work as an editor and anthologist, Braithwaite was able to promote the avant garde while also supporting African-American writers because he operated from a clearly stated premise: "to respect the vitality and variety of present-day poetry" while carefully understanding its place in an ancient tradition (*Braithwaite Reader* 91). And, of course, he encouraged all efforts that were consistent with his vision of social justice and racial equality.

The type of race consciousness that shaped both Braithwaite and the emerging "New Negro" at the turn of the century gave rise to two distinct but related strategies. One, of course, was the type of political activism and social-commentary literature practiced by William Monroe Trotter, W. E. B. Du Bois, Ida B. Wells-Barnett, J. Max Barber, and others. It was this approach—and these very individuals—that established first the Niagara Movement and then the NAACP. The second approach was more personal and was expressed as an engaged and committed desire to live one's own life free of the bonds of a racist system. Both of these approaches, of course, would be the driving forces of the Harlem Renaissance of the 1920s. Indeed, Benjamin Brawley's 1915 essay "The Negro Genius," first published in the Hampton Institute's *Southern Workman* magazine, is an early statement of an aesthetic argument that would often be repeated by Du Bois, James Weldon Johnson, and Alain Locke. Brawley suggested that "America should realize that the Negro has peculiar gifts which need all possible cultivation, and which will one day add to the glory of the country. Already his music is recognized as the most distinctive that the United States has yet produced. The possibilities of the race in literature and oratory, in sculpture and painting, are illimitable" ("Negro Genius" 330–31). A writer such as Braithwaite hoped that this realization would be possible without rancorous conflict; that it might be spurred by the example of artists, like himself, who genuinely believed—though socially and politically hampered by racial discrimination—that their artistic possibilities could not be segregated. It was, in fact, on the strength of such a personal credo that W. S. Braithwaite was able to achieve his unprecedented position of literary eminence at the Boston *Evening Transcript*.

The adolescent "Willie" Braithwaite, reading his way through the great Boston Public Library, would have shared Du Bois's epiphany about the power of art. "I sit with Shakespeare," Du Bois wrote in *The Souls of Black Folk* (1903), "and he winces not. Across the color line I move arm in arm with Balzac and Dumas. . . . they come all graciously with no scorn nor condescension" (76). After having experienced overt racial discrimination while seeking a job in the book business in New York in 1900, Braithwaite became determined, as William H. Ferris noted, "to make his living solely with his pen" (*African Abroad* 869). "The resolution I formed," Braithwaite recalled in 1941, "was to express myself on the common ground of American authorship, to demonstrate, in however humble a degree, that a man of color was the equal of any other man in possession of the attributes that produced a literature of human thought and experience, and to *force* a recognition of this common capacity and merit from the appreciation of the reading public and the authority of critical opinion" (*Braithwaite Reader* 179, emphasis added).

It is this resolve—and the fact that William Stanley Braithwaite was able, over five decades, to bring that dream close to reality—that marks him clearly as a philosophical mentor to the Harlem Renaissance. Just as clearly, his efforts on behalf of the new poetry—whether we decide he was, as Conrad Aiken charged, more of a drum major than a critic—were essential to making viable James Oppenheim's hope that America could be "regenerated by art" (Kazin 172) or Wallace Stevens's belief that poets, indeed, *can* change it all.

Works Cited

Abbott, Craig S. "Magazine Verse and Modernism: Braithwaite's Anthologies." *Journal of Modern Literature* 19 (1994): 151–59.
Aiken, Conrad, ed. *Modern American Poets*. London: Martin Secker, 1922.
———. "Prizes and Anthologies." *The Poetry Journal* 4 (1915): 95–100.
———. *Scepticisms: Notes on Contemporary Poetry*. 1919. Rpt., Freeport, N.Y.: Books for Libraries Press, 1967.
Aly, Lucile F. *John G. Neihardt: A Critical Biography*. Amsterdam: Rodopi, 1977.
Bacote, Clarence A. *The Story of Atlanta University: A Century of Service*. Atlanta, Ga.: Atlanta University, 1969.

Bérubé, Michael. *Marginal Forces/Cultural Centers: Tolson, Pynchon, and the Politics of the Canon.* Ithaca, N.Y.: Cornell University Press, 1992.

"Books of Literary Interest." *The Stratford Journal* 1 (1916): 86.

Braithwaite, William Stanley. *The House of Falling Leaves.* 1908. Rpt., Miami, Fla.: Mnemosyne, 1969.

———. "Introduction." In *Anthology of Magazine Verse for 1913.* Cambridge, Mass.: W.S.B., 1913. v–xiii.

———. "Introduction." In *Anthology of Magazine Verse for 1958.* New York: Schulte Publishing, 1959. xxxix–lxxv.

———. "Some Contemporary Poets of the Negro Race." *The Crisis* 17 (1919): 275–80.

———. *Victory! Celebrated by Thirty-Eight American Poets.* Boston: Small, Maynard and Co., 1919.

———. *The William Stanley Braithwaite Reader.* Ed. Philip Butcher. Ann Arbor: University of Michigan Press, 1972.

Brawley, Benjamin. Letter to William Stanley Braithwaite. 16 November 1919. William Stanley Braithwaite Papers. Schomburg Center for Research in Black Culture, New York Public Library. Box 1, folder 21.

———. "The Negro Genius" (1915). In *Black Nationalism in America.* Ed. John H. Bracey Jr., August Meier, and Elliot Rudwick. New York: Bobbs-Merrill, 1970. 327–31.

———. *The Negro in Literature and Art in the United States.* New York: Duffield, 1918.

Clement, Rufus E. Letter to William Stanley Braithwaite. 17 September 1940. William Stanley Braithwaite Papers. Schomburg Center for Research in Black Culture, New York Public Library. Box 1, folder 24.

Earle, Ferdinand, ed. *The Lyric Year: One Hundred Poems.* 1912. Rpt., Freeport, N.Y.: Books for Libraries Press, 1971.

Ferris, William H. *The African Abroad—Of His Evolution in Western Civilization.* 2 vols. 1913. Rpt., New York: Johnson Reprint, 1968.

———. "Negro Composers and Negro Music—Is There Race in Music? Is There Race in Art?" (1922). In *African Fundamentalism: A Literary and Cultural Anthology of Garvey's Harlem Renaissance.* Ed. Tony Martin. Dover, Mass.: Majority Press, 1991. 299–302.

Fox, Stephen R. *The Guardian of Boston: William Monroe Trotter.* New York: Atheneum, 1970.

Gioia, Dana. "Can Poetry Matter?" *The Atlantic* 267 (1991): 94–106.

Handlin, Oscar. *Boston's Immigrants: A Study in Acculturation.* Rev. ed. New York: Atheneum, 1977.

Harmon, Judith E. B. "A New Negro: James Weldon Johnson Re-Viewed." *The Griot* 12 (1993): 1–12.

Holmes, Oliver Wendell. "Dorothy Q" (1871). In *Harper American Literature.* Ed. Donald McQuade et al. 2 vols. New York: Harper and Row, 1987. 1:2182–84.

Johns, Orrick. "Second Avenue." In Earle, *The Lyric Year,* 132–37.

———. *Times of Our Lives: The Story of My Father and Myself.* 1937. Rpt., New York: Octagon Books, 1973.

Johnson, Abby Arthur, and Ronald Mayberry Johnson. *Propaganda and Aesthetics: The Literary Politics of Afro-American Magazines in the Twentieth Century.* Amherst: University of Massachusetts Press, 1979.

Kazin, Alfred. *On Native Grounds: An Interpretation of Modern American Prose Literature.* New York: Reynal and Hitchcock, 1942.

Markham, Edwin. "The Man with the Hoe" (1896). In *American Poetry: The Nineteenth Century.* Ed. John Hollander. 2 vols. New York: Library of America, 1993. 2:496.

McKay, Claude. "In Bondage." In *The Passion of Claude McKay: Selected Poetry and Prose, 1912–1948.* Ed. Wayne Cooper. New York: Schocken Books, 1973. 122.

Mearns, Hughes. *Creative Youth.* Garden City, N.Y.: Doubleday-Page, 1927.

Millay, Edna St. Vincent. "Renascence." In Earle, *The Lyric Year,* 180–88.

Monroe, Harriet. *A Poet's Life: Seventy Years in a Changing World.* New York: Macmillan, 1938.

———. "Sir Oracle." *Poetry: A Magazine of Verse* 9 (1917): 211–14.

———. "Tradition." *Poetry: A Magazine of Verse* 2 (1913): 67–68.

Monroe, Harriet, and Alice Corbin Henderson, eds. *The New Poetry: An Anthology.* Rev. ed. New York: Macmillan, 1924.

Myers, D. G. *The Elephants Teach: Creative Writing since 1880.* Englewood Cliffs, N.J.: Prentice-Hall, 1996.

Nadel, Ira B., ed. *The Letters of Ezra Pound to Alice Corbin Henderson.* Austin: University of Texas Press, 1993.

Nielsen, Aldon Lynn. *Reading Race: White American Poets and the Racial Discourse in the Twentieth Century.* Athens: University of Georgia Press, 1988.

Poston, Robert L. "Dunbar, Braithwaite, McKay—An Analysis" (1925). In *African Fundamentalism: A Literary and Cultural Anthology of Garvey's Harlem Renaissance.* Ed. Tony Martin. Dover, Mass.: Majority Press, 1991. 69–70.

Redding, J. Saunders. *To Make a Poet Black.* 1939. Rpt., Ithaca, N.Y.: Cornell University Press, 1988.

Rittenhouse, Jessie B. "Contemporary Poetry." *The Bookman* 46 (1918): 678–83.

———. *My House of Life: An Autobiography.* Boston: Houghton Mifflin, 1934.

Rogers, J. A. "William Monroe Trotter." In *World's Great Men of Color.* 2 vols. 1947. Rpt., New York: Collier Books, 1972. 2:399–405.

Sandburg, Carl. *The Letters of Carl Sandburg.* Ed. Herbert Mitgang. New York: Harcourt, Brace and World, 1968. 123–25.

Schnittkind, Henry Thomas. "The Aims of *The Stratford Journal.*" *The Stratford Journal* 1 (1916): 3–7.

Spingarn, J. E. "The New Criticism" (1910). In *Criticism in America: Its Function and Status.* New York: Harcourt, Brace, 1924. 9–45.

"Statement of the Ownership, Management, Circulation, Etc." *The Stratford Journal* 1 (1916): 86.

Thompson, Lawrence. *Robert Frost: The Years of Triumph, 1915–1938.* New York: Holt, Rinehart and Winston, 1970.

Wagner, Jean. *Black Poets of the United States: From Paul Laurence Dunbar to Langston Hughes.* Trans. Kenneth Douglas. Urbana: University of Illinois Press, 1973.

Wattles, Willard. "On Reading the Braithwaite Anthology for 1916." *Poetry: A Magazine of Verse* 10 (1917): 52–54.

Weiss, Nancy J. "The Negro and the New Freedom." In *The Segregation Era, 1863–1954.* Ed. Allen Weinstein and Frank Otto Gatell. New York: Oxford University Press, 1970. 129–42.

Williams, Ellen. *Harriet Monroe and the Poetry Renaissance: The First Ten Years of "Poetry," 1912–22.* Urbana: University of Illinois Press, 1977.

Williams, Kenny J. "An Invisible Partnership and an Unlikely Relationship: William Stanley Braithwaite and Harriet Monroe." *Callaloo* 10 (1987): 516–50.

4

Poetics of the Americas

Charles Bernstein

Speaking in Buffalo in 1994, the Argentinean poet Jorge Santiago Perednik ended his talk on cultural resistance to the recent reign of terror in his country by saying, "the struggle is impossible and for that reason it took place." Without wanting to violate the cultural specificity of Perednik's comment, I understand this also to mean that poetry, insofar as it resists reification as culturally sanctioned Poetry, is also impossible—and for that reason takes place. For the sake of this collection, I would like to add America to this list, for America is impossible; and for this reason, also, it exists.

Or Americas, for it is in the resistance to any singular unity of identity that the impossibility of America, of a Poetics of the Americas, may be said to dwell. The cultural space of this impossible America is not carved up by national borders or language borders but is transected by innumerable, overlaying, contradictory or polydictory traditions and proclivities and histories and regions and peoples and circumstances and identities and families and collectivities and dissolutions—dialects and ideolects—not national tongues—localities and habitations—not states.

Such an America, however, is imaginary, for everywhere the local is under fire from the imposed standard of a transnational consumer culture and undermined by the imperative to extract it and export it as product.

In the United States, we are particularly bedeviled by our own history of cultural resistance, often confusing the struggles for cultural legitimation of the last century with our own reversed roles in this one. I am thinking of the specific needs, a century ago, that gave rise to the invention of American literature as an academic category within the university system that had only recently countenanced English, or British, literature as a suitable appendix to the study of the classics (primarily Greek and Roman works). At that time, there was a clear necessity for breaking away from the perceived limitations of "island" English literature to build an audience for, and give a measure of respectability and legitimation to, certain New England, Middle Atlantic, and southern English-language texts. In this context, "American" was a strategic rather than an essential category; as a result, the multiethnic and polylinguistic reality of the United States was not accented in early formations of American literature. By 1925, William Carlos Williams, with *In the American Grain*, had given new breadth to the concept of America; yet his related insistence on an American speech suggested a false essence to a concept useful only as a negation: *not* English verse diction. That is, as a negative category, American literature was a useful hypothesis. In contrast, for the present, the idea of American literature understood as a positive, expressive totalization needs to continue to be dismantled.

The problem here is twofold: the totalization of America and the globally dominant position of the United States. Since the United States is the dominant English-language nation in the political, economic, and mass-cultural spheres of the West, its monopolizing powers need to be cracked—from the inside and outside—as surely as one version of England's grip on our language's literature needed to be loosened in the nineteenth and the early twentieth centuries. The same logic that led to the invention of American, as distinct from English, literature now leads to the invention of, on the one hand, an English-language literature not centered in America and, on the other, a poetics of the Americas. Any unitary concept of America is an affront to the multiplicity of Americas that make U.S. culture as vital as it is. America is, to echo Perednik, an "unclassifiable" totality. For there is no one America. The United States is less a melting pot than a simultaneity of inconsolable coexistences—from the all-too-audible spokespeople of the state to the ghostly voices of the almost-lost languages of the sovereign nations of Arapaho, Mohawk, Shoshone, Pawnee, Pueblo, Navaho, Crow, Cree, Kickapoo, Blackfoot, Cheyenne, Zuni, . . . ; though in truth, there are no sovereigns, only sojourners.

For writing, or reading, to assume—and consequently express or project—a national identity is as problematic as for writing to assume a self-identity or group identity. However, in jettisoning such presumptions, some sense of what such entities might be may be revealed. Such exploratory writing does not escape from its sociohistorical situation but rather contributes to an interrogation and reformulation of the *description* of that sociohistorical situation, foregrounding heterogeneous and anomalous elements rather than homogenizing ones. In contrast, attempts to represent an already constituted idea of identity may preclude the possibility of encountering newly emerging identity formations.

I feel much closer to the concerns of some small press magazines in the United Kingdom, Canada, New Zealand, Ireland, and Australia than to most poetry magazines in the United States or the Americas. I would say that *L=A=N=G=U=A=G=E* and *Xul*, the magazine with which Perednik is associated, probably share more than *L=A=N=G=U=A=G=E* shared with most other poetry magazines published in New York.[1] The national focus of "American poetry" tends to encamp poets who would do better to share work and readership; similarly, it tends to arbitrarily limit the horizons of much current criticism of poetry. At the same time, "internationalism," like its Anglophonic cousin the "trans-Atlantic," has provided models of connoisseurship that have removed poems from the local contexts that give them meaning while at the same time developing a canon of works that undervalues the untranslatable particularities not only of given poems but also of the selection of poets. (A related problem of decontextualization is apparent in the reception of "Latin American" fiction in the United States.) Perednik speaks of the serendipitous colliding of different poetries as the "law of poetic coincidence"; this poetic law provides a way to navigate between the universalizing humanisms of internationalism and the parochialism of regionalism and nationalism.

This is not to say that our different national and cultural circumstances are not marked in our poems; on the contrary it is the insistence on registering these social circumferences in the forms of our poems that may be our shared methodological approach. I am also conscious that U.S. poets tend to be less aware of developments in other English-writing countries than the other way around. Often, our boasting about the significance of a non-European American poetry has deafened us to the newness of English language poetries and non-English language poetries even further from Europe than our own, including some being written right in the heart of that "old" world.

The impossible poetics of the Americas does not seek a literature that unifies us as one national or even continental culture: America (the United States), North America (the United States and Anglophonic Canada), multicultural North America (Canada, Mexico, and the United States), Latin America (south of the United States), South America (the "seventh" continent, since in the United States we learn that the Americas are two separate continents). Rather, the impossible poetics of the Americas insists that our commonness is in our partiality and disregard for the norm, the standard, the overarching, the universal. Such poetry will always be despised by those who wish to use literature to foster identification rather than to explore it.

So I hope it will be apparent that while I welcome the challenge of multiculturalism as it has entered U.S. arts and education in the past decade, I continue to find many of its proponents more interested in reinforcing traditional modes of representation than allowing the heterogeneity of forms and peoples that make up the cultural diversity of the Americas to transform poetic styles and personal and group identities. Yet it is hardly surprising that static conceptions of group identity represented by authentic spokespersons continue to ride roughshod over works and individuals whose identities are complex, multiple, mixed, confused, hyperactivated, miscegenated, synthetic, mutant, forming, or virtual.

American literary multiculturalism, insofar as it seeks to promote representative figures, runs the risk of becoming a kind of domestic "internationalism." When we seek representativeness from a poet we often do so at the cost of misrepresenting the poem. At the same time, official verse culture remains dominated by a poetics of individuality and subjectivity that has tried to remain resistant to (not to say "above") not only questions of identity politics but also aesthetic position, a double evasion often expressed, apparently without irony, as "disaffiliation." The result is a homogenization of poetic values and practices undreamt of among poets willing to acknowledge their affiliations.

The problem is how to pursue affinities while resisting unities and how to resist unities without losing the capacity to be poetically responsible—that is, responsive to and supportive of those poetic tendencies and affiliations that deepen, intensify, and extend the activity of poetry. And that means enacting poetry's contemporaneity—the willingness of poets and ability of poems to act on and in the present social and cultural circumstances, including working with the cultural forms and linguistic materials specific to the present. The point is to pursue the collective and dialogic nature of poetry without necessarily defining the nature of this collectivity—call it a virtual collectivity or, to appropriate Stanley Cavell's phrase for Emersonian moral perfectionism, "this new yet unapproachable America," this unrepresentable yet ever presenting collectivity.

\|\|\|

In *Modernisms: A Literary Guide,* the British critic Peter Nicholls schematically contrasts two modernisms that may be applied to American poetry. The first and more familiar kind, associated with a partial reading of Ezra Pound and T. S. Eliot, "rests upon assumptions of a unitary self that carefully differentiates itself from the world of the Object and thus asserts codes of mastery" (200).[2] In this type of modernism, the poem imposes a (masculine) order and form on the (feminine) flux of the modern world; the self is imagined as closed, autonomous, distant, and antagonistic in its effort to establish stable authority. Another modernism can be associated especially with Gertrude Stein and her nonsymbological or constructive practice. In Nicholls's words, this poetic practice is "preoccupied with what seems other but turns out to be the same," thus unsettling the autonomy of the self that is central to the first type of modernism. "Stein shares with H.D. the desire to move beyond the object-based poetics which derives its force from the repudiation of the feminine, and to discover in its place a form of writing that reveals continuities between self and world" by opening the self to that which is outside it (202).

I would propose at least three modernist projects: subjective, objective, and constructive. By nonsymbological or constructive, I am referring to the fact that in many of her works, Stein does not depend on supplemental literary or narrative contexts to secure her meaning but enacts her subjects as continuously actualized presentations of meaning. Unlike Pound or Eliot—with their myriad literary and other references—or Joyce—with his etymological anaphora—with Stein, you are left with the words on the page and the Imaginary structures they build.

In the poetry of the past two decades, we have moved away from the choice of subjective, objective, or even constructive and toward a synthesizing or juxtaposing of these approaches. Here the influence of the dialect poetries of the modernist period gives way to a dialectical poetry that refuses allegiance to standard English without necessarily basing its claim on an affiliation with a definable group's speaking practice. The norm enforces a conduct of representation that precludes poetry as an active agent to further thought, unbound to the restrictions of rationalized ordering systems. Poetry can be a process of thinking rather than a report of things already settled; an investigation of figuration rather than a picture of something figured out. Such ideologically informed, nonstandard language practice I call *ideolectical,* and I find it equally present in U.K. poets such as Maggie O'Sullivan, Tom Leonard, and Tom Raworth; in U.S. poets such as Susan Howe, Bruce Andrews, Lyn Hejinian, Leslie Scalapino, Harryette Mullen, and Clark Coolidge; in Canadian poets such as Steve McCaffery, Deanna Ferguson, Nicole Brossard, Christopher Dewdney, Karen Mac Cormack, Lisa Robertson, and Catriona Strang; or in such South American poets as Perednik and Cecilia Vicuna.[3]

The invention of an ideolectical English language poetry as a poetry of the Americas involves the replacement of the national and geographically centered category of English (or Spanish) poetry not with the equally essentialist category of American poetry but with a field of potentialities, a virtual America that we approach but never possess. English languages, set adrift from the sight/sound sensorium of the concrete experiences of the English people, are at their hearts uprooted and translated: nomadic in origin, absolutely particular in practice. Invention in this context is not a matter of choice: it is as necessary as the ground we walk on.

The impossible poetics of the Americas of which I speak has, in the United States, a history of breaks from the received literary language of England. The vernacular was a crucial factor in many of those breaks, particularly as explored by such African-American poets as Paul Laurence Dunbar, Langston Hughes, Sterling Brown, J. W. Johnson, and Melvin Tolson. At the same time, the American language was being transformed by the "bad" or "broken" English of the European immigrants from the 1880s through the early years of the new century: "new" syntaxes and new expressions came to the New World. Here it is significant that Williams, Stein, Louis Zukofsky, and other makers of a new American poetry were themselves second-language speakers of English, while others were children of second-language speakers, as Peter Quartermain notes in the introduction to *Disjunctive Poetics*. So for these children of immigrants, English became less transparent, more a medium subject to reforming. Correlatively, on the other side of the Atlantic, the explorations of dialect traditions by Basil Bunting in the north of England and Hugh MacDiarmid in Scotland and in the Caribbean by Claude McKay and more recently by Linton Kwesi Johnson, Louise Bennett, Michael Smith, or Kamau Brathwaite (who rejects the term dialect, preferring "nation language"), become a source of shared language resources among English-language poetries.

I realize that my emphasis on nonstandard language practices makes for unexpected affiliations. Tony Crowley, in *Standard English and the Politics of Language,* points to two senses of "standard." A standard is a rallying point for the forward movement of an ideology or group by means of which a unity is invoked—as, for example, a flag in battle. But a standard is also an objective unit of measure and regulator of uniformity; and, as such, it is a product of normalization and averaging. Standard American English involves both these senses: it is a sociohistorical construction—embedding class, ethnic, and racial preferences—that serves to build national unity; and it is also a regulator of language practices, serving to curb deviance. Under the aegis of standardization, problems of social coherence are displaced onto questions of linguistic correctness:

> The search for linguistic unity and identity is one that is founded on acts of violence and repression: a denial of heteroglossia—discursive and historical—in favor of centralizing, static forms. And the victory of one dialect or language over others produces a hierarchy, an ordering of discourse which excludes, distributes and defines what is to count as discourse and what is to be relegated to

oblivion. It brings into being the 'authoritative word' [that in Bakhtin's words] 'is located in a distanced zone, organically connected with a past that is felt to be organically higher. It is, so to speak, the word of the fathers.' There is then no possibility of challenging this discourse. . . . Its authority is already borne along with it and it is the authority of the ruling patriarchal tradition. (Crowley 9–10; Bakhtin 217)

In "our" "own" literature, the most significant past debates on these issues took place in two distinct quarters. Disowning and deflating the "authoritative word" was a central project for Stein and other constructivist poets of the modernist period. Even more explicitly, however, standard English was the center of a debate that took place under the frame of the Harlem Renaissance, itself a geographic displacement of what is more accurately described as African-American arts of the 1920s and the 1930s. Writers such as Hughes and Brown invented and defended a vernacular poetry that refused the standards of literary English advocated by poets such as Countee Cullen. This resulted in a controversy that in complicated ways echoes the debate between Booker T. Washington and W. E. B. Du Bois. The issue in both controversies is the nature, terms, and price of assimilation.

As our literary history is usually told, the nonstandard language practices of the radical modernists (and their descendants) are not linked to the dialect and vernacular practices of African-American poets.[4] But the construction of a vernacular poetry was a major project for many poets, black and white, during the modernist period, and the fact that these developments often took place without reference to each other—the fact of the color line—should not now obscure their intimate formal and sociohistorical connection. Stein's breakthrough into the ideolectical practice of *Tender Buttons*, for example, was prepared by her problematic improvisations on African-American vernacular in "Melanctha." A generation later, both Melvin Tolson and Louis Zukofsky used complex literary framing devices as a means of working with and against—torquing—vernacular linguistic materials. By linking dialect and ideolect, I wish to emphasize the common ground of linguistic exploration, the invention of new syntaxes as akin to the invention of new Americas—or possibilities for America. In Brathwaite's account, however, dialect is better called "nation language." If that is the case, it would seem to run counter to ideolect, whose nations may be described, in Robin Blaser's phrase, as image nations, imaginary, ideological; dialectical in that other sense. I do not wish to relieve this tension so much as to locate it as pivotal to our literary history and contemporary poetics. I am convinced, however, that nonstandard writing practices share a technical commonality that overrides the necessary differences in interpretation and motivation, and this commonality may be the vortical prosodic force that gives us footing with one another.

In *History of the Voice,* Brathwaite's 1979 talk about the "process of using English in a different way from the 'norm'," Brathwaite speaks of the break with the pentameter metric of English verse as decisive in establishing a distinct Caribbean "nation language" rooted in an oral tradition:

> It is *nation language* in the Caribbean that, in fact, largely ignores the pentameter.... English it may be in terms of some of its lexical features. But in its contours, its rhythms and timbre, its sound explosions, it is not English, even though the words, as you hear them, might be English to a greater or lesser degree.... But it is an English which is not the standard, imported, educated English.... It is what I call, as I say, *nation language.* I use the term in contrast to *dialect.* The word "dialect" has been bandied about for a long time, and it carries very pejorative overtones.... Nation language, on the other hand, is the *submerged* area of dialect which is much more closely allied to the African aspect of experience in the Caribbean. (Brathwaite 13)

Brathwaite's nation language is as much a new standard to rally national spirit as it is a break from standardization. Any comparison of ideolectical and dialectical poetry must confront this obvious contradiction: dialect, understood as nation language, has a centripetal force, regrouping often denigrated and dispirited language practices around a common center; ideolect, in contrast, suggests a centrifugal force away from normative practices without necessarily replacing them with a new center of gravity (at least as defined by self or group). Furthermore, the social positions from which these practices emerge will often be quite distinct. Dialect poets may be regarded by the dominant literary culture as outsiders, but they are often also at the center of collective formations that are struggling to obtain self-respect and cultural legitimacy. Ideolect poets often eschew the center with which they may be associated by education or social position to the point of refusing the collective identities with which they might otherwise be affiliated. The point of a social reading of these forms is neither to elide nor reify such differences but to bring them into con*ver*sation. The meaning of poetic forms can never be separated from the social contexts in which they are used since meaning is never uniform but always informed by time and place. My emphasis is on how poetic forms can be used to question, rather than reinforce, the representations and, one might say, the enactments of these social contexts. For the social meaning of these forms is not given but made.

The works of Bunting and MacDiarmid are useful to consider in this respect, for they are both poets whose work, dialect and not, insisted on a "northern" identity—Northumbrian and Scottish—while rejecting closed forms of Northumbrian or Scots nationalism. MacDiarmid's sympathy for but ultimate rejection by both communist and nationalist political parties is exemplary of the tension between localism and socialism or anarchism. Writing next to the island center of traditional English verse, the poetry of MacDiarmid and Bunting skirts the distinction between dialect and ideolect in a continuing dialogue between language and place that dances around and within such ideological fractures and fractals, exposing the materiality of sound patterns to the territorialization of desire. MacDiarmid and Bunting had to invent aspects of the Scots and Northumbrian in *A Drunk Man Looks at the Thistle* and *Briggflatts* (although the inventions were quite different in each case). *Briggflatts* is more a work of constructed syntax than an idiomatic reconstruction of an oral tradition; aurality is its most salient feature.[5] If we understand the direction of "English" away from its island English center as a structural question, then we can begin to see links between poetic projects involving secession, dispersal, and regrouping. We may understand disparate practices as sharing a poetic space that is grounded not in an identical social position but in the English language itself as the material with which we make our regroupings and refoundings. Never just English but always a new English that is an object and a subject of our verse. As Louise Bennett[6] so eloquently and hilariously points out in her 1944 poem "Bans o' Killing," this issue is as much one of the past as of the present and future:

So yuh a de man, me hear bout!
Ah yuh dem sey dah-teck
Whole heap o' English oat sey dat
Yuh gwine kill dialect!

Meck me get it straight Mass Charlie
For me noh quite undastan,
Yuh gwine kill all English dialect
Or jus Jamaica one?

Ef yuh dah-equal up wid English
Language, den wha meck
Yuh gwine go feel inferior, wen
It come to dialect?

Ef yuh kean sing "Linstead Market"
An "Wata come a me y'eye",
Yuh wi haffi tap sing "Auld lang syne"
An "Comin thru de rye".

Dah language weh yuh proad o',
Weh yuh honour and respeck,
Po' Mass Charlie! Yuh noh know sey
Dat it spring from dialect!

Dat dem start fe try tun language,
From de fourteen century,
Five hundred years gawn an dem got
More dialect dan we!

Yuh wi haffe kill de Lancashire
De Yorkshire, de Cockney
De broad Scotch an de Irish brogue
Before yuh start to kill me!

Yuh wi haffe get de Oxford book
O' English verse, an tear
Out Chaucer, Burns, Lady Grizelle
An plenty o' Shakespeare!

Wen yuh done kill "wit" an "humour"
Wen yuh kill "Variety"
Yuh wi haffe fine a way fe kill
Originality!

An mine how yuh dah-read dem English
Book deh pon yuh shelf
For ef yuh drop a "h" yuh mighta
Haffe kill yuhself. (Bennett 209–10)

Bennett's wit makes all the more disturbing her point that suppression of "variety" in language produces the cultural suppression of a people: "Bans o' Killing." A people invents and sustains itself through its shared language, so it is not surprising that colonial governments have often prohibited the use of native languages, dialects, patois, creoles, and pidgins in an effort to maintain social control. Bennett, whose poetry is written in Jamaican idiom, points to, and defuses, the stigma attached to dialect use; but she also makes patent the deep social scar left by the denigration of a particular language practice as inferior. In this sense, dialect becomes the verbal equivalent of skin color: an objective mark of alterity.

The explicitly political use of dialect in contemporary poetry is apparent in the work of Jamaican dub poet Michael Smith,[7] even as he toys with old English rhymes:

Say
Natty-Natty,
no bodder
das weh
yuh culture! (Smith 50)

Or consider not only Linton Kwesi Johnson's deforming spelling "Inglan" but also these raucous lyrics from "Fite Dem Back" in *Inglan Is a Bitch*:[8]

we gonna smash their brains in
cause they ain't got nofink in 'em . . .
fashist an di attack
noh baddah worry 'bout dat[.] (Johnson 20)

Here, Johnson switches from a quoted dialect that he mocks—the first two lines are in the voice of the neofascist "paki bashah"—back to his own dialect voice. Note that brains, in the quoted dialect, is spelled in the standard fashion but that *nothing* manages to suggest *fink* and, more tellingly, in Johnson's comment, *fascist* manages to suggest *shit*. Similarly, in "Sonny's Lettah," Johnson can use a traditional, heavily rhyming prison-letter form more effectively than any contemporary poet I can think of. "For these inheritors of the revolution," says Brathwaite, "nation-language is no longer anything to argue about or experiment with; it is their classical norm and comes out of the same experience as the music of contemporary popular songs: using the same riddims, the same voice-spreads, syllable clusters, blue notes, ostinado, syncopation, and pauses" (45–46). The British poet John Agard puts the case directly in "Listen Mr Oxford Don":[9]

I ent have no gun
I ent have no knife
but mugging de Queen's English
is the story of my life

I don't need no axe
to split / up yu syntax
I dont need no hammer
to mash / up yu grammar[.] (5–6)

As Brathwaite puts it: "It was in language that the slave was perhaps most successfully imprisoned by his master, and it was in his (mis-)use of it that he perhaps most effectively rebelled" (qtd. in Chamberlin 67).[10]

But rebelled into what? Not, I think, a more authentic representation of speech but an even more marvelous realization of the yammering gap between speech and writing (the stammering gaps among speeches and writings).[11] "Writing wrongs speech," as Neil Schmitz puts it in *Of Huck and Alice* (97). In these senses, the nonstandard spelling of dialect writing does not so much transcribe words as underscore the sensuous/sinuous materiality of language. The pleasure is in this play between the written word and the impossible objects of its desires.[12]

Little has been written about Claude McKay's early dialect work, no doubt due to the ambiguous status of certain literary dialect practices even for such eloquent proponents of nation language as Brathwaite:[13] "McKay's first two books of poetry (1912), written in Jamaica, are unique in that they are the first all-dialect collections of an anglophone Caribbean poet. They are however *dialect* as distinct from *nation* because McKay allowed himself to be imprisoned in the pentameter; he didn't let his language find its own parameters" (20). Dialect practice can appear to be a form of self-deprecation as it approaches blackface—the minstrel-mocking of black vernacular by white as well as black performers. As Brathwaite remarks: "Dialect is thought of as 'bad English.' Dialect is 'inferior English.' Dialect is the language when you want to make fun of someone. Caricature speaks in dialect. Dialect has a long history of coming from the plantation where people's dignity is distorted through their language and the descriptions which the dialect gave to them" (13). The anxiety of dialect is inscribed already in Paul Laurence Dunbar's work, where poems in plantation dialect are placed side by side with poems in standard English, both sharing the heavily accented pentameter that Brathwaite marks as problematic but which nonetheless makes Dunbar's *Complete Poems* (1913) one of the most unsettling and provocative works of early modernism. Brathwaite goes on to criticize McKay for his turn to the sonnet in the poems for which he is most famous, noting the heavy cost of McKay's desire for universality. This echoes the debate between advocates of standard literary verse such as Countee Cullen and practitioners of the vernacular such as Sterling Brown, a debate that is at the heart of Houston Baker's *Modernism and the Harlem Renaissance*. Baker identifies the controversy as between "mastery of form" and the "deformation of mastery" (21–22, 31–32, 37, 49, 85–86). In contrast to my approach here, Baker champions the assimilationist poetics of Cullen and Washington, arguing for the longterm efficacy of using dominant cultural forms, as one would a mask, to provide camouflage while precluding total identification. At the same time, he rebukes—unfortunately so, in my view— what he calls the "guerrilla" tactics (77; also 49–52) of resistance and secession represented by Dunbar and others involved with "sounding deformation," a position he associates with Du Bois (51, 93).

The use of dialectical or ideolectical language in a poem marks a refusal of standard English as the common ground of communication. For poets wishing to obliterate or overcome such marks of difference, the choice of the conventional literary language, whether understood as mask or not, reflects a willingness to abide by the linguistic norms of a culture and to negotiate within these norms. Nonstandard language practice suggests an element of cultural resistance that has—as its lower limit—dialogic self-questioning and—as its upper limit—secession and autonomy.

Cullen took up the forms valued as universal by a dominant culture in which the use of African-American dialect—as opposed to those of the Midwest or Northeast—was taken to be a mark of inferiority; his work wears its humanity on its sleeve, the only place where it could be seen in a society defined in large measure by the color line. In such a reading, Cullen can be understood as an American pragmatist par excellence.

Brathwaite, an advocate of nation language—that is, of linguistic autonomy and self-sufficiency—makes an argument against the compromised form of dialect practiced by McKay, seeing it as, at best, the beginning of a cultural practice that comes to fruition, in the Caribbean, with Bennett, Smith, Johnson, and his own work. In the United States during the modernist period, Sterling Brown is probably the foremost practitioner of such a poetics. For Brathwaite, nation language is not a deformation of mastery but the sign of a newly forming collective identity. It moves beyond critique and subversion to positive expressivity, beyond a bogus universality to what Brathwaite—problematically, in my view—understands as a genuine locality.

The tension between universality and locality is not simply a deformation or an embryonic phase of group consciousness to be shed at maturity. As against the positive expressivity of nation language, I would speak of the negative dialectics of ideolect, where ideolect would mark those poetic sites of contest between the hegemonic and the subaltern, to use the terms of Antonio Gramsci. Here would be a poetics of compromise and dependency—of hybridization, contradiction, and multivocality. Under this sign of radical modernism, I would include not only Dunbar and McKay but also Hughes, Jean Toomer, and Tolson. In the United States, I would add, among others, Louis Zukofsky, Hart Crane, and Abraham Lincoln Gillespie; in United Kingdom, I would include Bunting and MacDiarmid.

One thing many of these poets have in common is the influence of Marxism on their poetic practice (Toomer may be the exception.)[14] Marxism is a universalist philosophy with a checkered history of (often contradictory) critiques of nationalism as well as ethnic and racial and sexual essentialisms.

Perhaps the most useful approach to this issue is found in the work of Gramsci, a Sardinian Marxist whose critique of hegemony is grounded in his own experience as a subaltern Italian southerner whose language was marked as inferior by its dialectical difference from the Italian of the North.

In considering the internal contradictions between the local and the universal, the subaltern and the hegemonic, I turn to McKay, who, in poems of breathtaking duplicity and paradox, uses proto-Marxist ideas of universalism to contest the hegemony of British culture in Jamaica. In 1912, when he was twenty-two and still living in Jamaica, McKay published two collections of dialect poetry, *Songs of Jamaica* and *Constab Ballads*. No one reading or commenting on these poems can fail to note the many compromising aspects of this collection. Most obvious are running translations and glosses at the foot of each page, providing unnecessary and misleading translations of dialect words and often giving blatantly, not to say comically, ameliorist interpretations of the poems. Like Dunbar's *Complete Poems,* McKay's dialect poetry is a schizophrenic presentation, foregrounding two unequally powerful readerships, black and white. Given McKay's association with, as Brathwaite puts it, "a Svengali like Walter Jekyll," the controlling hand of white editorial authority is always present on the page.[15] Another equally marked gesture of complicity is the title *Constab Ballads* itself, for what kind of poetic autonomy can we expect from poems written from the point of view of a Jamaican native working for the British as a police constabulary?

How is it possible for an act of linguistic defiance bordering on revolt to appear in a cultural space that would suppress any explicit expression of political opposition? In *The Practice of Everyday Life* (*Arts de faire,* literally "the art of doing"), in a section titled "a diversionary practice," Michel de Certeau speaks of an "enunciative" tactic he calls "*la perruque,*" or "the wig":

> *La perruque* is the worker's own work disguised as the work of his employer. It differs from pilfering in that nothing of material value is stolen. It differs from absenteeism in that the worker is officially on the job. . . . the worker who indulges in *la perruque* actually diverts time (not goods, since he uses only scraps). . . . for work that is free, creative, and precisely not directed toward profit. . . . to deal with everyday tactics in this way would be to practice an "ordinary art," to find oneself in the common situation, and to make a kind of *perruque* of writing itself. (de Certeau 25, 28)

In McKay's 1912 collections, pentameter dialect is the ruse or wig that allows a running double play of ingratiation and defiance. For the white audience, the dialect plays as minstrel show: charming, even ingratiating in its gratuitous nods to British sentiment and in its self-glossing self-deprecations. At the same time, the poems compose a song to the aesthetic power of difference of the sonic and semantic richness of vernacular Jamaican; in their themes, they corrode the very authoritativeness to which they appear to be kowtowing, accumulating a counterhegemonic force that mocks every surface pretense of accommodation. This double play brings to mind Melville's *Benito Cereno,* which, as Aldon Lynn Nielsen points out, "is a dramatization of the white racist mind *not reacting* in the face of a slave insurrection; for the dramatic irony of the novel derives from Delano's inability to recognize that which is palpably before him. He is so much inhabited by the discourse agreements of white mythology" that he misinterprets "the actuality of the slave revolt" as stereotypical gestures of "servile loyalty" (16–18).

Certainly, the most ingratiatingly Anglophilic, doggedly iambic, and apparently self-deprecating poem in *Songs of Jamaica* is "Old England":

Just to view de homeland England, in de streets of London walk . . .
I would see Saint Paul's Cathedral, an' would hear some of de great
Learnin' comin' from de bishops, preachin' relics of old fait';
I would ope me mout' wid wonder at de massive organ soun',
An' would 'train me eyes to see de beauty lyin' all aroun'
. . . .
I'd go to de City Temple, where de old fait' is a wreck
An' de parson is a-preachin' views dat most folks will not tek;
I'd go where de men of science meet togeder in deir hall,
To give light unto de real truths, to obey king Reason's call. (63–74)

On the surface, this is a poem of nostalgia and complacency, even ending on the subservient note of the native returning home from the mother country, resting "glad an' contented in me min' for evermore" (65). No wonder Brathwaite points to this poem as an example of McKay's "literary colonialism in the primordial (?) anglicanism" (20). But the poem overplays the sentiment in a way that, at least at the distance from which I am reading it, calls attention to itself or calls for a different kind of attention, a reading between the lines. What, after all, is this "great learning" coming from "relics" of an "old fait'" but the old *fate* of racism and colonialism; what is this "beauty lyin' all aroun'" but more relics of lying beauty overturned by the "real truths," or Reason. For this poem, after all, is unambiguous in enforcing the truths (plural) of Reason: the cant of the preachers is a lying beauty, a wreck of learning that appears beautiful or truthful only with eyes "trained." (But by whom?) Read as wig, the poem begins to destabilize, although a line like "I would ope me mout' wid wonder at de massive organ soun'" remains difficult, as far as I can see, to turn around. Yet even the textual glosses can seem to take on significance; here, only two words, among a number that are equally nonstandard, are singled out for definition: "t'o't"("thought") and "min" ("mind"). It is as if we are to be reminded that the native has thoughts and a mind of his own: in this sense, *mine* is synonymous with *mind*. Perhaps this poem is not so far from Louise Bennett's work after all, considering that McKay's work was Bennett's first example of Jamaican dialect poetry (Brathwaite 28). Even the "old" in "Old England" begins to seem more ominous.

Am I overreading? McKay is careful to note in *A Long Way from Home* that he became a "free-thinker" before he was thirteen, discovering "like a comet . . . the romance of science in Huxley's *Man's Place in Nature* and Haeckel's *The Riddle of the Universe*" (12). By the time he was writing *Songs of Jamaica* and *Constab Ballads,* McKay was steeped in Spinoza (for a while he considered himself a pantheist), Schopenhauer, and Spencer (and, by extension, Darwin).

Consider McKay's "Cudjoe Fresh from de Lecture" about "How de buccra te-day tek time an' bégin teach / All of us dat was deh in a clear open speech" (*Songs* 55). The buccra's, or white's, "open speech" is about evolution, a humanist scientific theory that, in Cudjoe's interpretation, undermines the racist ideas that are lived out in the plantation system reflected in the "imprisoned pentameter," the closed (constrained) speech, of the poem: "Him tell us 'bout we self, an' mek we fresh again" (55). This idea of being made "fresh" (not used, exploited) is what Cudjoe tells as the urgent "news" from this lecture: "Me look 'pon me black 'kin, an' so me head grow big, . . . / For ebery single man, no car' about dem rank, / Him bring us ebery one an' put 'pon same plank" (55). Looking upon his black skin, he also sees his black *kin* in this collective vision of the equality of "ebery man." On one reading, "me head grow big" has the same stereotyping gesture of self-patronization as "ope me mout wid wonder"; but, taken literally, it means the opposite—the news reverses the patronizing of him and his kin, returns heads to actual size. If evolution "tell us 'traight 'bout how de whole t'ing came" (56), then Christianity, which preaches that blackness is a "cuss," tells it crooked: "An' looking close at t'ings, we hab to pray quite hard / Fe swaller wha' him say an' don't t'ink bad o' Gahd" (56). Is ingratiation or defiance hidden in a smirk as broad as the face of "Gahd"? If evolution preaches chance rather than predetermination, then the scenario of *Benito Cereno* is closer to hand, for no natural law precludes the justice of insurrection (the hound, let us say, being on the other tooth): "But suppose eberyt'ing could tu'n right upside down, / Den p'rhaps we'd be on top an' givin' some one houn'" (57). The very next stanza quells such an interpretation, noting that were the Africans not brought to the Americas, they might still be "half-naked . . . tearin' t'rough de bush wid all de monkey"—"Wile an' uncibilise', an' neber comin' tame" (57). Yet the poem is not about the taming effect of this "clear open speech" but how this way of thinking inspires strong feelings that lead to Cudjoe's *own* uncorked "talk." Acknowledging that his talk is going in two directions, Cudjoe then says maybe not:

> Yet both horse partly runnin' in de selfsame gallop
> For it is nearly so de way de buccra pull up:
> Him say, how de wul' stan', dat right will neber be,
> But wrong will eber gwon till dis wul' en' fe we. (58)

The buccra stops the gallop of Cudjoe's racing thoughts by saying right will never be. But the last line of the poem is ambiguous: for if wrong will grow till this world ends *for us,* does that not mean that we will have to end it ourselves, so that we may establish the truth of a new world? I hear this, anyway, with all the doubling I have so far noted, in the title of a poem that might be read as a hymn to accommodation, "Whe' Fe Do?" The gloss provided for this title encapsulates the issues sharply; it runs like this: "What to do?—equivalent to 'What can't be cured, must be endured'" (27). Each stanza of the poem ends with a variation on the title's question: "All we can do" (27); "Dat we might do" (27); "For dat caan' do" (28); "Whe' else fe do?" (28); "De best to do" (28); and, finally, "But whe' fe do?" (29). But cannot (caan') the title also mean "What Is to Be Done?"—all that can be done, what is best to do, what must be done?

What to make of this? In McKay's Jamaican poems, iambic pentameter is made the metrical mark of colonialism, the chains around a corrosive dialect. Pentameter is used to serve as the acoustic trapping of "old England," yoked to a diffident creole, the weird ordinary of verse dialect. It is an oxymoronic form. In this sense, the dialect poems have a similar implosive power to McKay's "If We Must Die," written five years after his move to the United States in 1914, which creates a tension between the conventional expectations of the Elizabethan sonnet form and its violent and unsettling subject matter.

Claude McKay's Jamaican poems are not free verse. They are marked by their uneasy relation to the cultural regime under which they were written. But what is the natural form for a vernacular poetry?[16] MacDiarmid and Bunting offer a radically modernist setting for their dialect works, which are far cries from the more direct, sometimes ethnographic, representations of Sterling Brown. Hughes's style is fluid but often sets itself apart from the quoted vernacular that peoples his work (as in "The Weary Blues"); unlike Brown, identification with the demotic voices is not total. In his *Harlem Gallery: Book I, The Curator*, Melvin Tolson chooses a radically defamiliarizing form to set his multilectical excursions:

> High as the ace of trumps,
> as egghead says, "'The artist is a strange bird,' Lenin says."
> Dipping in every direction like a quaquaversal,
> the M.C. guffaws: "Hideho, that swig would make
> a squirrel spit in the eye of a bulldog!"
> Bedlam beggars
> at a poet's feast in a people's dusk of dawn counterpoint
> protest and pride
> in honkey tonk rhythms
> hot as an ache in a cold hand warmed. . . .
> A Creole co-ed from Basin street by way of
> Morningside Heights . . .
> brushes my shattered cocktail glass into a tray . . .
> O spiritual, work-song, ragtime, blues jazz—
> consorts of
> the march, quadrille, polka, and waltz! (82–83)

This is neither universal poetry nor nation language. It is "quaqaversal poetry," a close relative to ideolect. Tolson's hybridization of discourse, featuring the music of shattering glass (pentameter, anyone?) on the tray of a "Creole co-ed" from New Orleans by way of the Upper West Side, mixes cultural references with the sophisticated elan of a poet who makes language his home: the poet's feast, this counterpoint of contrasting rhythms, protest and pride. It is not that the indigenous cultural forms of African Americans—spiritual, work song, ragtime, and blues, so remarkably and directly charted in Brown's poetry—are the same as the European dance forms; but a process of creolization is underway: they consort with each other in the dance of America.

The closest thing I can think of to Tolson's dazzling mix of citations and refutations, discourse as concourse, is Zukofsky's collage poems, from "Poem Beginning 'The'" to "*A*." I think the "Creole co-ed" may even be a kissing cousin to Zukofsky's "A Foin Lass" in his translation into Brooklynese of "Donna mi Prega," "A Foin Lass Bodders." Zukofsky's use of slang is not, to be sure, an instance of cultural identification, and his sense of his Jewishness reflected the ambivalence of many leftists of his generation. He had, after all, chosen not to write in his native tongue—or at least the language of his parents, Yiddish—specifically deciding not to join with some of his differently radical contemporaries, who wrote Yiddish poetry as an assertion of what could well be called Jewish nation language. But Zukofsky's ear was tuned to the local and the vernacular; and even as he transforms the demotic into his own brand of ideolect, the origin in the ordinary is patent.

When de Certeau writes of the practice of the wig as "an ordinary art," he provides a reminder that dialect and ideolect practices are practices of the ordinary and, in this way, are linked to other demotic literary practices; but de Certeau also also indicates that the ordinary grounds itself in provisional constructions, not natural facts. The ordinary eludes fixed forms of representation; it can be evoked, not captured. For the ordinary captured becomes merely captions on a vanished object, an evacuated site for the residual rubbernecking of exhausted passersby. The poetic practice of the ordinary is synthetic and synthesizing, not essentializing. Verse dialect, like any representation of speech in writing, is always a form of invention.

One of the extraordinary things about the poetics of the ordinary is that it can make poems that look so strange. Any approach to the ordinary is partial because the ordinary, like materiality itself, is inexhaustible. The poetics of the ordinary can set its sights on a series of aspects—meter, diction, theme, lexicon. Poetic attention to any one of these aspects may make a poem that will seem alien to those accustomed to different literary conventions. Transcribed speech, for example, may seem more unnatural than the idealized conventions for representing speech. Dialect, because it uses a nonstandard lexicon, can look as odd as the zaum or neologistic poems of Velimer Khlebnikov, David Melnick, Abraham Lincoln Gillespie, or P. Inman, even to the native speaker of the represented idiom. The ordinary erodes and resists the standard, just as standard English and normative verse forms exoticize and defamiliarize the ordinary. There can be no completely ordinary poetry because there can be no poetry without style or form. "We fling ourselves, constantly longing, on this form" (Stevens 470).

Very little has been written about the ideolectical writing of Gillespie.[17] His pervasively neologistic work bears some resemblance to *Finnegans Wake;* certainly, Gillespie knew Joyce's work. Unlike Joyce, Gillespie was not interested in maximizing the etymologic resonances of words but rather in creating a kind of scat writing, with jazz as a significant influence. American identity, along with self-expression, is certainly under erasure, more likely actively being erased, in "Expatracination" (out from fatherland and race/roots), Gillespie's response to a 1928 *transition* questionnaire on Americans living in Europe:

> the Spiritual Future of America is not to evolve till a present diabetes is admit > removed, t'wit: America's total lack of parent-sagacity to exprimply an especially-while-correcting them goodwill toward, and to cull an early admiration from the children ... THEN—the American Spirit will commence-sing as naive-direct-

elimgoalpursue-clearly as its present FolkMelod—"PopularSong," frequently as blare-OutréFruct-freely as its dynaSaxophoneyc. . . . (i.e. Fair, groove-compulsed into an inevitaBanter-Fair—we *are* a Good Will-Collective—will assume social sensitude, a BodyClap-RazzCourtly deft-joice-skew-Apply-akin (somehow) to the finesse of France's Golden period. . . . Semitised Russia will certainly psychYap doubly, its individuentsremainingscorn-evadedDefeatists, speaking their present flapdoodleNonDigninholdLiable'd rushout-heedless-O-Self!-stuff. (17–18)

If dialect poetry seems to foster group identification, ideolect poetry may seem to foster the opposite: a rejection or troubling of identity structures—whether group or individual. Yet the rejection of received ideas of identity can also be understood as the continuation of the politics of identity by other means. The poetics of identity cannot be symmetrical for the subaltern and for that which it is subaltern to. For every poetics of cultural legitimation, might not there also need to be a poetics of delegitimation? (As in, "Please move over." Or else we fall in the "groove-compulsed . . . Banter" of America as [we are not] "Good Will-Collective.") This passage from Gillespie reminds me of nothing so much as one of Bruce Andrews's "dynaSaxophoneyc" riffs of invented slang in *I Don't Have Any Paper So Shut Up (or, Social Romanticism)*, which, like Gillespie's work, approaches the vernacular question from the other end of the stick—that is, none too pretty out there. The evisceration of a preassigned cultural identity, as in Andrews (a son, like Gillespie, of affluent white America), is also a form of identity politics.

Khlebnikov's *zaum,* or transense poetry, was made to transcend the divisions of national languages; he wanted to write an ideolect that all could understand. *Zaum*'s desire for universality is marked by its high coefficient of weirdness—which is to say, its abiding and enchanting peculiarity. At another subdivision of this spectrum, David Melnick's homophonic, and therefore ideolectical, translation of Homer, *Men in Aida,* may first be read for the sheer pleasure of its sonic plenitude; but after a while, the playful signification of both a gay and poetic *sub*culture, an erotic and writerly community, is unmistakable:

Ache I on a rope alone, guy guard on a wreck, day oh say sting.
Hose cape pee, oh tit, toes on echo sat. O Phoibos Apollo. . . .
Egg are oh yummy. Andrews call o' semen hose Meg a pant on.
Argue on, critic. All high pay, then tie Achaioi. (n.p.)

No more a poet of the Americas than Bunting or MacDiarmid, Javant Biarujia, an Australian poet, has embarked on the most systematically and literally ideolectical poetry of which I am aware. Over the past twenty-five years, since he was a teenager, Biarujia has been working with an invented language that he calls

Taneraic; he also edits a poetry magazine, *taboo jadoo,* dedicated to "the discussion and expression of private language (*langue close*)," which is in the process of publishing an extensive Taneraic-English dictionary:

> MEPA. 1. present (n.). 2. being in the process of. 3. in (*often with gerund*). A
> *mepa* xirardi celini armin. A is wearing a beautiful shirt. Vadas ibescya
> *mepa* avi bouain. I failed *in* my attempt. Anqaudi rasra ilir *mepa* virda.
> There's no point [*in*] waiting.
>
> *mepaceti.* nowadays
> *mepadesqesati.* this morning
> *mepadesqovati.* this evening; tonight
> *mepadesusati.* this afternoon
> *mepaiveti.* today
> *mepajabeti.* up-to-date; modern
> *mepanintati.* for the night; tonight
> *mepa yu.* whereas
> *mepeili.* in every place: everywhere
> MEPIR. imagination. *mepirdi.* imagine. *mepiri.* imaginary. *mepirocya.*
> imagination; fantasy; hallucination. *mepirsya.* fancy . . .
> *mepir rin.* delusion. *das mepir rindi.* delude
> *mepir tane.* vision.
> *mepir troutou.* fancy.
> *mepir uza.* vision, foresight. *das mepir uzadi.* envision; visualize, envisage
> MEQA. sexual prowess *or* potency. (94)

This is from a dream recorded in Biarujia's diary: "Mepadesqesati, vamahusatta ye trahemoqá e *Abdeleslam.* . . . Ayoi vasyenda, tusqeriaru yole bayada e tusqer yoca, busai go ayoi vajesda vaireubda yole ayoi qussada. Vasezoqda gon. . . . Oubqendiyo. Amahusatta, busai sezoqiaru duvondi aiban desqes."[18]

As dialect becomes vernacular, as the demotic is traded for ideolect, we may hear a complication, evasion, or erasure of identity more than a celebration of it: an exploration of the space between identities more than the establishment of a primary identity. Then again, perhaps what we hear is a writing that moves beyond the present definitions and inscriptions of collective and individual identifications and toward a virtual or coming identity about which these confusions and comminglings—call them confabulations—hint; as if such writing leaves room for readers' multifoliate projections.

I am conscious that an ideolectical poetry, insofar as it may dismantle whatever self or group identities we may have already developed, risks making us more atomized and so more passive. In this state of postmodern paranoia, all collective formations—real or imagined—are ironized or aestheticized, that is, debunked as arbitrary codes, with fashion and market ascendant as the arbiters of value. If social identities are to be made problematic as part of the poetic process, this may be in order to forge new collective identities that will enable a more resourceful resistance to rigidly territorializing clannishness and paralyzingly depoliticizing codicity.

The problem is how to be resistant to the reductiveness of all forms of positivism without succumbing to the relativistic erosions of market value that transform poetry from an arena for social exploration or expression to an empty marker of subjectivity in designated free-trade zones (to which both poet and reader are subject). That is, to presume a realm of social truths against the one truth of technorationality and its schizoid doubles, triumphalist capitalism and religious fundamentalism.

Blake remains the greatest emblem of this "Mental Fight" in the English poetry traditions, and Blake's active, oppositional Imagination—"Image Nations"—is a vital source for a poetics of the Americas.

The point is not to display imagination but to mobilize imaginations.

How, though, can we mobilize imaginations, those imaginary nations, when, for the most part, imagination and subjectivity have become housepets of the personal lifestyle industry, cousins to a creativity that seems to apply more to earrings than to hearing? This is no doubt Adorno's fear in questioning the historical role of lyric poetry in the wake of a systematic extermination process that seems to show up all our means of representation as thin, palely inadequate to the realities at hand.

For most conventional verse practices, like many other forms of cultural production, are more the products of an ideological system than of any putative author. As a result, they can be read as cultural symptoms rather than as the inspired and original works of an autonomous author. However, the current movement of cultural studies risks leveling all art to the status of symptom. For poetry can, even if it often does not, resist absorption into the zeitgeist. No artist can remain entirely free from collaboration with the society in which she or he works—history is too consuming for that—but relative degrees of resistance are possible. Art can provide a means—cognitive maps, if you will—by which to read culture. New forms provide new methods of critique.

Surely, the subjectivized, gutted lyric that dominates poetry today proves Adorno's point. Nonetheless, from this same historical point of view, I would say that poetry is the most necessary form of language practice after the wars: but a different poetry than we have known. The task of creating this poetry is impossible and, for that reason, takes place.

Notes

An initial version of this essay was prompted, in part, by a panel on the "Poetics of Americas" organized by Ernesto Grosman and presented at New York University in March 1994. Much of the material in this essay was presented in a series of seminars at the Poetics Program at SUNY-Buffalo. I am indebted to many of the participants for their comments.

1. A *Xul* reader, edited by Ernesto Grosman, was published in 1997 by Roof Books. *L=A=N=G=U=A=G=E* was a magazine I coedited with Bruce Andrews from 1978 to 1981.

2. The formulation here is Peter Quartermain's, from a letter (17 May 1994).

3. For a related discussion of the multiplicitous chartings of American identity in Lyn Hejinian, Haryette Mullen, and Theresa Hak Kyung Cha, situated in the context of a reading of Stein and Dickinson, see Juliana Spahr, "Re Letter and Read Her: The Reader-Centered Text in American Literature," Ph.D. diss., State University of New York at Buffalo, 1995.

4. A new and important exception is North's *Dialect of Modernism*. North contrasts the mimicry of black dialect by white modernists and the skepticism of some African-American poets toward dialect. "Linguistic imitation and racial masquerade are so important to transatlantic modernism because they allow the writer to play at self-fashioning. Jazz means freedom to Jakie Rabinowitz [the Jolson character in *The Jazz Singer*] partly because it is fast and rhythmically unrestrained but also because it is not ancestrally his. . . . For African-American poets of this generation, however, dialect is a 'chain.' In the version created by the white minstrel tradition, it is a constant reminder of the literal unfreedom of slavery" and what followed (11). This reflects, in part, the view of James Weldon Johnson, who, in his preface to *God's Trombones*, underscores that dialect verse is a "limited instrument . . . with but two complete stops, pathos and humor" (7; see also note 13).

North goes on to scrutinize dialect and "primitivist" elements in such modernists as Eliot, Stein, Williams, and Loy, which he sees not as forging a new poetics of the Americas but as trapped in a racist ventriloquism. Indeed, North suggests that "white interest in African-American language and culture was, if anything, more dangerous than indifference" (11)—a conclusion that is sucked into the very vicious circles North's book sets out to critique.

5. Peter Quartermain, in a letter (18 March 1995), comments: "The new English that each uses is inescapably itself, a shade alien to the ear and at the same time a shade more 'authentically' English, because it departs from the koine, standard English, even though it is comprehensible in an ordinary English context and to an ordinary English ear (whatever ordinary means there—one used to 'standard' I suppose, but that concept has been decaying for the last forty or so years I think). You'll have noted that I'm saying nothing about what sort of syntax that is, but I do think it cultivates tur-

bulence and roughness to the ear and tongue because the smooth and the graceful and the beautiful . . . are not only 'southron' but also 'literary', gesturing lazily as they do to a pitifully limited concept of what constitutes the sublime. Like Mina Loy, they cultivate 'gracelessness' (but then one has to define 'grace,' no?) and might indeed be said to share with her the project which says 'I do not write poetry'—if what the centre produces is poetry, then they want none of it, reaching to another definition of sense and discourse, derived from dialect/ideolect speech, and from prose."

6. Bennett, a popular performer in Jamaica, was born in 1919.

7. Smith, who was born in Kingston, Jamaica, in 1954 was killed in 1983.

8. The distinction between the two voices is even more marked in Johnson's performance. Thanks to Nick Lawrence for his comments on this poem/song, as well as other comments on the manuscript.

9. It is significant that Agard's poem opens the anthology *The New British Poetry* as well as the section of black poets, which includes Johnson and several other poets working with dialect (or nation language): Valerie Bloom, Jean Binta Breeze, Merle Collins, Grace Nichols, Levi Tafari. Mottram's and Edwards's sections in the anthology specifically chart poets working in the wake of Bunting and MacDiarmid. Thus, at least in the United Kingdom, the two streams I navigate in this essay are brought into close proximity.

10. In the United States, the explicitly political dimension of these issues emerges in the "English First" movement as well as in confrontations over the use of black English.

11. On the poetics of limping, staggering, stuttering, and stammering, see Mackey, "Sound and Sentiment, Sound and Symbol."

12. This is a good place to thank Robert von Hallberg for his detailed reading of the manuscript and for his many helpful suggestions.

13. North's *Dialect of Modernism* includes a chapter on McKay, "Quashie to Buccra: The Linguistic Expatriation of Claude McKay," which begins with a discussion of his dialect poetry.

14. Peter Quartermain, in a letter (18 March 1995), notes that Bunting had read *Capital*. Despite his often stated antipathy to Marx "as economist and call it historian—it's the Hegelian side of Marx, the notion of that historical dialectic which will inevitably (or not) bring about historical change, the withering away of the state . . . Bunting had great sympathy for Marx as social critic, as let's say 'humanist,' and was especially taken with [his] diagnoses of the conditions of the working (and unemployed) poor."

15. According to McKay in his autobiography *A Long Way from Home,* Jekyll "became my intellectual and literary mentor and encouraged me to continue writing verses in Negro dialect" (13). Jekyll, McKay continues, "had gone among the peasants and collected their field-and-yard songs (words and music) and African folk tales and published them in a book called *Jamaica Song and Story* [1907]." Jekyll "became interested when he first saw my verses—enthusiastic really—and said they sounded like the articulate consciousness of the peasants" (13).

16. Lorenzo Thomas points to the significance of James Weldon Johnson's *God's Trombones: Seven Negro Sermons in Verse* (1927) as "an attempt to distinguish an au-

thentic African-American vernacular from dialect stereotypes using Modernist poetic form" in a review of Eric J. Sundquist's *Hammers of Creation: Folk Culture in African-American Fiction*. I am grateful to Thomas's discussion of Johnson as part of a Poetics Program lecture on Melvin Tolson at SUNY-Buffalo on 14 November 1991.

17. Gillespie was born in Philadelphia in 1895; he died in 1950.

18. Biarujia provides the translation in an offprint from *Vehicle* 3 (1992): "This morning I awoke from a nightmare about Abdeleslam.... I ran to him, moving in slow motion, and when I reached him I cried out that I loved him. I cried.... I kissed him. I woke up, and spent breakfast in tears" (n.p.). In a letter (23 May 1995) responding to a draft of this essay (and correcting a few typos I had made in his Taneraic), Biarujia says he has translated the word ideolectical into a Taneraic paraphrase: "*aspelasi remou abaq sancyab e sava mamale* (lit., nonfigurative thought-basis-way and personal-speech)."

Works Cited

Agard, John. "Listen Mr Oxford Don." In *The New British Poetry*. Ed. Gillian Allnutt, Fred D'Aguiar, Ken Edwards, and Eric Mottram. London: Palladin, 1988. 5–6.

Andrews, Bruce. *I Don't Have Any Paper So Shut Up (or, Social Romanticism)*. Los Angeles: Sun and Moon Press, 1992.

Baker, Houston A., Jr. *Modernism and the Harlem Renaissance*. Chicago: University of Chicago Press, 1987.

Bakhtin, M. M. *The Dialogic Imagination*. Trans. Caryl Emerson and Michael Holquist. Austin: University of Texas Press, 1981.

Bennett, Louise. *Jamaica Labrish*. Kingston, Jamaica: Sangster's Book Stores, 1966.

Biarujia, Javant. *Nainougacyou Tanerai Sasescya Sepou E–Na/Taneraic-English Dictionary E–Na*. Ser. 6 of *taboo jadoo*. Melbourne: Nosukomo, summer 1992/1993.

Brathwaite, Edward Kamau. *History of the Voice: The Development of Nation Language in Anglophone Caribbean Poetry*. London: New Beacon Books, 1984.

Bunting, Basil. *Briggflatts*. London: Fulcrum Press, 1966.

Cavell, Stanley. *This New Yet Unapproachable America*. Albuquerque: Living Batch Press, 1989.

Chamberlin, J. Edward. *Come Back to Me My Language*. Urbana: University of Illinois Press, 1993.

Crowley, Tony. *Standard English and the Politics of Language*. Urbana: University of Illinois Press, 1989.

de Certeau, Michel. *The Practice of Everyday Life*. Trans. Stephen Rendall. Berkeley: University of California Press, 1984.

Dunbar, Paul Laurence. *Complete Poems*. New York: Dodd, Mead, 1913.

Gillespie, Abraham Lincoln. "Expatracination." In *The Syntactic Revolution*. Ed. Richard Milazzo. New York: Out of London Press, 1980. 17–18.

Grosman, Ernesto Livon, ed. *The "Xul" Reader: An Anthology of Argentine Poetry, 1980–1996*. New York: Roof Books, 1997.

Johnson, James Weldon. *God's Trombones: Seven Negro Sermons in Verse.* 1927. Rpt., New York: Penguin, 1990.

Johnson, Linton Kwesi. *Inglan Is a Bitch.* London: Race Today Publications, 1980.

MacDiarmid, Hugh. *A Drunk Man Looks at the Thistle.* In *Selected Poetry.* New York: New Directions, 1993. 24–113.

Mackey, Nathaniel. "South and Sentiment, Sound and Symbol." In *The Politics of Poetic Form: Poetry and Public Policy.* Ed. Charles Bernstein. New York: Roof Books, 1990. 87–118.

McKay, Claude. *A Long Way from Home.* New York: Harcourt, Brace and World, 1970.

———. *Songs of Jamaica.* In *The Dialect Poems of Claude McKay.* Plainville, N.Y.: Books for Libraries Press, 1972. 1–134.

Melnick, David. *Men in Aida, Book One.* Berkeley, Calif.: Tuumba, 1983.

Nicholls, Peter. *Modernisms: A Literary Guide.* Berkeley: University of California Press, 1995.

Nielsen, Aldon Lynn. *Reading Race: White American Poets and the Racial Discourse in the Twentieth Century.* Athens: University of Georgia Press, 1988.

North, Michael. *The Dialect of Modernism: Race, Language, and Twentieth-Century Literature.* New York: Oxford University Press, 1994.

Quartermain, Peter. *Disjunctive Poetics: From Gertrude Stein and Louis Zukofsky to Susan Howe.* New York: Cambridge University Press, 1992.

Schmitz, Neil. *Of Huck and Alice: Humorous Writing in American Literature.* Minneapolis: University of Minnesota Press, 1983.

Smith, Michael. *It a Come.* San Francisco: City Lights, 1989.

Stein, Gertrude. *Tender Buttons.* Los Angeles: Sun and Moon Press, 1994.

Stevens, Wallace. "An Ordinary Evening in New Haven." In *Collected Poems.* New York: Alfred A. Knopf, 1978. 470.

Thomas, Lorenzo. Review of *The Hammers of Creation: Folk Culture in African-American Fiction,* by Eric J. Sundquist. *American Book Review,* March–May 1995, 4.

Tolson, Melvin. *Harlem Gallery—Book I: The Curator.* New York: Twayne Publishers, 1965.

Williams, William Carlos. *In the American Grain.* New York: New Directions, 1933.

5

"THE STEP OF IRON FEET":
CREATIVE PRACTICE IN THE WAR SONNETS
OF MELVIN B. TOLSON AND GWENDOLYN BROOKS

Maria K. Mootry

The literary careers of two mid-twentieth-century black poets, Melvin B. Tolson and Gwendolyn Brooks, were shaped by the poets' perceptions of a crisis in creative practice in black poetry. During interviews, Tolson and Brooks have discussed their efforts to illuminate black experience by new poetic modes, not only out of an art-for-art's-sake commitment but also in an effort to honor the complex reality and poetics of black life.[1] As mature poets, Tolson and Brooks used an eclectic practice that would simultaneously answer modernism's stringent demands *and* black values, hopes, and dreams. In their initial publications, Tolson's *Rendezvous with America* (1944) and Brooks's *A Street in Bronzeville* (1945), the authors' series of war sonnets serve as models for the genesis and evolution of their respective ideas about creative practice in relation to social issues.

Nowhere are black values, hopes and dreams more problematic than when black Americans are faced with the issue of war. Phillis Wheatley, Frances E. W. Harper, and Paul Laurence Dunbar had expressed the powerful reactions of blacks to the Revolutionary War and the Civil War in standard poetic forms. Their poems reflected the dual black response to these times of upheaval— fierce loyalty was invariably yoked to hopes for increased equity and inclusion in the American community. Accordingly, the poets cheered or chided, critiqued or collaborated, as the times fluctuated. In the social consciousness of their war poetry, Tolson and Brooks carry on this African-American tradition of social poetry. Additionally, what Tolson and Brooks do with their war sonnets illustrates, in microcosm, the progress of the black sonnet and the richness and diversity of craft within the black poetic tradition. Building on the social-protest sonnets popular among 1920s Harlem Renaissance poets, Tolson and Brooks enrich the sonnet by infusing it with elements from a variety of "low" cultural traditions in new, unexpected ways. Their sonnets reflect the contemporary impulse, also found in such modern poets as e. e. cummings and Robert Lowell, to wrest aural and visual creative practice from sonnet conventions. In Tolson's war sonnets, for example, creative practice unites the hyperbolic conventions of American folktales with contemporary propagandist mass-art techniques. In Brooks's sonnets, however, creative practice lies in the rich vocative and visual architecture she achieves when she joins her twelve sonnets into an impressionistic sequence. In short, Tolson, through his use of vivid personal landscapes, narrative, and epigraph, creates a kind of popular-art or poster sonnet; while Brooks, using the same elements, creates an intricate collage-like assembly by adding visual prosody and shifting voice. Both poets illustrate what Raymond Williams has acutely observed about the evolution of art forms: "Creative practice is . . . of many kinds. . . . It can be the long and difficult remaking of an inherited (determined) practical consciousness. . . . It can be more evident practice; the reproduction and illustration of hitherto excluded and subordinated models; the embodiment and performance of known but excluded and subordinated experiences and relationships; the articulation and formation of latent, momentary, and newly possible consciousness" (212).

When Tolson and Brooks published their first volumes of poetry in the mid-1940s, America and most of the rest of the world was involved in the cataclysmic struggle against racism and fascism of World War II. Denis Judd's *Posters of World War II* reproduces posters that urge Americans to "AVENGE DECEMBER 7," join the U.S. Army, or support the war effort in other ways. In fact, the dust jacket of *A Street in Bronzeville* carries a plea (under a photo of Brooks) for the public to purchase war bonds.[2] Jack D. Foner documents the irony of black men being called on to risk their lives in the war effort while the American armed forces routinely practiced the most racist policies of American society. In 1939, as World War II approached, the National Association for the Advancement of Colored People's publication *The Crisis* had issued a dire, but soon-to-be-fulfilled, prediction concerning military segregation and discrimination: "Judging from prevailing Jim Crow practices in the armed forces of the United States today, the next war . . . will see the same gross maltreatment of the Negro soldiers seen in World War [I]" (qtd. in Foner 132). By the war's end in the fall of 1945, another observer, writing in *Commonwealth* magazine, summed up the fate of black American servicemen during the war: "Perhaps the sorriest chapter in the story of the war which has just come to an end is the treatment accorded Negroes in the American armed forces. In a war ostensibly fought against a racist ideology we ourselves have practiced the same ideology" (qtd. in Foner 133). Both of these comments suggest the disappointment of black Americans who felt that America once again had failed to fulfill its social contract with its minority citizens. Thus, Tolson and Brooks faced the Ellisonian "complex fate" of many black artists. They needed to construct a responsible art that could combat fascism *and* carry the burden of their love of democracy and their criticism of democracy's failure in America. Their war sonnets developed a uniquely coded aesthetic with varying success.

Tolson's War Sonnets: The Sonnet as Poster Art

Robert Farnsworth has noted the indirect relationship of Tolson's *Rendezvous with America* to the Second World War by observing that "the arrangement of the poems within the book contains a message aimed at a world at war" (77). Indeed, "Rendezvous," the lengthy title poem, climaxes with a stanza condemning the bombing of Pearl Harbor and denouncing "fascist spawn." "Rendezvous" thus operates diachronically by naming, in the manner of a praise song, historical sites such as Plymouth Rock and Valley Forge; but its synchronic function is to rededicate the speaker ritually to a fresh place and event. For example:

> The traitor's ruse
> And the traitor's lie,
> Pearl Harbor ruins
> Of sea and sky,
> Shall live with me
> Till the day I die.
>   *Here,*
>   *Now,*
> At Pearl Harbor, I remember
> I have a rendezvous at Plymouth Rock and Valley Forge
> This Seventh of December. (10–11)

In these lines, vistas of American landscape, past and present, become a "charged field"[3] saturated with meaning and full of nuance. More importantly, the speaker's focus and his speaking posture constitute a trope, a figure that supersedes narration or discourse. "*Here, / Now, /* At Pearl Harbor, I remember" incorporates space, image, time, speaker, and the speakerly text into a single charged metaphor.

When Tolson again turns to the theme of war in his sonnets, however, he usually abandons the first-person mode and adopts a combination of bestiary, fable-like narration, hyperbolic symbolism, and sloganistic use of the epigraph.

His sonnets seem to speak textually, not only to the literary tradition of protest and satire but also to the twentieth-century art form often associated with war—poster art. Widely used in all countries during World War I and World War II, poster art was a form of propaganda that varied but which often followed several conventions. Among the posters collected in Judd's *Posters of World War II,* the heavy use of tropes, including synecdoche and symbolism, was often united with caricature, distortion, and the hyperbolic rendering of recognizable personalities. Over metonymic landscapes and against a montage of backgrounds, personae such as Winston Churchill were often juxtaposed with aphoristic text (sometimes ironic) reading "*tout va trés bien,*" or "better an honest death than a life of shame" (Judd C.3, C.30).

A particular form of symbolism, the bestiary, was not uncommon in poster art. In one example, France's collaboration with Nazi Germany is portrayed as a relationship between two dogs: standing over a lapdog with a swastika on its collar (France) is a larger dog that wears a Hitler mustache (Germany) (Judd 9.8). The smaller dog tries desperately to bark like his superior. In another poster, Germany is a tigerish creature with a knife stuck through its tongue (Judd C.36). And, in a Henri Guignon poster, Churchill, a favorite of illustrators, is a stern bulldog standing staunchly above a motto in bold capital letters: "HOLDING THE LINE" (Judd 2.6). In Tolson's war sonnets, lions, tigers, eagles, and ants are part of a bestiary that metaphorizes relations between the powerful and the weak.

Other poster conventions found in Tolson's sonnets are onomastics (the use of proper names), which reflect topicality and historical consciousness; expressionistic landscapes that symbolize nations and places of martial conflict; synecdochic parts of the human body (especially hands and booted feet) to convey themes; and classical figures (such as the idealized female reminiscent of Helen of Troy, Dante's Beatrice, or Joan of Arc) employed as mobilizing techniques. In Tolson's sonnets, the use of proper names seen in references to Versailles, David Lloyd George, and Abraham Lincoln reflects his historical and topical sensibility. Similarly, Tolson infuses a powerful sense of setting by his reference to places, again by proper names (Versailles) as well as through stereotypical images of "icy wastes" or "jungles." The common synecdochic device of the hand, often shown smashing the enemy in war posters, appears as a central image in Tolson's sonnet "The Big Game Hunter." Similarly, an idealized figure of womanhood is central to Tolson's sonnet "A Traitor to France." In posters, this heroic image of the female is often juxtaposed with a vignette of marching troops and serves as a national symbol (Judd 1.7). In imagery, therefore, the overall aesthetic of war posters is a popular-art, comic-strip sense of energy, conflict, and hyperbolic personae; and in Tolson's war sonnets, this same aesthetic dominates.

On a semantic level, the heroic, satiric, and strident directness of poster art is reflected in its range of linguistic styles, which range from serious, dignified appeals to the public to the use of colloquialisms and slang. This eclectic mixture of levels of language allows for shock value. Puns and other forms of wordplay lend wit that holds an audience. In the Churchill poster mentioned earlier, for instance, the motto "HOLDING THE LINE" gains triple resonance, suggesting the specific geographical site of the Maginot Line, Churchill and Britain as America's first line of defense, and, finally, a general sense of firmness and fortitude. These elements of punning and disparate levels of language are found in Tolson's sonnets as well and represent yet another aspect of his creative practice. In his concluding sonnet, the parodic use of pseudoaphorisms in the first quatrain achieves an irony similar to the "*tout va trés bien*" text in the Churchill poster cited earlier: "*In the sweat of thy face shalt thou eat bread. / Rifle that basket that thy neighbor brings*" (Rendezvous 70).

Four of Tolson's war sonnets deal indirectly with the theme of war by focusing on human aggression in a Darwinian sense, while two of his sonnets are specifically concerned with the two world wars Tolson had lived—and was living—through. The four indirect war sonnets, "Inevitability," "The Braggart," "The Big Game Hunter," and "The Dictionary of the Wolf," include liberal use of the bestiary and other fable-like discourse on unequal relations. The two other sonnets, "A Legend of Versailles" and "A Traitor to France," use historical personae and situations as metaphors for the themes of duplicity and deception that Tolson associated with the world wars. In all his sonnets, Tolson limits visual prosody to the sporadic use of italics and direct quotations. In general, on the visual level, he relies on Shakespearean sonnet conventions or setting off the concluding couplet to underscore its summarizing or commentating function.

As has been noted, on an imagistic level, Tolson often incorporates landscape figures (space or setting) into his text as a trope for national identity or ideology. In "Inevitability," action takes place on a "winter's day that / Entombs a cosmic waste of hill and vale," suggesting the sterility and impending death of Nordic supremacist ideologies. Similarly, a story is told to a captive audience in "The Braggart" in another cold, inhuman setting; the narrator begins: "As snowdrifts moored [them] at the cabined hearth" (68). The personae are forced to listen to the diatribe of a smug, philosophizing bigot whose racist "reading" of nature's "figures" will soon be refuted. The landscape shifts to an iconic African jungle in "The Big Game Hunter." There, a tale of heroic encounter and individual valor on behalf of the group suggests both the Harlem Renaissance's "African ideal" and comic-strip depictions of good and evil. A forest-like setting is suggested in Tolson's concluding war sonnet, "The Dictionary of the Wolf," to underscore its American flavor. In this poem, Abraham Lincoln tells a fable about wolves, sheep, and social justice, thus offering a bestiary to a "grizzled axman" who represents the American Everyman in his quest for understanding true liberty. For Tolson, these landscapes become "charged fields" of meaning, as in his title poem. They embody his preoccupation with fascist claims of Aryan superiority. In "The Braggart," for instance, the first speaker is a "Blond magnificence" who tries to intimidate his captive audience, described as "sea fish caught within the damning earth," with his own interpretation of landscape:

> "The eagle kings the realm of birds," he said,
> "The lion monarchs the jungle; the world of trees
> kneels to the redwood; Everest's imperial head
> Outdazzles the peaks; the Pacific queens the seas." (68)

The poem concludes: "Elite and mongrel! That is Nature's plan / . . . / The Nordic is the zenith rung of man" (68). In the concluding couplet, trope answers trope when another speaker replies: "I saw a horde / Of ants unflesh a lion as he roared" (68). "The Braggart," while rather simple in its structure of a tale within a tale and its use of character, dialogue, and concluding homily, achieves perhaps inadvertent complexity in its reversal of call-and-response patterns in the premodernist, black oral tradition. Here the call (the braggart's trope of eagle and lion over underlings) is met with a counterresponse, the second speaker's answering trope of a mighty lion downed by lowly ants.

Returning to a comparison with the graphic arts, in this response, the image of the lion destroyed by ants recalls the poster-art tradition of vilifying and traducing one's enemy by placing him in an absurd position. A dual commentary is made on the very nature of the interpretation of figures. The braggart has interpreted nature's figures one way; the other speaker has read them the opposite way. Tolson suggests that the figurative, the symbolic, the metaphorical, and the tropological are alike arbitrary, particularly in their functions. This self-reflexive commentary on the entire process of fable making complicates and enriches Tolson's intended didactic conclusion about the inevitable doom of "fascist spawn."

If the bestiary functions tropologically and provides images or metaphors as figures in the text, then Tolson's plots provide a central mimetic element that is also symbolic, achieving the status of a parable. "The Traitor to France," for example, is a parable for the French who deserted Free France during World

War II and let their country of *liberté, egalité, fraternité* fall into the hands of Marshal Petain's collaborative Vichy government. The entire sonnet rests on the idea of France as an iconic virgin, in an erotic conceit recalling simultaneously the Petrarchan and Donnean tradition and popular-art renderings of virtue and constancy, the Statue of Liberty being an excellent example. The entire sonnet is a "speakerly text" voiced by the husband persona, who describes his violation of the marriage contract and the consequences of that transgression. The first quatrain presents an overview:

> This land is mine, for better or for worse
> *Let no man put asunder* sealed the pledge.
> We who betrayed her freedoms cajoled and curse
> And drag her virtues through the marsh and sedge. (64)

The next two quatrains describe the deceived virgin's new condition in rather garish language. "*Mon Dieu*! she is a bawling Magdalene," begins the section; a series of hyperbolic alternative appellatives for her state follows: she is a "taxi dancer," a "Jezebel," a "wench" (64). The concluding couplet explains exactly why the heroine left virginity for whoredom: "She was a virgin till my deception led / Her to the harlotry of Vichy's bed" (64). The netherworld of a cityscape functions as the tropological background of this "fall." Driven to the ugly, nightmarish part of the city, the woman "Seduce[s] apaches and paillards and guttermen / Beyond the gaslights on a byway bench" (64). This simple narrative, then, presents the fall of a pure woman brought about by the betrayal of the marriage contract in two opposite images of womanhood, the virgin and the whore. Although no bestiary is used in this story, the narrative's use of the female as icon recalls poster-art conventions and, as will be shown, offers an interesting contrast to Brooks's own use of the same conventions in her sonnets, especially in "love note II: flags."

Tolson's historical consciousness and topicality are given a fable-like quality in "A Legend of Versailles," a sonnet about the meeting between David Lloyd George, Woodrow Wilson, and Georges Clemenceau after World War I. In this sonnet, the principal characters are given the qualities of beasts: Clemenceau is called the tiger; Lloyd George, at one point, shakes a "shaggy head." Since the three powerful personae meet with the articulated goal of making the world "safe for democracy"—but are, in reality, preparing to divide it up among themselves—this dramatic text rests on an ironic base. Landscape, for instance, functions only referentially, but with a telescopic thrust, because the principal actors are in the act of carving up an entire globe. In a sense, the whole world is a landscape of imperialistic and colonial intrigue. If Tolson's discourse in "The Traitor to France" was couched in the confession of the traitor and in the contrasting female symbols, in "A Legend of Versailles," it appears in the conversation between Wilson, Lloyd George, and Clemenceau. The tiger's clever and academic question, "Do you really want a lasting peace?" (65), underscores the gaming aspect of language often found in poster art. Tolson achieves wit and satire when he shows the tiger manipulating his colleagues into agreeing with his own selfish interests, which are really their own interests as well.

Another bestiary poem, "The Dictionary of the Wolf," opens with two personae, a listener and a speaker, and an implied landscape—the quintessential American woods. This time, the first quatrain is a vocative spoken by a historical figure associated with war (Abraham Lincoln) to a "grizzled axman." The landscape of a forested, new America is suggested in the clothing and the appearance of these two woodsy characters, iconic folk figures representing America's historical Everyman. Described as "homespun"—with "hands to split a log" and a "cracked palm hat"—Lincoln begins in medias res, presumably in answer to a query:

> "We all declare for liberty..."
> "We use the word and mean all sorts of things;
> *In the sweat of thy face shall thou eat bread.*
> *Rifle the basket that thy neighbor brings.*" (*Rendezvous* 70)

Following this philosophical and tongue-in-cheek observation about the relationship between human beings and language, Lincoln launches into a vividly imagined fable to illustrate his point:

> "The wolf tears at the sheep's throat; and the sheep
> Extols the shepherd for cudgeling tyranny;
> The wolf, convulsed with indignation deep,
> Accuses the shepherd of murdering liberty." (70)

Within this fable, we see that the question of language and the interpretation of words are presented in a bestiary. Verbs such as "tear," "convulsed," "accuse," and "murder" infuse a violent element into the tale. The sonnet's couplet, in which Lincoln interprets the dilemma for the puzzled woodsman, adds a discursive element to the poem that underscores its didactic and rhetorical purpose with a vivid image. Lincoln summarizes: "But the dictionary of the wolf is writ / In words the rats of time chew bit by bit" (70). The vernacular diction here, as in the word "chew," is unflinchingly placed alongside the archaic "writ," indicating an intentional mixing of rhetorics—Tolson's bravado in the face of an urgent social issue. It also anticipates, perhaps more importantly, Tolson's continued mixture of such high and low forms in his mature, modernist work. Here, Tolson's greatest urgency seems to be to drive home his message that the forces of social justice, imaged in the tiny but efficient rats (akin to the ants in "The Braggart"), will destroy all nonauthentic word systems (covenants, dictionaries, etc.), just as the forces of social justice bring into being documents that buttress human freedom. By making the speaker of this fable the man who presided over the Civil War and helped to end slavery, Tolson gives his narrative a device often used in poster art to sway the audience—diachronic as well as synchronic resonance.

In a reversal of his previous sonnets, landscape, narration, and discourse preempt the vocative in "The Big Game Hunter." With a historically conscious celebration of African greatness reminiscent of the Harlem Renaissance, negritude, and the later Black Arts movement, Tolson places his heroic personae, members of the warrior Zulu peoples of Southern Africa, in a "charged field," the soil of Africa itself. In this sonnet, blackness is a trope for natural heroism, the focus of which is appropriately the group rather than the individual. The chief's ebony "fisted hand," a synecdochic image recalling the iconic hands often found in war posters, darts forward to choke a charging lion that threatens to wipe out his band. In the second quatrain, words and phrases such as "giant chief," "wiped out," "terror," "iced," "jungle king," "fisted hand," "shot," "cavern mouth" and "ebony dart," create a sense of violent motion. The monosyllabic active verbs ("shot," "iced") combine with powerful images of heroic struggle ("giant chief," "jungle king") and stark visual images ("cavern mouth," "ebony dart") to lend a cartoon-like, poster-art quality to the poem:

> The *giant chief* saw that his rooted band
> Would be *wiped out.* Though *terror iced* his heart,
> He charged the *jungle king,* the *fisted hand*
> *Shot* into the *cavern mouth* like an *ebony dart.* (69; emphasis added)

In spite of his own fears, the Zulu warrior obeys the terms of the natural social contract that Tolson evidently felt was embedded in the very forces of nature. The concluding couplet states explicitly the moral of this fable of human valor: "The flower of sacrifice blooms the lunar year, / And conscience serves as pallbearer of fear" (69). The high tone of this couplet presents another leap of rhetoric from the commonplace vocabulary that preceded it; yet, even here, the idea of conscience being imaged as "pallbearer" is almost self-parodic in the popular arts conventions of graphic arts. Yet through the metaphor of self-sacrifice as a flower that blossoms under the laws of astral influences, Tolson makes nature itself a *figure* of human empathy and homeostatic accountability.

Tolson's use of sonnets to express or embody his ideas about war and the struggle of man against man is highly propagandistic, approaching hyperbole and parody. Yet, at the height of the Harlem Renaissance, W. E. B. Du Bois, one of the major black intellectuals of the era, declared: "All art is propaganda" (296). Tolson's use of popular language, imagery, and overt sloganeering, while tendentious and crude to some readers, was one aspect of his bold approach to creative practice. Although he abandoned the sonnet form after *Rendezvous with America,* he went on to use many of the techniques found in his sonnets: the hyperbole, the caricatured personae, the shifting of "charged" landscapes, the ironic dialogue, and, above all, his unique combination of historical consciousness with cutting social commentary on contemporary events.

Brooks's "Gay Chaps": The Sonnet Sequence as Collage

As was Tolson's intent in his poems, Brooks's war sonnets critiqued America's war effort from the perspective of those who were subject to the vagaries of racist ideologies, at home and abroad, even as they fought. Like Tolson, Brooks exposes myths through satire and reversal, but her fragmented and elliptical symbolic systems contrast with Tolson's bold aesthetic. While Tolson uses starkly drawn, overstated figures, Brooks's sonnet sequence is a collage of fragmented voices and images, oral and visual patterns. Some are variations on a theme, and others are oxymoronic, creating a vast text of multiple meanings.

In interpreting Brooks's poems, then, it is not enough to read them simply as the words appear on the page. One must consider what Gerard Genette has called the "gap" (*écart*) between the text's figures and implied context. The total universe of discourse for Brooks's war sonnets encompasses not only the intertextual patterns of puns and recurrent imagery but also her use of varied typography, the interstices between the titles and the bodies of the sonnets, and the visual structuring of white space. It is from this perspective that "Gay Chaps" may be seen as a collage with a modernist aesthetic of indeterminacy, fragmentation, multilocused meaning, and difficulty of interpretation. According to Janis and Blesh, the word "collage" derives from *coller,* meaning to paste or glue. The word initially carried with it a shock, because its slang meaning was "to have an illicit love affair." Thus, the term itself carries connotations of rebellion. Moreover, the past participle, *collé* (pasted or glued), when used in its slang sense, means faked or pretended. The essence of collage, then, as introduced by the great modernists Picasso and Braque, was to bring together disparate elements "coupled in surprising and revealing combinations" (Janis and Blesh 21). Puns, both visual and verbal, in the medium of commonplace, found objects, especially scraps of newspaper, were used to set up a dialogue between reality and illusion. In this visual prosody, the paradox between the true and the false induces equivocal resonances that involve the metamorphosis of one reality into another. The result is a message—indirect, witty, and shocking—fit to convey the complexities of the modern world.

The interplay of sequence title, dedication, and epigraph at the beginning of Brooks's sonnet sequence offers a good example of her attention to the visual prosody of her work. The bold capitals of the sequence title are followed by the dedication in contrapuntal lowercase, additionally set off by indentation. Continuing the same indentation, but with intervening blocked white space, the title of the first sonnet appears, repeating the dedication's lowercase, but in a darker type. The repetition of the title in bold uppercase and in lowercase sets up a visual pattern of repetition and variation. Implied in this repetition is the idea that the sequence presents both the heroic (bold uppercase) and the ordinary (lowercase).

The first sonnet's title appears over an epigraph that is set off and framed by ellipses after being further indented than the dedication above, emphasizing the epigraph's fragmentary status and underscoring its reflexive role. Comparable to the scraps of newscopy typical of plastic collage, this fragment from a friend's letter injects a private, almost confessional, voice into the collage of sounds that will structure the text. It also undercuts the bold public ethos suggested by the title. Further, the identification of the letter writer's location ("LIEUTENANT WILLIAM COUCH / in the South Pacific") elliptically establishes the text's shifting geographical imagery. The non-Western, the tropical, the exotic are juxtaposed with the American, the urban, the commonplace. Such protean landscape imagery matches the voices that will reverberate throughout the sonnets.

Brooks's capacity to establish "surprising and revealing combinations" of ethos and their attendant imagery in her sonnets, as well as her visual prosody, is the major difference between her creative practice and Tolson's. For instance, the title of the sonnet sequence itself is highly equivocal. "GAY CHAPS AT THE BAR" suggests, at first glance, the quintessential image of America's unique hero, the cowboy. In the early 1940s, Brooks's favorite diversion was attending the movies, as she admits in her autobiography, *Report from Part One* (72). Outfitted literally in chaps (thus the title's pun), the cowboy as rough rider ideally brought justice to America's own exotic territory, the Wild West, but he did so in his own wild way. The cowboy as cinematic hero emerged in the 1930s. Then, in the 1940s, this western image shifted into the image of the American soldier as hero, as Randolph Scott's and John Wayne's film careers illustrate. Thus, Brooks contrasts the commonplace reality of her black soldiers with the larger-than-life mythos of the WASP heroes who reigned in the mass media. In so doing, Brooks sets up an "equivocal vibration" between reality and illusion and an implied dialogue concerning "the paradox between the true and the false."[4]

Popular-culture imagery, coupled with Brooks's altered Shakespearean and Petrarchan sonnet conventions, constitutes yet another layer of disparate materials thrown together in surprising combination. Continuity, however, is established when the first-person voice in the epigraph is continued in the first sonnet. Between the title, epigraph, and sonnets, a complex interplay of voices acts as a kind of glue that holds the sonnet sequence together. Among the sonnets themselves, titles constitute another layer. In lowercase, but in boldface type, they are sometimes fragments ("still do I keep my look, my identity") that seem to move forward the implied discourse of the sequence; or, in another case, the title is a fragment from a hymn ("God works in mysterious ways") that functions oxymoronically with the poem it introduces, since that sonnet expresses grave religious doubts brought on by the exigencies of war; as the final couplet warns: "Step forth in splendor, mortify our wolves / Or we assume a sovereignty ourselves" (56). Or again, titles suggest a thematic pairing of fragments, as in "love note I: surely" and "love note II: flags" (the tenth and eleventh sonnets), in which the term "note" creates the image of a tacked-on item, a small letter or a fragmentary message.

Opening phrases among the sonnets also set up a variety of implied relationships. Some sonnets begin in medias res, as in the sixth ("mentors"), which begins, "For I am rightful fellow of their band" (53), suggesting the continuation of an argument established in the preceding sonnet, "piano after war." Another example is the ninth sonnet, which begins with a conjunction, "*But* often now the youthful eye cuts down its own dainty veiling. Or submits to winds" (56; emphasis added), reversing the preceding sonnet's argument. The fragmentary status of the last two sonnets is established by the repetition of the word "still" in their opening lines: "Still, it is dear defiance now to carry" (58); "And still we wear our uniforms"(59). The repeated word underlines Brooks's theme of continuity and commitment amid change and chaos.

Similarly, voice functions contrapuntally and as an element of continuity among the sonnets. Voice in the sonnets varies. There is a third-person, impersonal, narrative voice in the seventh sonnet ("the white troops"). There is apostrophic address in second-person voice in the third ("looking"), tenth ("love note I: surely"), and eleventh sonnets ("love note II: flags"). But in the first and last sonnets, voice most clearly emerges as the glue that holds the sequence together. In them, the first-person plural voice ("We knew just how to order"; "And still we wear our uniforms") establishes the commonality of the personae and their perspectives.

On an imagistic level, throughout the sonnets, images of weather, domicile, dress, social rituals, landscapes, and even food generate a theme-in-variation pattern of "equivocal vibrations between reality and illusion." One reality is metamorphosed into another as images shift from seasonal icons (spring, summer, autumn), symbolic times within the diurnal cycle (midday, sunset, darkness, midnight), open spaces (castle, shack, school, mansion), symbolic social rituals (baseball, courting, a piano recital, banquets, and balls), symbolic foods (honey, bread, an apple), and symbolic containers, from the quotidian to the somber (jars, cabinets, coffins).

A more shocking example of a surprising and revealing combination is seen in "love note II: flags," in which Brooks's coupling of the female icon with patriotic symbols, particularly the flag, is done to further the dialogue between reality and illusion. Like Tolson's "A Traitor to France," Brooks's sonnet turns on the conceit of a woman as symbol of "motherland," of freedom and justice (often draped literally in a flag), who demands defense and unswerving loyalty. Because Tolson's sonnet follows the conventional iconography of woman, tragedy in his poem lies in the betrayal of the icon. In Tolson's sonnet, woman is shown as unmalleable: she must be either virgin or properly married; otherwise, she is a whore. Brooks scrambles this iconic convention in "love note II: flags." Here the woman-flag equation achieves surprising meaning when the soldier makes the equivocal gesture of taking the flag he has carried with "dear defiance" and pulling it down into his foxhole, then releasing it to flutter again, "crumpled and wan" against his passion. Here womanliness is associated, as in tradition, with the lovely, the privileged, the capricious, and the weak, but it is also a symbol the black soldier must appropriate even as he defends it. Brooks thus suggests that an illicit sexual act, if not a love affair, is necessary between a black man and his "fair" democracy. For a black man to put a white woman on a pedestal is *collé,* a fake gesture whose meaning must be exposed to render one reality into another. Thus, the soldier's "dear defiance" does not lead to the "fair" lady's whoredom but converts to metaphor the black man's continuing struggle for social justice as the ongoing war between the sexes. The soldier's love-doubt relation with a vacillating America is seen when he describes the flag-woman to herself: "The blowing of clear wind in your gay hair; / Love changeful in you" (58).

Finally, throughout "Gay Chaps," sound and silence form patterns of intertwined reality and illusion, alternations of false and genuine. In her first sonnet, the soldiers are rendered mute by the enormity of their situation: "We brought / No brass fortissimo, among our talents, / To holler down the lions in this air" (48). But their silence is more eloquent than the banal phrases uttered by well-meaning civilians who shout "come back" or "careful" to them in the fourth sonnet. Likewise, in the fifth sonnet ("piano after war"), the music that suffuses the chambers of the soldier as his lover plays the piano with "Cleverly ringed" fingers must give way to "cries and whispers" of "reproving ghosts"—the soldier's dead comrades. Thus, from the "cracked cry of bugles" to the "step of iron feet," a collage of sounds and silences reifies the soldiers' metaphysical and sociopolitical condition. In the sound image of the iron feet, Brooks creates a brilliant, final, equivocal vibration. Are these the marching boots of democracy or of Nazi Germany? Or are they the homegrown sound of American racism? The step of iron feet becomes a somber pun, suggesting even the iron feet of metrical conventions—the tyranny of poetic practice matching the tyranny of political relations. Little wonder that the concluding couplet of the sequence's last sonnet breaks down metaphorically and syntactically into off-beat fragmentary phrases and culminates in a final interpolated white space that sets apart the last fearful word the soldiers utter. And little wonder that it is presented not as a declamation but as a final determinate interrogative: "How shall we smile, congratulate: and how / Settle in chairs? Listen, listen. The step / Of iron feet again. And again wild" (59).

In March 1969, Brooks told an interviewer that she would not be writing many sonnets from then on (*Report* 157). She needed, she said, a new voice, with new cadences and new rhythms, to express the new order of her time. Interestingly, Tolson had already abandoned the sonnet in quest of new creative practices. In his *Libretto for the Republic of Liberia* (1948) and in *Harlem Gallery* (1965), he would employ a variety of prosodic techniques, including visual prosody, with an effectiveness that would never have been possible within the confines of the sonnet. Nevertheless, in their use of the sonnet form in their initial volumes, Brooks and Tolson had played off its conventions of stanzaic structure, rhyme, meter, and poetic argument against their own creative practices. In so doing, they demonstrated that their ongoing concerns were not only the issues of race and war but also the problematic of the relationship between art and life—and the nature of art itself.

Thus, throughout their writing careers, Brooks and Tolson insisted on seeking a creative practice that would make their craft accountable to their ideas, just as they wanted their society to be accountable to its citizens.

Notes

1. See, for example, the Tolson interview "A Poet's Odyssey," in *Anger, and Beyond*. Also see Brooks's March 1969 interview with George Stavros and her April 1971 interview with Ida Lewis, reprinted in Brooks's autobiography, *Report from Part One*.

2. See the dust jacket for the 1945 edition of *A Street in Bronzeville*. Under oversized type (reading "BUY WAR BONDS"), the copy anticipates Brooks's structure in her sonnet sequence and includes quotations from a soldier (though not identified as black) about the "illusory" news from the front proclaiming "laudatory accounts" that do not really amount to victories. Here also is Brooks's emphasis on the end to hostilities and hope for "that international health and quiet sure, one day, to come."

3. Robert Stepto has pointed out the importance of Victor Turner's "charged field" concept in many other black American texts. See, for example, Stepto's essay "After Modernism, after Hibernation: Michael Harper, Robert Hayden and Jay Wright," in *Chant of Saints*.

4. The terminology in this paragraph derives from Harriet Janis and Rudi Blesh and is quoted to highlight Brooks's artistic affinity with collage technique.

Works Cited

Brooks, Gwendolyn. *Report from Part One*. Detroit: Broadside Press, 1972.

―――. *The World of Gwendolyn Brooks*. New York: Harper and Row, 1971.

Du Bois, W. E. B. "Criteria of Negro Art." *The Crisis* (October 1927): 296.

Farnsworth, Robert M. *Melvin B. Tolson: Plain Talk and Poetic Prophecy*. Columbia: University of Missouri Press, 1984.

Foner, Jack D. *Blacks and the Military in American History*. New York: Praeger Publishers, 1974.

Genette, Gerard. *Figures of Literary Discourse*. Trans. Alan Sheridan. New York: Columbia University Press, 1982.

Janis, Harriet, and Rudi Blesh. *Collage: Personalities, Concepts, and Techniques*. New York: Chilton Books, 1967.

Judd, Denis. *Posters of World War II*. New York: St. Martin's Press, 1973.

Stepto, Robert Burns. "After Modernism, after Hibernation: Michael Harper, Robert Hayden, and Jay Wright." In *Chant of Saints*. Ed. Michael Harper and Robert Stepto. Urbana: University of Illinois Press, 1979. 470–86.

Tolson, Melvin B. "A Poet's Odyssey." In *Anger, and Beyond*. Ed. Herbert Hill. New York: Harper and Row, 1966. 181–95.

―――. *Rendezvous with America*. New York: Dodd, Mead, 1944.

Williams, Raymond. *Marxism and Literature*. New York: Oxford University Press, 1977.

6

BLACK MARGINS:
AFRICAN-AMERICAN PROSE POEMS

Aldon Lynn Nielsen

> In this inert town, this strange throng which does not pack, does not mix: clever at discovering the point of disencasement, of flight, of dodging. This throng which does not know how to throng, this throng, clearly so perfectly alone under this sun, like a woman one thought completely occupied with her lyric cadence....
> —Aimé Césaire, "Notebook of a Return to the Native Land"

> For you have seen it all, all presenting itself to you not flamboyantly scribbling itself across the evening in archaic calligraphy like a gold tooth in the mouth of a Nashville Negro, but subtly shaping itself to you, waiting this exact moment and this year to manifest itself for you to see, as long ago in the confusion of scribbling you first recognized your name.
> —N. J. Loftis, *Black Anima*

In the last of the small hours, to borrow from Aimé Césaire, in the waning dawn of a new epoch, the notebook of our returns appears, as it did at the beginning of the century, to have failed in its full accounting, to have expelled to the margins much of what has made our narratives what they are, even as we have increasingly construed our studies as studies of the marginal or as readings in the margins. When we shape our accounts of our recent past, we find once more that the margins of our ledgers are more constricting than commodious. As Richard Yarborough has observed, "only twenty years since the end of the sixties, it is already necessary to salvage the work of important writers of that era.... Not to place the recovery of such texts high on our scholarly agenda is to participate in canonization by default: If the texts are not in print, they will not be bought or taught" (108). Not only writers but forms must be recovered; not only forms but the ruptures of form must be historicized. It proves too often the case that when recovering one set of texts for our accounts we occlude others, that our progressive reopening of the textual past of literary studies reenacts a reactionary closure we had thought to overcome. This is currently happening in the midst of our reformist recastings of American literary canons. What is needed additionally is a nomadic form of critique as interdiction. If we are not to replicate the critical, racial caste systems of past American literary studies, we require a criticism that acts always as an intervention in the reconstitution of racial significations, an interethnic and interracial reading that inserts itself in the junctures between "races" and "ethnicities," diverting the signifying motions of race and refusing to continue on a path that will inevitably reproduce the tar baby of American Africanist subjectivity historically imagined by white readings. What is needed is an array of intertextual reading strategies that will open themselves to the possibilities latent in the interstices of race and form, of genre and color.

When Donald Allen published his remarkable anthology of the *New American Poetry*, an anthology valuably implicated in the reading pasts of many of the most interesting postmodern poets experimenting in prose genres, there was only one African-American poet represented among the varied geographies of that collection, the young LeRoi Jones, who was even then undertaking the audacious prose works found in *The System of Dante's Hell* and *Tales*. In Allen's later, expanded version of his anthology, retitled *The Postmoderns: The New American Poetry Revised,* the revisions include the addition of several writers, more women notably, but Jones, now known as Amiri Baraka, remains the sole representative of black writing. Seemingly even in Allen's retrospect, Baraka was all there was to be found that was African American among those new poetries and poetics that developed at mid-century. Even more striking is the restricted universe described in the original and second editions of Stephen Fredman's indispensable study *Poet's Prose: The Crisis in American Verse*. While one might suspect that it is always a moment of crisis for African-American writing, this appears to be an invisible crisis; no black writers are discussed in Fredman's text. In compiling his "suggestive list of poets who have written poetry in prose" in the twentieth century, Fredman suggests by omission that black writing has not assumed this shape. When he goes on to describe a "new generation of poets . . . for whom verse has given way almost wholly for new forms of prose or to non-versified performance texts," the impressive list again includes no black writers (2). Why, we must ask, is there no mention in this volume of Jean Toomer, Melvin B. Tolson, Baraka, Bob Kaufman, Stephen Jonas, Oliver Pitcher, Julia Fields, Tom Postell, Henry Dumas, Clarence Major, Larry Neal, David Henderson, Lorenzo Thomas, Alexis Deveaux, Erica Hunt, Nathaniel Mackey, or other

African-American poets who have produced significant texts as poets writing between justified margins? Even when discussing the influence of French surrealism, Fredman strangely omits mention of Aimé Césaire. And Fredman's omissions seem paradigmatic. Margueritte S. Murphy's more recently published volume *A Tradition of Subversion: The Prose Poem in English from Wilde to Ashbery* again finds no black writing in that subversive company. While Jonathan Monroe continued the elision of African-American prose poems in his studies of the genre, he has, in "*Mischling* and *Métis:* Common and Uncommon Languages in Adrienne Rich and Aimé Césaire," begun to pursue the incredibly vital communication between poets of the Caribbean and North America.

Particularly troubling is the fact that the disappearance of African-American prose poems from the critical discourse of American literary history is a relatively recent phenomenon. While it is true that most critical histories of American poetry written by white critics prior to 1950 ignored African-American writing entirely, there were those students of black writing who recognized the prose poem as a distinct genre practiced by prominent black writers. Most characteristic in this regard, perhaps, is Robert T. Kerlin's study *Negro Poets and Their Poems,* published in 1923. Kerlin's volume is more an appreciative tour of the available literature than a truly critical examination, but his devotion of a section of his book to prose poems, along with his inclusion of poets who were not generally known for their work in the genre, indicates the thoroughness of his survey. Kerlin remarks the fact that many chapters of W. E. B. Du Bois's *Darkwater* conclude with litanies, chants, and credos, specifically citing Du Bois's "Litany at Atlanta." According to Kerlin in 1923, "modern literature has not such another cry of agony" (202), and later readers must wonder if the repeated "*Selah*" of the litany might not be one of the sources for Melvin B. Tolson's use of the technique in *Libretto for the Republic of Liberia.* Kerlin also quotes at length from Kelly Miller's *Out of the House of Bondage,* which, in Kerlin's description, "concludes with a strophic chant, highly poetical, and poured forth with the fervor of some old Celtic bard" (206). Few readers today would think of Miller, better known for his work in sociology, as a poet; fewer still will recall the names of the remaining authors of prose poems discussed by Kerlin. Charles H. Conner, a Philadelphia shipyard worker and the author of *The Enchanted Valley,* is noted for the "mystical and philosophical quality of his writings" (210), and William Edgar Bailey is cited as the author of *The Firstling,* which includes a prose text. Robert Kerlin confuses matters a bit as he closes out his collection of African-American prose poems with a selection of V. R. Nathaniel Dett's blank verse, suggesting that the prose poem—even such lyric and rhetorical examples of the form as those offered in *Negro Poets and Their Poems*—was finally nearly too great a departure from normative meters for Kerlin.

Given the fact, then, that the African-American prose poem had been critically acknowledged as early as the second decade of the twentieth century, it is all the more remarkable that there is a complete absence of poet's prose by black writers—or, indeed, of most formally adventurous verse—from the majority of the multicultural anthologies and readers currently flooding the academic market, an absence echoed, if an absence might be said to produce an echo, in the preponderance of critical works being published in ethnic studies and African-American literature by university presses and mainstream commercial houses. Others have remarked the low level of attention given to contemporary poetry among even the most theoretically engaged of American critics, yet even more problematic is the nearly universal critical silence about contemporary black poets who might be considered in any way experimental or whose writing doesn't conform to standard M.F.A. program expectations. Indeed, the emphasis on the cultivation of the individual voice as the expressive manifestation of a preexisting, coherent subjectivity in American writing classrooms has coincided in recent decades with a critical emphasis on a politics of identity in the ethnic-literature classroom at predominantly white universities in a way that virtually precludes the study of writing that formally and thematically interrogates the presuppositions of essentialist views of race and poetry.

The result has been that in the very moment of the universities' resolution to reform their curricula by taking their students into the geography of the racial and ethnic margins, they have covertly prepared the way by presupposing what could or should be found in the margins. At the very moment that English departments combined an interest in the marginal with an emphasis on the individual voice of personal experience, literary criticism and education produced a desired subjectivity that spoke only and always of the always-waiting-to-be-found experience of identity that the newer criticism was prepared to celebrate. (Meanwhile, poststructuralist critiques were regularly taken to task for denying the privilege of such subjectivities.) Speaking in a quite different context, Lawrence S. Rainey has asserted: "Cognition of the Other turns out to be a mirror in which, dimly discernable at the margins, we also find its uncanny double the Self of current criticism" (117). It is the integrated racial self that the ethnographic gaze of much current curricular reform seeks in the mirror of its self-constituting anthologies. Hence, even something as marvelously reformed as the current *Heath Anthology of American Literature* offers a second volume in which black writing that deconstructs the assumptions of identity politics is disappeared. Current American literary discourse is constructed in such a way as perpetually to deny justifications to the margins of black writing. Thus we are not likely to find in any multicultural readers marketed today the following paragraph from Bob Kaufman's poem "Second April," which, significantly for my purposes, takes as its epigraph a line from another piece of poet's prose, the twelfth chapter of the New Testament book of Romans, which advises: "Be ye not conformed to this world: but be ye transformed by the renewing of your mind."

Kaufman's paragraph contains a desiring body that speaks in the first person, but it satisfies few of the usual demands for a coherent marginal self that speaks with the authoritative voice of its own experience, demands that guide the decisions of most contemporary anthology editors. This poem, even with its insistent pronoun, follows none of the dictates of the fashionable "voice" poem (in this it clearly resembles William Carlos Williams's improvisations in *Kora in Hell*), and the poem is undeniably justified and rectangular, if not actually square:

> Session semi-zero before inverted fraction . . . is a five thing and strategic incisions, one-o, two-o, three-o, four-o, five-o snips for veal cutlets, paper signing papas . . . a thing, O god, let me use your library card, I want the OxforD BooK oF ModerN JazZ . . . I want Baudelaire's Denunciation of Moses, I want Ezra Pound's Life of George Washington, I want Starkweather's Biography of Billy Graham, let me steal James Dean's suicide note from the film division, I need the Intelligent Woman's Guide to Mongrelism, I need Greenwich Village Novels to wipe me with, I need New York Times Index to count the murders, I need to talk with fly pages, that's a thing now, fly pages . . . o fly, o so higho fly, they watch, put spaghetti in the octane, the new bomb is clean, thank God for soaP. (*Solitudes* 67–68)

Prose such as this is difficult to read as the transparent ethnographic report so eagerly sought by some white readers searching for their empathic double in the Other of the margins. Kaufman's work thus becomes a suppressed margin that the center of acceptable verse rejects with violence.

That violence is felt by artists as a repetition of segregationist aesthetics. In an interview with Manthia Diawara, the filmmaker Sonia Boyce says: "Whatever we black people do, it's said to be about identity, first and foremost. It becomes a blanket term for everything we do, regardless of what we're doing" (194). Boyce is attempting no escape from what she is and what her experiences have been, but she is unwilling to be railroaded by the predictable and powerful desires of hegemonic criticism into creating art that is always and only to be read as a statement of who she is. Lorenzo Thomas, too, has reason to worry about that metaphorical engine. In "Hat Red," he writes: "when I woke up, all the lights were off and the train was deserted and I remembered Baraka's *Dutchman* and got scared and thought O shit can this be some kind of joke or is this the end of the line or the last stop or the world hunh" (113). Thomas's prose piece, which I have never seen in an anthology, no matter how multicultural, recalls—with its allusion to Baraka's play—the deadliness of force that white expectation may bring to black poetry. But, like Baraka's play, Thomas's "Hat Red" derails formal expectations, a derailment prefigured by the reproduction of James Farber's collage "After the Fall," which appears on the cover of Thomas's book *Chances Are Few*. Thomas's "Hat Red" refuses lyric constraints as powerfully as the crashed freight cars in Farber's collage refuse to be the vehicle for bad news.

In such acts of refusing the ease of association between tenor and vehicle, we may trace the functioning of poets' prose as critique. Even those prose poems whose diction and syntax are otherwise traditional may often be used by the poet as a space within which to resist American literary culture's apparatuses of interpretive discipline. Julia Fields's "What Donne Meant," included in her book *Slow Coins*, refuses to accept the subject position reserved for her in advance by the college poetry teacher who appears to proclaim: "I myself by order of the powers vested in me. I myself having the authority will tell you so that you will be certified to tell others what it was that Doon-Donne meant. We will confer upon you the meaning of what Donne meant, and in due time you will be able to tell others" (177). By refusing her place in this signifying chain of interpretive oppressions, Fields endangers her career as a teacher while at the same time refusing to accept her assignment, an assignment as teacher and black woman that it will be her "'job' to entertain and to mystify" (177). Poets' prose also performs acts of critical interdiction, disrupting the assumptions of poetic diction and line. If, as Margueritte Murphy argues, the prose poem is also a genre in which the poetic discovers and confronts its other within itself, if "the prose poem draws in and alters other genres or modes of discourse as part of its own peculiar self-definition" (3), then it may be that African-American poets' prose, writing from its still-marginalized margins, is a scene of interdiction wherein the thinking of race produces and undoes its Other in an ever-shifting dance of interruptions, a dance that derails race as a genre even as it refigures the dictions of race. The prose poem becomes an area of act in which the genre is transformed by black poets confronting ideologies of race and form *within* the existing space *of* the form. This mode of interdiction parallels the interruptions of European philosophizing made by Frantz Fanon. Writing of Fanon's interrogations of existentialism, Paget Henry argues that "it was a new move within the tradition. This existential coding liberated the zone [of the Afro-Caribbean psyche] from its invisibility and nonrecognition in dominant discourses of the tradition. It supplemented the emancipatory appropriations of European liberalism, socialism, constitutionalism, and surrealism that was evident in the works of Garvey, James, Césaire, and other Afro-Caribbean writers" (235). Henry contrasts Fanon's form of supplemental, emancipatory appropriation with the "repressive use to which some of these same philosophical appropriations were put by Euro-Caribbean writers" (235). In much the same way, a contemporary African-American poet such as Will Alexander will seize on the prose poem as a space in which to reassert the innovations of Césaire against more widely recognized forms of poet's prose while replicating Césaire's radical reappropriations of surrealism as a mode of interdiction against dominant conceptions of the "rational." Alexander's poem "Hypotenuse Shadows Shouting Buffalo Lyrics" begins: "This is the problem I propose to Mssrs. Whitehead and Russell; measure your deaths in terms of the leaps of your ashes. The logic of keeping your bones from skipping spaces, from popping through the grass of some buffalo's eyeball at mealtime" (12). Here, Alexander confounds the analytic modes of Russell and Whitehead and confronts them with the real surrealism of lynch mobs and the murderers of Emmet Till. But Alexander's work does not simply make an argument about race and reason; his prose poem appears within the mythmaking structures of literature as a means of disrupting the mythopoeism in progress: "Outside myself and bleeding on my own discoveries I discover in a cave Pythagorian lodestones broken in the air of Chaldean snake myths. These myths, burrowed in the fingers of the wandering poet who writes with the sweat of vituperative magic, who succumbs in the sentence to rifle and axe blade" (13). Where Charles Olson argued for a hands-on history in which the poet would find out the myths for himself (and for Olson it seemed very much to be a *him*self), Alexander makes these discoveries *outside* himself and reads in them a "vituperative magic." His is, if anything, a yet more projective verse.

In the early 1960s, Melvin B. Tolson, whose *Libretto for the Republic of Liberia* concludes with a series of justified verse paragraphs, wrote in his *Harlem Gallery:* "We who are we / discover *altérité*" (26). As Tolson's reformulations of modernist forms centered *altérité* as the one essential of black discovery, so have later African-American poets made use of the forms of poets' prose as a radical locus from which to challenge those very desires for lyric reproduction of self-identical presence and mimetic expression of always familiar personal experiences of the margins that have served to repress critical examination of radical experiment in black prosody. In his 1958 collection *Dust of Silence,* a volume that has fallen into the deep critical silence that surrounds experimental black poetry, Oliver Pitcher describes a spiritual moment in which art and identity are parted from themselves and from one another, a moment in which a "Stygian traffic" passes between the artist and his future: "This is the hour young men with store houses congested with empty picture frames for heads, walk the dusty roads in stocking feet. Their canvasses are tattered to cards of identity scattered upon the sea" (9). In a 1973 book titled *Black Anima*, N. J. Loftis asks readers to "suppose a bright billboard appeared on the sky reading: THIS IS YOUR IDENTITY" (21). One senses that some of our students and colleagues read contemporary poetry as if it were just such a billboard, but Loftis's *Black Anima* works to make such literalism difficult to sustain. This difficulty may in part account for the absence of Loftis from most accounts of his period and for the fact that his reputation seems to have derived no benefit from recent restructurings of canon and curricula. *Black Anima* is long out of print. It was published by a major commercial press, Liveright, which featured Loftis in its Liveright New Writers series, with words of praise collected from W. H. Auden (who appears in the poem) and John Ashbery. But even these desirable trappings of a market commodity have not been sufficient to land Loftis's work in major anthologies. His book promises a discovery of black identity, but it guarantees that the discovery will be unsettling: "You must know how to wait until memory seeks and exhausts herself in you. Thus putting aside your Blackness momentarily, you grow, discovering a black identity the fashionable publicity sheets neither imagine nor know" (109).

The altering forms of *Black Anima* would have appealed to audiences weaned on modernist juxtaposition and palimpsest. The work is divided into sections titled "Changes," "Hell," "Birth and Rebirth," and "Black Anima." These last two segments are composed almost entirely of justified paragraphs, and the initial section combines prose poems with free verse. In Loftis's cosmology, though, "Hell" is made up entirely of lyric verse. In *Black Anima*, Loftis draws a parallel between his readiness to jettison the generic expectations of verse and his assault on the givens of a racialized Cartesian subjectivity. He describes a "striptease of the ego" in which we view "cumbersome mental furniture removed from a privileged position in mental cavity and placed on the lawn like a housewife doing spring cleaning" (18). His domestic metaphor describes the altering forms of his own work. *Black Anima,* for all its reliance on modernist recourse to myth, resembles a yard sale in which all the poetic modes have been set out on the grass, none being privileged, so that something new can be done in the house. Even with its occasional pomposities, *Black Anima* remains a significant moment of alterity in black writing, one that will not conform itself to the ethnographic gaze. "You pause at daybreak," Loftis writes, "staring the moment calmly through and through, tracing each vein that might lead somewhere, yet leaves you where you were, each hollowing that may contain some hidden meaning, yet never does" (98).

Nathaniel Mackey's *Bedouin Hornbook,* published as a volume in 1986 (portions had been appearing in journals for some years), follows Loftis's procedures of utilizing the shapes of prose precisely to engage a radical interrogation of dominant views of race and identity as well as prevailing conceptions of the individual lyric voice. The hornbook, despite its title, takes the form of an epistolary experiment, a series of letters from a nomadic correspondent who signs himself "N." The letters are addressed to an "Angel of Dust," and they are as formally fluid as the African-American musics that are so often their subject. A letter dated 28 August 1980, begins:

> Dear Angel of Dust,
> Perhaps I can put it across this way: "Public" and "private" are now disjunctive, now convergent masks for the featureless cave or the evaporative curve of an elapsed interiority, non existent self. They cohabit so as to woo, so to speak, an otherwise involuted, apparitional pigment, a profoundly suspect, deeply pre-political "taint." Though I may not be saying this with all the elaboration it deserves, a timely enough illustration of it took place a few nights ago. The Art Ensemble of Chicago came to town for a concert over at UCLA. As you've probably heard they sometimes do, they came onstage with their faces painted. To me it made perfect sense. I saw line, spotting effects and color taken on as though they were voluntary, self-contracted stigmata, emanations of the flesh as though it were a canvas or a cave-wall, gaudy with aboriginal paint. The band seemed to revel in the imposition of a public, admittedly masklike face, but only to ambush, it turned out, the public's nonchalance toward its own deep investment in "smeared" paints, "painted" snares or self-wielding "strokes." . . . The emphasis seemed to fall on an identity not as entity so much as enmity, self not as substance but as auto-constitutive stress. To me it made perfect sense. (61)

The allusion to the Art Ensemble of Chicago carries with it an inescapable reference to one of the best-known poems of an earlier African-American poet whose loyalty to the lyric was in part a refutation of white expectations of black poetic diction. In "We Wear the Mask," Paul Laurence Dunbar speaks of how, behind "the mask that grins and lies," the wearers of the mask "mouth with myriad subtleties" (71), and any who have read or recited Dunbar's dialect *Lyrics of Lowly Life* will recognize that just as the persona who speaks in those poems is a mask, so the very forms of his lyrics are masks of an autoconstitutive self formed to answer the self constituted for him by a white readership. The paint on the faces of the Art Ensemble of Chicago (always excepting Roscoe Mitchell, who masks himself within the ensemble by not wearing paint or costume) ambushes the desires of their audiences, interrogating the audiences' investments in African accoutrements and spectacle. Similarly, writing from behind the orthographic mask of the initial "N," Mackey creates a form, a poet's fictive epistle, that deconstructs generic expectations of epistolary presence. We are accustomed by now to view poets' letters as potential commodities to be published in collected editions; but in Mackey, we find a poet who devotes much of his career to the creation of these fictive epistles that combine discourses of philosophy, musicology, narrative, lyric, and anthropology with cosmological diagrams and general jazz gossip. We would probably not unproblematically take "N" to be the author of Mackey's poems, as we take the man who signed his letters "Wallace Stevens" to be the author of *Harmonium*, and this curious signature on these letters to the Angel of Dust is, like the Art Ensemble's masks, an instance of identity as enmity that complicates our reading of the music of African-American prose poems. In *Harlem Gallery*, Tolson's curator notes: "Black Boy often adds / the dimension of ethnic irony / to Empson's classic seven" (122). Mackey's work demonstrates that literary forms themselves are implicated in a racial history whose ironic masks linger in the margins of our readings.

One source of that ethnic irony is the intertextual motion of racial differences as texts from various traditions pass between readings inflected as white and those inflected as black. Among Bob Kaufman's most effective late prose poems, the title poem of his collection *The Ancient Rain* rereads Federico García Lorca against the background of racial discourse in America. Kaufman's prose poem brings together issues of race and representation, linking white insistence on a monological reading of race and history to what Kaufman views as an inability to read adequately one of García Lorca's major texts. "The Ancient Rain is falling on America now. It shall kill D. W. Griffith and the Ku Klux Klan" (76). Griffith reported that as he read Thomas Dixon's novel *The Clansman*, the source for *The Birth of a Nation*, he "skipped quickly through the book until [he] got to the part about the Klansmen, who according to no less than Woodrow Wilson, ran to the rescue of the downtrodden South after the Civil War" (qtd. in Rogin 346). Wilson, as it happens, had been a fellow student of Dixon's at Johns Hopkins University. All three men reproduced and circulated a view of American Reconstruction history that, as W. E. B. Du Bois notes in *Black Reconstruction in America*, was purveyed by powerful historians at Columbia University (719). Griffith, prior to producing *The Birth of a Nation*, had acted in one of Dixon's touring companies. Dixon proposed Wilson for an honorary degree at Wake Forest. Wilson completed the circuit by screening *The Birth of a Nation* at the White House; and thus the first cinema screening in White House history rewrote the official version of post–Civil War history as Southern racist triumphalism.

This is the racist history that Bob Kaufman sets out to destroy by completing another intellectual circuit within the texts of García Lorca. García Lorca, whose command of English was so nearly nonexistent that he would have been unable to attend to such histories, studied briefly at Columbia University in the midst of Harlem and wrote his *Poet in New York*. Kaufman reimagines García Lorca in a manner that most white poets have not: "The Ancient Rain is falling on the intellectuals of America. It illuminates García Lorca, the mystery of America shines in the Poet in New York. The Negroes have gone home with García Lorca to the heaven of the lady whose train overflows. Heaven" (79). Home with García Lorca is home to Harlem. Kaufman is not the only black American poet to have found his way home in the company of the Spanish poet of *duende* and deep song; N. J. Loftis also is haunted by García Lorca and finds his way back to Whitman in part through García Lorca's ode written in depression-era New York. Stalking another form of depression, Loftis asks, in one of the verse sections of *Black Anima:*

> Is it you, Federico Garcia
> walking these mean streets
>   where a skyful
>   of visionary birds
> strike at you
> along the corners of fear
> You who taught us to sing
> the poet among his people[.] (36)

It is a poet who is not among his people, García Lorca among the blacks of New York, who helps Loftis find a way to sing among his people. García Lorca, whose writing bears accents of a Moorish past, writes a new kind of American poem in his New York dormitory room. Loftis, wandering the same streets, reads the absence of the displaced García Lorca as a sign. Likewise, García Lorca's voice comes through the rain to Bob Kaufman:

> I walked off my ship and rode the subway to Manhattan to visit Grant's tomb and I thought because Lorca said he would let his hair grow long someday crackling blueness would cause my hair to grow long. I decided to move deeper into crackling blueness. When Franco's civil guard killed, from that moment on, I would move deeper in crackling blueness. I keep my secrets. I observed those who read him were not Negroes and listened to all their misinterpretation of him....
>
> I remember the day I went into crackling blueness. His indescribable voice saying Black Man, Black Man, for the mole and the water jet, stay out of the cleft, seek out the great Sun of the Center. (*Ancient Rain* 81)

Kaufman, probably reading Ben Belitt's translation of García Lorca's "*Norma y paraiso de los negros,*" with its repeated intonation of "*azul crujiente*" (García Lorca 16), reads the historic racial difference of American consciousness as the dividing point of reading—and of readings of García Lorca. Kaufman in effect becomes his reading of García Lorca, responding to a call that is filtered through a translation, as indeed García Lorca's experience of black America was mediated by multiple translations.

Harryette Mullen's turn to prose forms in her more recent volume *Trimmings* enacts a wondrously overdetermined set of such ironic readings. The title itself is a critical interdiction of dominant modes of racial signifying: for with her title, Mullen finds ways to reread the influence of Gertrude Stein while depriviledging the racist markings so often found in Stein's texts. If, as Mullen suspects, American signs of gender are overironized constructions, then race, too, may be considerably less of a cultural given than Stein supposes in *Melanctha, The Autobiography of Alice B. Toklas,* and elsewhere. Mullen, exploring "the ways that the English language conventionally represents femininity," finds that, as a black woman writer, she has "an ironic relationship" to the constant remarkings of the feminine as pink and white. "Of course if I regard gender as a set of arbitrary signs," she remarks in her note on the text, "I also think of race—as far as it is difference that is meaningful—as a set of signs" (69).

The relationship between Mullen's book and Stein would already have been unmistakable without her title, for here is a work of poet's prose arranged in short paragraphs and published by a press called Tender Buttons. Not only do we then tend to read each of the prose poems as "tender buttons"—with the sexual and literary connotations of that reading—but we must also read the pun of Mullen's title as one that carries us intertextually and intersexually across an arbitrary divide of racial signifying. This volume renders central and primary all that which is normally considered supplementary and decorative, the trimmings that are added to the otherwise already finished, by naming itself with a black pun, by naming itself for the very anatomy of tender buttons, by naming itself for a center of erotic experience. "Trim" thus names the center as black woman's sexuality and playfully refuses, in *Trimmings,* to allow that trim to be read only as filigree. As William Carlos Williams, in *Spring and All,* rescues the obsolete rose so that it again may stand for and with love in verse, Mullen retrieves black sexuality from Stein's texts, in which it is determined and determining, so that she can again write the erotics of black women's lives: "Holes breathe and swallow. Openings, hem, sleeve. Borders on edges where skin stops, or begins. Fancy trim. Sew buttons on, but they are slow to open flowers—imagine the color. Loose skirt, a petal, a pocket for your hand. My dress falls over my head. A shadow overtakes me" (33). We could say here that Mullen stages invagination. In Paule Marshall's novel *Praisesong for the Widow,* Avey Johnson recalls the days when language and sex mixed ecstatically, when she and her husband conversed, "his voice a whisper, of her trim, gently bringing his hand there to touch her in the way she had taught him; her lovely, still incredibly tight trim" (127). The tight paragraphs of Mullen's poems make trim figures ready to hand, and Stein's buttons keep reappearing: "Tender white kid, off-white tan. Snug black leather, second skin. Fits like a love, an utter other uttered. Bag of tricks, slight hand preserved, a dainty. A solid color covers while rubber is protection. Tight is tender, softness cured. Alive and warm, source animal hides. Ghosts wear fingers, delicate wrists" (9). Stein's buttons made it impossible for readers ever again to read cookbooks unproblematically by foregrounding an erotics of cuisine. Mullen's texts reproblematize the erotics of fashion and race, making poetry in prose from the same materials that fashion concerns use to fashion advertising in commercial verse. Mullen sees "a body wearing language as clothing or language a body of thought" (66) and always sees the erotics of language as a meeting of trimmings. Perhaps most importantly, Mullen casts her prose poems as the scene of "an utter other uttered," the place where race is constructed, reproduced, taken in for alterations. In one poem, we read: "Hannah's bandanna flagging her down in the kitchen with Dinah, with Jemima. Someone in the kitchen I know" (11). There always is someone in the kitchen I know; there is always someone I know in the kitchen, cooking.

Mullen's strategy—like Kaufman's, like Loftis's—is to make an intertextual music in prose that denies the stability of racial identities as it denies the stability of lyric voice and the verse line. She reads African-American vernacular tradition and the modernism of Gertrude Stein as kissing cousins in a paragraph that confounds ruling assumptions about black culture and black writing, most notably those assumptions of Stein herself. Mullen's is a poetry that finds in its margins the available space for the uttering Other, a capacious space formed out of the available discourses of race, gender, mothering, and literary history, a space in which Hawthorne's *Scarlet Letter* and Stein's *Tender Buttons* read each other and are read into black song. Indeed, Mullen's *Trimmings* makes us think of Billie Holiday and what a little moonlight could do: "What a little moonlight inside her pink silvery is softness condensing a glaze to repair a blister. Itches sit and silken, growing dearer to the wearer. Who would wear a necklace of tears. Inside her moonlight lining, tears were shed. Smooth tears, bitter water, a salted wound produced a pearl. A mother's luster manufactured a colored Other. Pearl had a mother who cried" (64).

We have come to read poets' prose as a text in which verse constructs and confronts its Other as radical alterity. American discourse has produced race as its manufactured, colored Other, as the defining horizon of identity that a politics of identity cannot unread, as the utterance of the utterly Other that may one day present itself as the telos of American writing. But the blackness against which white American discourse defines itself as discourse as such will not stay in its assigned place, and the African-American prose poem, the black margins of American writing, may be, as Harryette Mullen suggests, a pearl of great price that still awaits its reading in the last of the small hours.

Works Cited

Alexander, Will. *Vertical Rainbow Climber.* Aptos, Calif.: Jazz Press, 1987.

Allen, Donald, and George F. Butterick, eds. *The Postmoderns: The New American Poetry Revised.* New York: Grove Press, 1982.

Boyce, Sonia. "The Art of Identity: Interview with Manthia Diawara." *Transition* 55 (1992): 192–201.

Césaire, Aimé. *The Collected Poetry.* Trans. Clayton Eshelman and Annette Smith. Berkeley: University of California Press, 1983.

Du Bois, W. E. B. *Black Reconstruction in America, 1860–1880.* 1935. Rpt., New York: Atheneum, 1977.

Dunbar, Paul Laurence. *The Complete Poems of Paul Laurence Dunbar.* New York: Dodd, Mead, 1913.

Fields, Julia. *Slow Coins: New Poems (and Some Old Ones).* Washington, D.C.: Three Continents Press, 1981.

Fredman, Stephen. *Poet's Prose: The Crisis in American Verse.* 2d ed. Cambridge: Cambridge University Press, 1990.

García Lorca, Federico. *Poet in New York.* Trans. Ben Belitt. New York: Grove Press, 1955.

Henry, Paget. "Fanon, African and Caribbean Philosophy." In *Fanon: A Critical Reader.* Ed. Lewis R. Gordon, T. Denean Sharpley-Whiting, and Renée T. White. Oxford: Blackwell Publishers, 1996. 220–43.

Kaufman, Bob. *The Ancient Rain: Poems, 1956–1978.* New York: New Directions, 1981.

———. *Solitudes Crowded with Loneliness.* New York: New Directions, 1965.

Kerlin, Robert T. *Negro Poets and Their Poems.* Washington, D.C.: Associated Publishers, 1923.

Loftis, N. J. *Black Anima.* New York: Liveright, 1973.

Mackey, Nathaniel. *Bedouin Hornbook.* Lexington: University Press of Kentucky, 1986.

Marshall, Paule. *Praisesong for the Widow.* New York: Putnam, 1983.

Monroe, Jonathan. "*Mischling* and *Métis:* Common and Uncommon Languages in Adrienne Rich and Aimé Césaire." In *Do the Americas Have a Common Literature?* Ed. Gustavo Pérez Firmat. Durham, N.C.: Duke University Press, 1990. 282–315.

Mullen, Harryette. *Trimmings.* New York: Tender Buttons, 1991.

Murphy, Margueritte S. *A Tradition of Subversion: The Prose Poem in English from Wilde to Ashbery.* Amherst: University of Massachusetts Press, 1992.

Pitcher, Oliver. *Dust of Silence.* New York: Troubador Press, 1958.

Rainey, Lawrence S. "Canon, Gender, and Text: The Case of H.D." In *Representing Modernist Texts: Editing as Interpretation.* Ed. George Bornstein. Ann Arbor: University of Michigan Press, 1991. 99–123.

Rogin, Michael. "'The Sword Became a Flashing Vision': D. W. Griffith's *The Birth of a Nation.*" In *The New American Studies.* Ed. Philip Fisher. Berkeley: University of California Press, 1991. 346–91.

Thomas, Lorenzo. *Chances Are Few.* Berkeley, Calif.: Blue Wind Press, 1979.

Tolson, Melvin B. *Harlem Gallery.* New York: Twayne, 1965.

———. *Libretto for the Republic of Liberia.* New York: Twayne, 1953.

Yarborough, Richard. "The First Person in Afro-American Fiction." In *Afro-American Literary Studies in the 1990s.* Ed. Houston A. Baker Jr. and Patricia Redmond. Chicago: University of Chicago Press, 1989. 105–21.

7

Bob Kaufman, Sir Real, and His Revisionary Surreal Self-Presentation

Kathryne V. Lindberg

> But in the main, I feel like a brown bag of miscellany propped against a wall. Against a wall in company with other bags, white, red and yellow. Pour out the contents, and there is discovered a jumble of small things priceless and worthless.
> —Zora Neale Hurston, "How It Feels to Be Colored Me"

> In a universe of cells—who is not in jail? Jailers.
> In a world of hospitals—who is not sick? Doctors.
> A golden sardine is swimming in my head.
> —Bob Kaufman, "#3, Jail Poems"

Risking the always disingenuous gesture of self-abnegation, let me say that I claim no special knowledge—neither on account of my Ph.D. nor on account of the San Francisco Beat aspirations of my thirteenth to sixteenth years. I am, in any case, late—now as I was in 1964, but, fortunately, not so late as to have missed Kaufman completely. And, now, I can set about saving him posthumously from the critical strictures that ensnare him and me—and do not. Invited or compelled to reread Kaufman on hearing the rumor that he was to be excluded from *The Norton Anthology of African-American Poetry* and, already distressed by the short shrift he gets in *The Beat Reader*, a text I was teaching, I am late to the recuperative enterprise,[1] even after Amiri Baraka's recent poem "A Meditation on Bob Kaufman," an ambivalent filiation with an old, black, Beat fellow traveler.[2] Anyway, if sometimes cryptically, I will reread *Bob Kaufman*—that is, read the books of poetry that appear under his name as well as my recollections of the man who haunted my North Beach youth. Now, geographically and perhaps occupationally far from listening directly to reading recommendations from the poetically sad character who guided me through the philosophy and politics sections of the now-defunct Phoenix Books, I nevertheless strip back my academic shell long enough to open this essay in this unwonted autobiographical fashion. I remember Kaufman. I need to drill through quite a bit of political and critical self-interest to let Kaufman's poetry speak for itself. Alas, I know that I will not get to his voice; I will only offer another (de)legitimation routine.

Before getting down to business, I acknowledge that, at the time of this writing, the most serious challenge to my reopening of Kaufman comes from Barbara Christian. She protests Kaufman's marginalization as an exemplary case of both mainstream and Beat dismissals of black poets as innovators. In 1972, Christian wrote a short protest or manifesto to reclaim Kaufman as a founding Beat and prodigious black poet.[3] I endorse Christian's strategic correction of the nearly exclusive focus on Kerouac and the white antiestablishment, who weirdly float, rebels without a cause, above race and class and beyond history. I do not want Kaufman excluded from the black—or any other—pantheon. However, his still-obstinate refusal to fit into anthologies ordered around fixed categories of race and class and sexuality and region and (life)style needs also to be prized.[4] Consider, in this vein, the treatment Kaufman has received from Beat survivors and anthologists, who, perhaps under the corrective of belated political pressure, have found Kaufman a useful race poet. In a similar way, Diane Di Prima is a woman among the Beats, a group otherwise newly and truly embarrassing as white boys with bad habits and worse politics.[5]

Kaufman quite deliberately refused the fixed racial and poetic identities required of a founding father or a romantic rebel. Indeed, his poetry, his few notes on poetics, and his variously recorded and remembered life rigorously interrogate the categories of identity that the Beats, much to their misogynist and apolitical misfortunes, failed to question. Without stacking up academic proof or analogues and parallels that sketch a Kaufman as drunk from serious reading in philosophy and politics and poetry as from white port and lemon juice and smack, I take Kaufman as a serious poet-critic. I will claim that Bob Kaufman's anatomizing of the category of race, his visceral and yet disembodied antipatriarchal poetics, is readable in terms of recent Third World, feminist, and/or identity politics.[6] More importantly, he was attuned to Frantz Fanon's theories of race—specifically, to Fanon's concern with seeing and being seen differently and his playing, as a black man, off Lacanian identity and/or the mirror stage. Kaufman might have known Fanon's texts well, since *The Wretched of the Earth* and *Black Skin, White Masks* were touchstones of the 1960s. Like the Hegelian, existentialist communist from Martinique, Kaufman surely resisted the fixed identities (Beat, African American/black/Negro, brown man, Jew, Native American, jazzman, merchant marine, loser) to which he had almost legitimate claims. Kaufman sometimes exercised such claims—if only long enough to empty out these categories by which bourgeois individuals measure Self and Other.

I want to bring Kaufman and Fanon into conversation over racialized yet potentially transformative *eyes* and *I*'s, over the constructed nature of identity. Fanon's mixed, generic *Black Skin, White Masks* (autobiography, Ph.D./ M.D. thesis draft, psychiatrist's case study, revolutionary handbook, book review, philosophical prolegomenon) and Kaufman's poetic corpus, fixated as it is on eyes and color and silence, cover the same terrain. They ask how the dominant subject position "I" makes the marginal or oppressed "Other" both instrumental and degraded or marginal. To begin, Fanon gives an account of racist stereotyping and the particular sexual objectification of black men: "The Negro . . . gives off no aura of sensuality either through his skin or through his hair. It is just that over a series of long days and long nights the image of the biological-sexual-sensual-genital-nigger has imposed itself on you and you do not know how to get free of it. The *eye* is not merely a mirror, but a correcting mirror" (201). I will look at Kaufman's similar refusal of the role of passive mirror. The antiracist as well as antiauthoritarian scopophobia in Kaufman's poetry is perhaps only superficially less polemical and less deconstructive than Fanon's treatment of Hegel's master-slave dialectic and Lacan's mirror stage (as compacted in the above quotation).[7]

Kaufman was indeed very much part of the Beat street scene from before the Gallery Six reading of *Howl* in 1955 through many nights of poetic and jazz/ musical and philosophical group effusions in San Francisco, on the Lower East Side, and in the Village from the mid-1950s until his death in 1986. At the risk of being unfair to his editors and other colleagues, and to abbreviate problematics of race and representation for Kaufman as the Black beat poet, I refer to the biographical-bibliographic note on the back flap of the jacket of *Golden Sardine:* "'GOLDEN SARDINE' scrawled on a scrap of brown wrapping paper found in a bundle of Bob Kaufman's manuscripts in a Moroccan-leather portfolio from which this second book of his poems is chosen—'Golden Sardine' floated loose in a stream of tattered papers & visions—'Golden Sardine' the image of the poet himself, brown paper skin torn & tossed South of Market, San Francisco, where he sleeps in a beat-up hotel."

My second epigraph—"A golden sardine is swimming in my head"—from the "Jail Poems" appearing in Kaufman's *Solitudes Crowded with Loneliness,* suggests the textual and imagistic source of Kaufman as "Golden Sardine." We might compare his golden sardine to his becoming, at the hands of editors, *the* representative golden sardine. He is posthumously transformed from a user of metaphors into a symbol. Rhetorically and/or politically significant differences separate *being*, by metonymic substitution, a golden sardine and *having* one, metaphorically, swimming in one's head. Kaufman is not a golden sardine, and there is something fishy about that color. The usual silvery gloss on live or fresh-killed sardines notwithstanding (instance Pound's "Say I dump my catch, shining and silvery / as fresh sardines flapping and slipping on the marginal cobbles"),[8] his "#3, Jail Poems" is not reducible to an instance of Kaufman's racial self-definition. Still, poem and metaphor become an interested appropriation and privileging of Kaufman as very beaten-down poet of color. The brown paper bag, oddly riffing or rhyming with Zora Neale Hurston's celebratory self-assertion of a *negritude* that scoffs at victimization and despair, was but one of the metaphoric identities—masks more than skin—that Kaufman constructed and, as quickly, deconstructed. My first epigraph, Hurston on "Colored Me," can be played alongside—and as grist for—the improvised self-reflexive solos in many of Kaufman's lines: "living in wrappers of jazz silence forever, loved. / . . . / My face feels like a living emotional relief map, forever wet" (*Solitudes* 6); "All losers, brown, red, black, and white" (*Ancient Rain* 37). Kaufman, even more or less than Hurston, refused to be fixed as a race poet—or a tragic mulatto, for that matter.

Let me stipulate that it is not my purpose to cast stones at, to *signify* on, such imagistic red herrings as Norman Mailer's "White Negro," or Rimbaud's "Vous etes de faux Negres"—that is, to accuse Kaufman's charitable and concerned forebears and friends of unkindness or political (in)correctness, at least not without noting that Kaufman was often a most unhappy and unhealthy user of drugs and alcohol whose friends and admirers generously helped him to food and into print.[9] Nevertheless, by a metonymic substitution or renaming, Kaufman, like other black jazzmen and hipsters, is made to represent his race and is represented—even textualized and fragmented—by his skin color. Referring, perhaps, to Whitman's well-known claim that "He who touches this book touches a man," the editors assign Kaufman "the text" and Kaufman "the author"—albeit, not Kaufman "*the movie*"—a title that marks an equation between the found and saved "scrap of brown wrapping paper" and "the poet himself, brown paper skin torn & tossed South of Market." Again, this is cryptic biography or ventriloquized autobiography, for Kaufman's poems vividly depict his friends and his life in the s.r.o. (single room occupancy) establishments "South of Market."[10]

Bob Kaufman did not supervise the publication of his works. This does not mean that he was casual about his poetry or that he tossed it off and away. He was, by turns, a spontaneous or performing poet and a silent presence. Courting a certain poetic anonymity more arduously than fame as a poet, Kaufman was, in any case, reticent and serious enough about immediacy and mediation to be chary about black marks on the white page. His reticence, which rather ironically shouts and echoes in his poems, had everything to do with his refusal of certain categories—which is to say, his categorical refusal to be fixed as a particular kind of poet, pinioned with a mastering adjective or even a string of generic modifiers. He was and was not black, Jew, Beatnik, hetero-/homosexual, American, African, Buddhist, junkie, drunk, jailbird, jazz poet, musician, minstrel, "Abomunist."

That last category was his coinage and the eponymous title of his one-man movement and manifesto. Abomunism sounds like abominable, as in snowman or cokeman: "Abomunists reject everything except snowmen" (*Solitudes* 78). Surely his movement is named after the atomic bomb: nuclear tests and Hiroshima and Nagasaki recur in Kaufman's poems as old plans, places, and physics dissolve.[11] To continue playing the old game of charades: the neologism sounds like abom-u-nism, parodically rhyming with comm-you-nism. Let us take a few moments over abomunism. First, we must grant that Kaufman, even more than other members of the Beat fraternity, refuses old-line or party political engagement in a world of radical relativity and nuclear madness. Also, there are no odds in looking to Kaufman for a straight tale of race or class victimage. In the long avant-garde tradition of sticking it to the bourgeoisie, Kaufman named a movement without a foundation or members. By way of parodying avant-garde gestures, his poetry was always para*citing*. Kaufman, sometimes signing himself "BOMKAUF," issued a series of statements, definitions, and mandates gathered together as the "Abomunist Manifesto" and reprinted at the end of *Solitudes Crowded with Loneliness* and, subsequently, in various anthologies.[12]

The "Abomunist Manifesto" shares the spirit of both the Futurist and Surrealist founding manifestos. Yet rather than issuing subsequent directives about technique and critique like those of earlier movements, Kaufman's playfully titled addenda—"Notes Dis- and Re- Garding Abomunism," "Boms," "$$Abomunus Craxioms$$"—fiddle Dada-like with the trappings of poetic identity and at resisting the inevitable fixity and fixtures of language. Or, more accurately, Kaufman sets words free to associate, through puns and sliding topical allusion, and to undermine the sexual and political repression that characterized the humorless strictures of Cold War behavior and ideology. Kaufman's favored "frinking," a portmanteau word for "fucking" and—with or while—"thinking," is hardly without political point, especially if we recall that J. Edgar Hoover's surveillance and blackmail tactics were as often focused on sex as on other subversions. Witness an excerpt from a whole—or purposefully open—piece called "Excerpts from the Lexicon Abomunon":

> At election time, Abomunists frink more, and naturally as hard-core Abo's, we feel the need to express ourselves somewhat more abomunably than others. We do this simply by not expressing ourselves (abomunization). We do not express ourselves in the following terms:
> Abommunity: n. Grant Avenue and other frinky places.
> . . . .
> Abomunate, the: n. The apolitical CORPUS ABOMUNISMUS.
> . . . .
> Abomunize: v. To carefully disorganize—usually associated with frinking.
> . . . .
> Abomunity: n. Regimentation. v. To impose organization from without, i.e. without oatmeal cookies.
> Frink: v. To (censored). n. (censored) and (censored). (*Solitudes* 80–81)

The interestedness of my own selection is rather mercilessly intended to hammer out Kaufman's point about strategic disorganization and diacritical or deconstructive quotation. I am just about willing to risk "Abomunosophy: n. Theoretical Abomunism" (81) in following Kaufman's movement, even as I hope to respect his silences and other occlusions. Note the warning implicit in the lexicon: "theoretical abomunism" at once distances me from poetic practice and abominizes theory; it frinks with the head. And Kaufman, both/neither Beat and/nor black, was, according to racist and authoritarian prejudices, overfrinked or was at least predisposed to self-destructive sexuality—and textuality. I would like to say that I, too, frink—and by all means necessary. Parodies, not to say puns, are, as Freud reminds us, always rather serious, and the "Abomunist Manifesto" is no exception to this condition.

First, abomunism announces the inescapability of certain filiations with old newnesses. As spontaneous as he could be, as automatic as he wanted his "exquisite corpse" or the performative corpus of his poetry to be, Kaufman acknowledges the revisionary nature of his project: "Abomunists spit anti-poetry for poetic reasons and frink" (*Solitudes* 77). Second, even as Kaufman forces his elusive and allusive jokes to carry a frightful freight of angst, abomunism opens onto both ridicule and pity: "Abomunists do not feel pain, no matter how much it hurts" (*Solitudes* 77). Kaufman's discursive and imagistic evasions of identity and identification—*I* and *eyeing* from within and without—both invite and indict the sort of romanticism and/or romantic racism that wraps him up as a "golden sardine" in "brown paper." I think of the romanticism of Mailer, whose "White Negro" brought down James Baldwin's justifiable wrath at the white writer's racist and homophobic depiction of black male's perceived sexual prowess.[13]

Kaufman easily, *abominably*, switched registers from somber to farcical—along a scale that was sometimes eloquently Ellingtonian, "Black, Brown & Beige." Some other quick switches are more disorienting, more critical and diacritical about Kaufman's race, sexuality, and politics. He sometimes announced that he embodied creolized America in a privileged way.[14] Outside his poems, as the son of a Jewish father and a black Catholic mother and as an adventurer who, in the manner of Kerouac if not Crane and Rimbaud, left for the sailor's life at an early age, Kaufman has a certain overdetermined authority to speak as a cultural and racial Other.[15] Read singly and theoretically, as they would be in an anthology of African-American or Jewish-American writers, several of Kaufman's poems represent and grant human dignity to peoples and traditions: "African Dream," "[Darkwalking Endlessly]," and "Sullen Bakeries of Total Recall" memorialize the African diaspora and Nazi Holocaust in exemplary ways; "Bagel Shop Jazz" has it both ways. Abomunism, taken philosophically or more destructively, opens more interesting possibilities by refusing to memorialize victimage. Moreover, as we shall see, "I Too Know What I Am Not" smashes readers' identitarian attempts to racialize and otherwise reauthorize the poet Bob Kaufman. In an uncharacteristically programmatic poem, "The Poet," Kaufman undermines even his own poetic authority.

> He speaks openly
> of what authority has deemed
> unspeakable, he becomes the
> enemy of authority. While the
> Poet lives, authority
> dies (*Ancient Rain* 70)

And, one might ask, does authorship expire with it?

⦀

Kaufman performed Dadaist and Surrealist raids on the sense and power of American identities and against constraints on his own fluid identifications. By the plural "identifications," I mean both how he was identified by the Beat circle or by squares and how he identified or refused fully to identify with groups by race, gender, politics, and other categories of social, artistic, and behavioral style. There's a good deal of play in his work, but it ain't funny. It's *black* humor worthy of Lenny Bruce, Kaufman's contemporary. Let me cite Kaufman's "Letter to the Editor" of the San Francisco *Chronicle*, dated 5 October 1963—which, above his cryptic signature, "Bob Kaufman, poet," now appears as the "last word" or authorizing signature of the collection *Golden Sardine*. This dead or rerouted "Letter to the Editor" is one way of addressing Kaufman's simultaneous refusal of fixed identity and final answers. He was, indeed, much more comfortable cataloging or listing what he was not. He was not white, for various reasons, including his own rebellion against social constructions, including biological models of race and color. Let me quote what he put on the page in and/or about "black and white" and about "passing" through life as Bob Kaufman, which meant being *between* and punning—or even "beating"—on blackness and privileges of whiteness: "Arriving back in San Francisco to be greeted by a blacklist and eviction I am writing these lines to the responsible non-people. One thing is certain I am not white. Thank God for that. It makes everything bearable" (*Golden Sardine* 80). Clearly, Kaufman exhibits what we would recognize as a bad *attitude;* not beatific, but still a kind of insistent presentness, a be-*at*-itude; a be-attitude; and, following out his puns on the rhythmic and downtrodden referents of "beat," a beat-attitude. Perhaps his beatness only seems more authentic than that of some of his cohorts—if only because of his early and beatnik-"beatified" (one would not want to say canonized) death, which was induced by (un)controlled substances and not a few police beatings.

Kaufman wrote insistently about what was in front of him and from himself, even insistently "through the body," according to the systole and diastole of the heartbeat—or so he figures the loudly silent "BEAT" in this letter. Unlike Kerouac, whose racial and sexual cruising white persona in *On the Road* travels around "wishing I were a Negro, feeling that the best the white world had offered was not enough ecstasy"[16] (148), Kaufman feigns that he is unconstrained by racial definition—although not exactly. On the one hand, he is constrained by virtue of his color: he cannot escape a certain "blacklist" (or "brownlist"). On the other hand, he does not have to wish to beat whiteness. In sum, Kaufman assumes the prerogative of the power (white?) position by moving in and out of color definitions made arbitrary in a way that Kerouac, always anxious about losing his self, would not have endorsed. The following passage bases Kaufman's name and/or Beat/poetic identity on puns, which are hardly a proper name or origin. Beat is a manifold and oft-explicated pun; but so is "blacklist," at least as Kaufman plays off it in the letter that one can hardly imagine William Randolph Hearst Jr., editor of the *Chronicle,* reading:

> To answer that rarely asked question. . . . Why are all blacklists white? Perhaps because all light lists are black, the listing of all that is listed is done by who is brown, the colors of an earthquake are brown, the colors of an earthquake are black, brown & beige, on the Ellington scale, such sweet thunder, there is a silent beat between the drums.

That silent beat makes the drum beat, it makes the drum, it makes the beat. Without it there is no drum, no beat. It is not the beat played by who is beating the drum. His is a noisy loud one, the silent beat is beaten by who is not beating on the drum, his silent beat drowns out all the noise, it comes before and after every beat, you hear it in beatween, its sound is

Bob Kaufman, poet . . . (*Golden Sardine* 81)

Protesting yet celebrating blacklisting or marginality and his overdetermined status as "nonperson" of various sorts, Kaufman insisted on being "in-beat-ween." In-*beat*-ween marks a characteristic silence or spacing in and beyond his poems. Rather like Derrida's notes on difference/*difference*, Kaufman's pun signifies a disturbance that writing causes in unmediated speech—and silence, the beat which isn't heard but by the Beats.

Silence is, along with Symbolist white writing, a trope for and of poetry. For Kaufman, a certain mystico-mysterious silence was also a posture or condition, one adopted from Hart Crane, the poet and poethood most cited by Kaufman. Not inappropriately, nostalgic commentators on Beatness make a good deal of Kaufman's apparently strategic silences. However one reads his reticence, one reason his publications and performances were so few and remained uncelebrated except by Beat and other fellow travelers is that twice—from 1963, the year of this letter, until 1973 and again from 1978 into the 1980s—Kaufman took oaths of silence. During these times, he effectively withdrew from the society of men and poets and biographers. The reason behind his silences is the stuff of rumor, of projected political protest and conjectural religious withdrawal. All are plausible.[17] New Directions' jacket note to *Ancient Rain: Poems 1956–1978* has him withdrawn into "disappointment, drugs, and imprisonment." Ann Charters has him silenced, in 1963, by Kennedy's assassination (32). His admirers tend to elevate or symbolically sacrifice Kaufman to a certain genealogy of Romantic suicides or self-annihilating victims of society. In his texts, in his life as text, we can trace a line of poetic martyrs: Keats, Crane, Kerouac, Caryl Chessman, perhaps Kennedy, and ultimately Christ make cameos as cacophonous presences in Kaufman's text or context. Seeming to affiliate with such a line, Kaufman himself salutes Hart Crane by allusive tributes in "Voyager" and in other poems addressed to a "Voyager." "Hart . . . Crane," the poem, is a graphically elliptical and surrealist affirmation of Crane's not-so-silent presence in America. For instance: "They hear you, Crane. . . . you are screaming from their turned-off radios"; "They deny you, Crane. . . . you are safely dead, but we know, / Crane you never were. . . . / They live you, Crane. . . . ON THE BRIDGE" (*Solitudes* 16–17). The dead poet can be made to speak the living hell Kaufman would at once escape and survive.

In this way, while pinning down Crane's identity, Kaufman nearly escapes.

Still, silence and giving voice to silent suffering offer the hope of transformation. More often than not, Kaufman tempers despair with resistance, taking up the poetic charge to transform reality. Beyond the poetic and heroic registers, Kaufman's poems frequently testify against genocide and racism. "Sullen Bakeries of Total Recall," in part a poem of Jewish identification, memorializes what continues to be unspeakable and unimaginable and thus a challenge to the efficacy of the very poetic traditions it appropriates:

> Sometimes I feel the ones who escaped the ovens where Germans shall
> forever cook their spiritual meals are leaning against my eyes.
>
> . . . .
>
> I acknowledge the demands of Surrealist realization. I challenge Apollinaire
> to stagger drunk from his grave and write a poem about the Rosenbergs' last
> days in a housing project. . . . (*Solitudes* 42–43)

Not without frequent and (sur)realistic touches—tending as much to Symbolist imagistic exaggeration as Surrealist incongruity—Kaufman proffers reminders of pain and voluminous notes toward suicide. Does he also allude to Jones's/Baraka's "Preface to a 20 Volume Suicide Note"? At least partially, Kaufman sides with subterranean or surreal joy, a condition he likens to jazz, which is ironically silent and usually misinterpreted. "Afterwards, They Shall Dance" tropes on jazz and dead poets, ending with a blues parody or signifying appropriation of Christic beatitude:

> Billie Holiday got lost on the subway and stayed there forever,
> Raised little peace-of-mind gardens in out of the way stations,
> And will go on living in wrappers of jazz silence forever, loved.
> My face feels like a living emotional relief map, forever wet.
> My hair is curling in anticipation of my own wild gardening.
>
> . . . .
>
> In order to exist I hide behind stacks of red and blue poems
> And open little sensuous parasols, singing the nail-in-the-foot song, drinking
> cool beatitudes. (*Solitudes* 6–7)

I take it that Christ, not Oedipus or Prometheus, is the ur-singer of that foot song, but the poem is about undoing fixed identity and spreading poetic sanctity along with anti-Oedipal blasphemy. Against origins, Kaufman offers the white noise of many possible allusions. Or so one imagines. You might recall Hart Crane's literary and personal Oedipal encounters on the subway (or the metro) that are further "finger pondered" (as Joyce would say) by William Carlos Williams. Kaufman often and subtly destroys traditional poetic genealogies and philosophical influences in palimpsestic allusions. He performs, improvises, or riffs others' tunes and themes.

As in that cryptic letter to the *Chronicle,* Kaufman's poems often aver his objectification into an Other(ness). Refusing to be other than what he is, which is both posture and process, he escapes and analyzes such positions as symbolic or representative black /man/Beat/poet. Nevertheless, this refusal of fixed identity is itself a mark of an identity, which he sometimes (im)properly names "Beat" and more often "jazz." *White* Kaufman was not. Whiteness/whites exist only because it/they can reflect and distort themselves against the blackness of racial Others. "Black, Brown & Beige," the colors of California earthquakes and the scale of blackness*es* (or nonwhiteness) inscribed in Ellington's tune and title, announce the impossibility of fixing and privileging whiteness without a stable *black*ground, if you will. Ellington and Kaufman expose the lie or construct that "whites" fix as whiteness against the mirror-opposite or Otherness of blackness. Note that it takes a "blacklist" to make Kaufman certain that he is not white.

By de-definition, rather than simple reversal, which might repeat the mirror-effect and the dialectic of master and slave, Kaufman subverts the binary logic of black and white. "Like Father, Like Sun," which is both anticolonial and autobiographical, paints an ironic victory or escape for a mixed race of rebels and artists in an America of unchained and unaccommodated difference:

> America is a promised land, a garden torn from naked stone,
> A place where the losers in earth's conflicts can enjoy their triumph
> All losers, brown, red, black, and white; the colors from the Master Palette.
> (*Ancient Rain* 37)

Just as he asserted "One thing is certain I am not white," Kaufman refused symbolic or generic blackness, refused to be fixed as symbolic victim or mirror by a racist and/or reductive gaze. Kaufman was in a dialogue—a sort of deconstructive conversation—with such fixed positions and definitions of beat-i-tude as LeRoi Jones's recuperation of Africa's musical and racial origins nuanced by black nationalism or Ted Joans's sexy self-assertion rap (in 1970's *Afrodesia,*). Kaufman de-defined his own beat, which is to say himself as a beat, in "I, Too, Know What I Am Not," which unmasks or remines the poet's mixed-race genealogy. Creolized and literally part Louisiana Creole— or "heterogeneous" in several senses—Kaufman places himself in and out of a Whitmanesque characterization of the singer and his song. He offers what might be called a "blacklist" or catalog of co-optated identities:

> No, I am not death wishes of sacred rapists, singing on candy gallows
> No, I am not spoor of Creole murderers hiding in crepe-paper bayous.
> . . . .
> No, I am not shriek of Bantu children, bent under pennywhistle whips.
> No, I am not whisper of the African trees, leafy Congo telephones.
> No, I am not Leadbelly of blues, escaped from guitar jails.
> No, I am not anything that is anything I am not. (Solitudes 28–29)

Number 7 of "Jail Poems" repeats the ambivalence of this self-assertion, this abnegation of packaged selfhood, if not of proper names and fixed categories more generally, including "beatnik":

> Someone whom I am is no one.
> Something I have done is nothing.
> Someplace I have been is nowhere.
> I am not me.
> What of the answers
> I must find questions for?
> All these strange streets
> I must find cities for,
> Thank God for beatniks? (*Solitudes* 58)

Not without reference to Emily Dickinson ("I'm Nobody! Who are you?") and Stein (who, on her deathbed, allegedly answered "What's the answer?" with "What's the question?") and Lear ("Nothing comes from nothing"), Kaufman noodles a cryptic answer—or is it a question?—in beatnik identity. Of course, he is being doubly ironic, since he names or identifies his own interrogation of identity with a famous, flexible, pejorative nonconcept: "beatnik." Elsewhere, as we have seen, he puts the epithet through various polyptotons: "beat," "beatitude," "beatness," and so forth.[18] Traveling beyond the ubiquitous male identity crises acted out over liminoid expressways and other tao-ways, Kaufman's beatnik(s) provided him a safe haven from fixed identity. "Some" and "no" are his favorite loci and foci—his sacred San Francisco spots.

\|\|\|

Let us return to Ferlinghetti's dust-jacket blurb—"South of Market, San Francisco, where he sleeps in a beat up hotel"—for a geographical signpost.

Not coincidentally, South of Market was the most romantic, the beatest zone on Kerouac's map. A recognizably metonymic strategy is at work in *On the Road*, where visiting a South of Market jazz joint, Kerouac projects "beat-i-tude" onto a black tenor-saxophone player. With deceptive specificity, Kerouac finds his own idealized or essentialized beat identity mirrored in a figure who is at once fully present and merely a stand-in for Billie Holiday in Harlem. Read slowly through what is a fast-moving but, I think, familiar riff; think back on Kaufman's version of Billie Holiday and his vision of jazz rebellion: "The girls came down and we started out on our big night, once more pushing the car down the street. 'Wheeoo!! let's go!' cried Dean, and we jumped in the back seat and clanked to the little Harlem on Folsom Street" (Kerouac 162). Note that Folsom Street stands in—as "little Harlem"—for New York's larger, perhaps less containable, and certainly more recognizable ghetto, which was but one popular site for several generations of white slummers. As Kerouac focuses in on the jazzman, he reads "beat life itself" in the player/singer's stage presence and delivery:

> Then up stepped the tenorman on the bandstand and asked for a slow beat and looked sadly out the open door over people's heads and began singing "Close Your Eyes.". . . . To sing a note he had to touch his shoetops and pull it all up to blow, and he blew so much he staggered from the effect, and only recovered himself for the next slow note. "Mu-u-u-usic pla-a-a-a-a-ay!" He leaned back with his face to the ceiling, mike held below. He shook and he swayed. Then he leaned in, almost falling with his face against the mike. "Ma-a-a-ake it dream-y for dancing"—and he looked at the street outside with his lips curled in scorn, Billie Holiday's lip sneer—"while we go ro-man-n-n-cing"—he staggered sideways—"Lo-o-o-ove's holida-a-ay"—he shook his head with disgust and weariness at the whole world—. (164)

For all Kerouac's fine details, including the frame drawn around the tenor player's world-weary beatness as we look out the door at the great American outdoors or the Beat provinces of anthropomorphized weary streets and sad roads, the player is only a mirror for the authorial spectator. The black jazzman is an authenticating symbol conjured up for Kerouac's readers: "and then he came to the end of his song, and for this there had to be elaborate preparations. . . . here we were dealing with the pit and the prunejuice of poor beat life itself in the god-awful streets of man, so he said it and sang it, 'Close—your—' and blew it way up to the ceiling and through to the stars and on out—'Ey-y-y-y-y-es.' . . . He looked down and wept. He was the greatest" (164). The object of Kerouac's camera-like gaze, an exemplary tenor player in an identifiable but also universal San Francisco joint, is the generic jazz musician translatable into a female blues singer. He/she/it is great because, not constrained by the tough-guy or cowboy ethic, *he* weeps. The lachrymose—which is to say feminized, objectified, perhaps suffering or victimized—Jazzman gives the Beat observer his identity and allows the writer safe distance from the undifferentiated condition of engulfing Beatness, of really being beaten. The tenor player is heroic or poetic victim, and, because he has both the beat of the music and the downtroddenness of Beat life, he is unwitting (?) prey to Kerouac's fetishistic gaze. Kerouac, legitimate founder or coiner of "Beat," spontaneous prose writer par excellence, is the star and doubly the *subject*/agent of that scene.

I admit to playing fast and free with Kerouac, whacking him with recognizable Lacanianisms, so let me *frame* (I hope not unfairly, but at least partially, in the sense of a frame-up) his programmatic identification *of* and *with* the jazz singer. On the one side, let me place Frantz Fanon's notion of the instrumentality of black skin to white self-definition and, on the other side, Kaufman's similar resistance to being objectified as racial or sexual Other that does not gaze or talk back. Thus, Fanon:

> It is always a question of the subject; one never thinks of the object. I try to read admiration in the eyes of the other, and if, unluckily, those eyes show me an unpleasant reflection, I find the mirror flawed: Unquestionably that other one is a fool. I do not try to be naked in the sight of the object. The object is denied in terms of individuality and liberty. The object is an instrument. It should enable me to realize my subjective security. I consider myself fulfilled (the wish for plenitude) and I recognize no division. The Other comes on to the stage only in order to furnish it. I am the Hero. (211–12)

With an abiding concern about being misread and a decided bias for the way Symbolists and Surrealists privilege the eye over the ear as the poetic and/or transformative organ—even hallucinations and moving pictures over mystic breath and bardic voice—it is hardly surprising to see Fanon's eyes all over Kaufman's poems. Not to miss a very American, Emersonian, and Whitmanesque pun, and with a nod toward Christopher Isherwood, Kaufman has a poem called "I Am a Camera." Further, the collection *Golden Sardine* includes a sort of cinema verité treatment cross cut with (other) media distortions of Caryl Chessman's execution. Indeed, troping tears of sorrow into corrective lenses, "Inquiry into a December Because" has "My eye leaks, dripping sight over my collar" (*Ancient Rain* 10). Another poem that finds Kaufman trapped in a body scarred and entropic or kippled and kudzued with memories, ends:

> My feet are covered with moss from bayous, flowing across my floor.
> I can't go out anymore.

I shall sit on my ceiling.
Would you wear my eyes? (*Solitudes* 40)

Naked and honest eyes are, for Kaufman, the poet's special responsibility and curse.

In addition to living and analyzing the categories of witness and seer, Kaufman is particularly concerned about becoming—personally and poetically—the degraded object of media scrutiny. Hollywood, in a poem of that title, is the "artistic cancer of the universe" (*Solitudes* 26). But more than that, Kaufman's *scopophobia* is connected to his terror of being fixed in a racist, sexist gaze, made a "symbol" and/or a *black* and/or a *poet*. In "A Terror Is More Certain," Kaufman evades the stares of a symbolic television audience of "cowboys" to perform his own sort of verbal—if not visual—terrorism: "publish fat books of the month & have wifeys that are lousy in bed & never realize how bad my writing is because I am poor and symbolize myself" (*Golden Sardine* 20). Keeping with the assertion—or is it abandoning hope?—that he can evade or at least determine his own symbolization, the piece ends with a terrifying yet funny vision of a television fixing and distorting Kaufman's image: "its [sic] no fun on top of a lady when her hair is full of shiny little machines & your ass reflected in that television screen, who wants to be a poet if you fuck on t.v. & all those cowboys watching" (*Golden Sardine* 20–21).

Similarly, Fanon insists that the racial Other, the marginal, is made to mirror and exhibit the master's repressed identity. *Black Skin, White Masks* poetically registers the hope that seeing differently, changing images—if not eyes—can transform the world. In a rather old-fashioned way, Fanon wants to turn the victim's cry into a triumphal ode. The Antillean Caliban transforms curses into high art: "The *eye* should make it possible for us to correct cultural errors. I do not say the *eyes*, I say the *eye,* and there is no mystery about what that eye refers to; not to the crevice in the skull but to that very uniform light that wells out of the reds of Van Gogh, that glides through a concerto of Tchaikovsky, that fastens itself desperately to Schiller's *Ode to Joy,* that allows itself to be conveyed by the worm-ridden bawling of Césaire" (202).

At this late date, we can surely go beyond Fanon's elitist eye-dentity, his attempt to transvalue the lowly. Avoiding that impulse to turn neocolonialism into another belated classicalism, perhaps I can avoid trying to make Kaufman legitimate along even these lines. Maybe not. But, by way of ending this call to begin again to reread his poems, I quote, from "Unanimity Has Been Achieved, Not a Dot Less For Its Accidentalness," another turn of his identity reel: "A beggar is the body of God-ness, come to shoot movies / with his eyes" (*Ancient*

Rain 16). At least you can't take that straight and/or as a simple projection of the need for poetical correctness.

Notes

I thank Joseph Donahue for his 1992 American Literature Association Panel on San Francisco poetry, which made me conjure memories that skirt this academic paper and still have me going. Thanks to Ed Foster for putting a version of this essay in good company in *Talisman* (Fall 1993), from which Aldon Nielsen was good enough to take it. Finally, thanks to Christopher T. Leland, novelist, for help improving the final version of this essay and to Murray Jackson, poet, for improving my reading and my life.

1. Since the first writing of this essay, Bob Kaufman's work is more readily available. Not only did the editors of the Norton *Anthology of African-American Literature* feel compelled to include several of his poems, but a volume of his selected poems—*Cranial Guitar*—is now available. Kaufman has long been recognized as a major poetic force, a symbol and coiner of symbols. Since the time that Herb Caen used the pejorative "beatnik" as epithet for Kaufman, who frequently got busted for performing his poems on unready San Francisco streets, he became known, in Paris, where *Solitudes Crowded with Loneliness* was reproduced, as the black Rimbaud (see Jacqueline Starer, for example). André Breton tagged him, along with Joans, a "Black Surrealist." This mainstream, avant-garde genealogy is being revised and (politically/racially/gender) corrected, but it should not be forgotten that Kaufman's political contributions have also been preserved in the African-American poetic tradition through anthologies and legend. I would mention here Kofi Natambu's "Bob Kaufman: A Great American Poet, 1925–1986," one indication of Kaufman's persistent influence on black poetics—in this case, on Natambu's now-defunct Detroit journal *Solid Ground*, which combined theory, labor activism, and political and avant-garde poetry.

2. Sometimes appropriating Kaufman's Abomunist coinages, signing his own name as "Bimgo," Baraka uses Kaufman as a bridge back to his own Beat playfulness—or at least to the origins of his own Black Arts movement. Baraka also ascribes an anger and victimage that Kaufman's Surrealist psychic transformations resisted.

3. Kaufman's early political, labor engagement with the militant National Maritime Union and the Progressive party and his later targeting by police and the mental heath establishment because of his unacceptable lifestyles, including his interracial marriage and public drunkenness, do not make him an ideal role model for any race or revolution. Instead, his ideas and art provide a still-potent critique of "institutionalization"— which for Kaufman meant literal incarceration as much as the strictures of canonization, the fate of textuality.

4. Maria Damon's chapter on Kaufman, "'Unmeaning Jargon'/Uncanonized Beatitude, Bob Kaufman, Poet," is to date the most comprehensive and sympathetic treatment of Kaufman's poetic performance. Damon records and corrects biographical and

performance details that have made Kaufman a mythic and perpetual outsider rather than a conscious(ness) activist and revolutionary. By recognizing both the virtues and the interested distortions of myth and the biography, Damon offers convincing readings of the poetry and several of Kaufman's epithets, "shaman," "griot," "voyager" (Damon 32–76).

    5. I think first of the early and understandably objectifying love tribute of Kaufman's wife, now widow, Eileen Kaufman, "Laughter Sounds Orange at Night." I must add that I was lucky enough to have several precious and critically enlightening conversations with Eileen Kaufman in Berkeley in 1996; these have enriched my ongoing project on black political lyrics. Michael Davidson was among the first academic critics to begin giving women, immigrant, and minority writers the attention often denied them by the work and canonizers of the small brotherhood around Kerouac (*San Francisco Renaissance*).

    6. For the sake of economy, I refer you to Chandra Mohanty's "Under Western Eyes." Closer to the Beat heritage, Charles Bernstein interrogates "identity," which he sees as too intact and patriarchal in Beat poetry (*A Poetics*).

    7. I am twisting "scopophobia" from the objectifying, sexist, and scopophilic "male gaze" named in E. Ann Kaplan's *Women and Film*.

    8. These are the first lines of Pound's original version of "Canto I," first published in *Poetry* and probably unknown as such to Kaufman.

    9. In giving context to his account of black identity politics' "postconsensus" Britain, Kobena Mercer provides a quick summary of Beat-related white maskings, racial crossings, and revisions of blackness. Kaufman seems to have played with, but also to have become the victim of, categories ambiguously redrawn by Beat adventure seekers. In any case, of Rimbaud's "false Negro" and Mailer's "White Negro," Mercer notes that "from noble savages to painterly primitives, the trope of the White Negro encodes an antagonistic subject-position on the part of the white subject in relation to the normative codes of his or her own society" (301). While I will not recite the now-long bibliography on white appropriations of blackness, it is worth noting that Caribbean writers, especially, have recently made heterogeneous populations and creolized culture a virtue, going so far as to create diasporic (normative-yet-non-normative?) nationalism and macaronic national languages out of African, Spanish, Asian, Carib, European peoples and cultures. Alongside Kaufman's rather more idiosyncratic and analytic or deconstructive racial personae, one might consider Derek Walcott's idea of "epic memory," Kamau Braithwaite's "nation language," and Stuart Hall's "new ethnicities."

    10. At once helpful and suspect along the lines mentioned, see Ferlinghetti's "Telegraphic Preface" to *The Ancient Rain* and the City Lights' editorial endnote (again written by Ferlinghetti) to *Second April*.

    11. If anything could be more explicit than A-bomunism, it is *Second of April*'s poetically prosaic mining of such coincidences as Easter/Passover, the poet's birthday, and A("pril is the cruelest month")-bomb, which would make Kaufman's poem join Wil-

liam Carlos Williams's *Spring and All* as a critique of Eliot. Kaufman suggests that in a postatomic or subatomic world, Aprils and quotations multiply exponentially to undo poetic origin-ality.

12. In effect, all of Kaufman's "books" are anthologies, since they collect poems titled and arranged by editors from the author's notes and magazine and broadside publications. Kaufman also thematized the thorny route from intention to execution, thought to action; he accepted as inevitable the contradiction of editorializing and improvising. We must thank Eileen Kaufman for preserving his memory and for depositing his transcribed works in archives in Paris and at Boston University. See Brenda Knight's recent edition, with commentary, of the works and (auto)biographical notes of Beat women, including Eileen Kaufman.

13. See Norman Mailer's "The White Negro" (reprinted in Charters's *Portable Beat Reader*) and James Baldwin's "The Black Boy Looks at the White Boy."

14. Creole/creolized in two senses: first, Kaufman was of Louisiana Creole descent; second, and more importantly, Kaufman represented and cultivated something close to José Martí's expanded notion of "creolized" America (indigenous plus waves of European and African immigrants). Martí says, for example: "The European University must bow to the American University. The history of America, from the Incas to the present, must be taught in clear detail and to the letter, even if the archons, of Greece are overlooked. . . . Let the world be grafted onto our republics, but the trunk must be our own. And let the vanquished pedant hold his tongue, for there are no hands, in which a man may take greater pride than in our long-suffering American republics. With the rosary as our guide, our heads white and our bodies mottled, both Indian and Creole, we fearlessly entered the world of nations" (88). My essay "'White Mythology' and/or Outside the Culture (Criticism) Industry" further considers Martí's "Our America" and Fanon's "masking."

15. Considering David Henderson's "Tribute to Bob Kaufman" (KPFA radio, 26 April 1986), one should note that, according to his brother George and several (even and especially nonpoetic) activists, Kaufman was not only well-read from his bourgeois early childhood, but he had been directly involved with organized labor and electoral actions from the radical National Maritime Union to the Progressive Party to the civil rights movement. That he chose what he could hardly have known would be such fatal and personally dangerous and damaging modes of protest and of assertion of revolutionary identity does not make him simply "the victim." See Maria Damon on this point; also Henderson's 1986 radio tribute, which dubs commentary by Maria Damon, Nathaniel Mackey, and others over earlier recordings, including a few of Kaufman's own readings.

16. This bald announcement of the Beat quest for black ecstasy is uncritically adopted by Mailer's "hipsters." Romantic racism, which reserves the privilege of return from primitivism to (white) conventionality and rationality, surely is the adequate term for such desire. John Waters's film *Hairspray* also comes to mind as a more self-consciously nuanced repetition of the same.

17. We should not forget, as Kaufman will not permit us to forget, the persistence with which law enforcers—from harassing street cops to the anonymous distributors of electrical torture and murder in the mental-health establishment and penal system—effectively pursued Kaufman. His poetry memorializes Chessman's as well as his own own prison pain. Even though his deceptive silences and the profound depths of his poems invite projection and romanticization of various sorts, it seems clear enough that Kaufman intended to protest injustice rather than to celebrate or canonize a heroic victimage, which can perversely augment the power(s) behind oppression and repression he suffered. Perhaps Kaufman, who experienced hundreds of prison stays and involuntary electric-shock treatments (ESTs), might now be more engaged by protest against the phenomenal current growth of the prison industry and the relegitimation of EST than interested by his growing poetic reputation. But, then, I do mean to close the book on the dialogue reopened over his important work.

18. The common definition of polyptoton, the Greek name for a rhetorical trope of revision and repetition, is the repetition of words with different endings and/or in different grammatical cases (Lanham 78). If "Beat," a noun, and "beat," a verb, can be a pun, "beat" in either sense and "beatitude" are a complex polyptoton and/or a compound of pun and polyptoton. The tropes that flower forth from Kaufman's wordplay on "beat" can be named with Greek or Latin names and with Beat or street argot. They are so full of coincidence and play, suggesting the syncopation, improvisation, and valences of jazz, that it might be best simply to say that Kaufman riffs on words; his poems are jazz riffs. Therefore, so do we riff on his words. By using "riff" and marking Kaufman's tendency to turn words loose from proper to active or diacritical forms—tropologically, if not also grammatically, nouns into verbs—I mean also critically to allude to the process of canonization Baraka names in his essay "Swing—From Verb to Noun." Poems performed by Kaufman, who sought anonymity and often did not write things down, cannot, by design, be pinned down.

Works Cited

Baldwin, James. "The Black Boy Looks at the White Boy." In *The Price of the Ticket: Collection Non-Fiction, 1948–1985.* New York: St. Martin's Press, 1985. 289–303.

Baraka, Amiri. "A Meditation on Bob Kaufman" (1989). In *Sulfur: A Literary Bi-Annual of the Whole Art* 29 (Fall 1991): 61–66.

———. "Swing—From Verb to Noun." In *The LeRoi Jones/Amiri Baraka Reader.* Ed. William J. Harris. New York: Thunder's Mouth Press, 1991. 33–50.

Bernstein, Charles. *A Poetics.* Cambridge, Mass.: Harvard University Press, 1992.

Charters, Ann. *The Portable Beat Reader.* New York: Viking, 1992.

Christian, Barbara. "Whatever Happened to Bob Kaufman?" In *The Beats: Essays in Criticism.* Ed. Lee Bartlett. Jefferson, N.C.: McFarland, 1981. 107–14.

Damon, Maria. *The Dark End of the Street: Margins in American Vanguard Poetry.* Minneapolis: University of Minnesota Press, 1993.

Davidson, Michael. *The San Francisco Renaissance: Poetics and Community at Mid-Century.* New York: Cambridge University Press, 1989.
Fanon, Frantz. *Black Skin, White Masks.* Trans. Charles Lam Markmann. New York: Grove, 1967.
———. *The Wretched of the Earth.* Trans. Constance C. Farrington. New York: Grove, 1968.
Henderson, David. "Tribute to Bob Kaufman." KPFA radio. Berkeley, Calif. 26 April 1986.
Kaplan, E. Ann. *Women and Film: Both Sides of the Camera.* New York: Methuen, 1983.
Kaufman, Bob. "Abomunist Manifesto." San Francisco: City Lights Books, 1959.
———. *The Ancient Rain: Poems, 1956–1978.* Comp. Raymond Foye. New York: New Directions, 1981.
———. *Cranial Guitar.* Minneapolis: Coffee House Press, 1996.
———. *Golden Sardine.* San Francisco: City Lights Books, 1967.
———. *Second April.* San Francisco: City Lights Books, 1959.
———. *Solitudes Crowded with Loneliness.* New York: New Directions, 1965.
Kaufman, Eileen. "Laughter Sounds Orange at Night." In *Beat Angels.* Ed. Arthur Knight and Kit Knight. California, Pa.: Faculty Scholarship Committee, 1982. 29–38.
Kerouac, Jack. *On the Road.* New York: Signet, 1957.
Knight, Brenda, ed. *Women of the Beat Generation.* Berkeley, Calif.: Conari Press, 1996.
Lanhan, Richard. *A Handlist of Rhetorical Terms.* 2d ed. Berkeley: University of California Press, 1991.
Lindberg, Kathryne V. "'White Mythology' and/or Outside the Culture (Criticism) Industry." *Emergences* 3–4 (Fall 1992): 170–92.
Martí, José. *Our America: Writings on Latin America and the Struggle for Cuban Independence.* Ed. Philip S. Foner. Trans. Elinor Randall. New York: Monthly Review Press, 1977.
Mercer, Kobena. *Welcome to the Jungle: New Positions on Black Cultural Studies.* New York: Routledge, 1994.
Mohanty, Chandra Talpade. "Under Western Eyes." In *Third World Women and the Politics of Feminism.* Ed. Chandra Talpade Mohanty, Ann Russo, and Lourdes Torres. Bloomington: Indiana University Press, 1991. 51–80.
Natambu, Kofi. "Bob Kaufman: A Great American Poet, 1925–1986." *Solid Ground: A New World Journal* 3.2 (1987): 28–30.
Starer, Jacqueline. *Les Écrivains Beats et le Voyage.* Études Anglaises 68. Paris: Didier, 1977.

8

Decolonizing the Spirits: History and Storytelling in Jay Wright's *Soothsayers and Omens*

C. K. Doreski

> The soothsayers who found out from time what it had in store certainly did not experience time as either homogeneous or empty. Anyone who keeps this in mind will perhaps get an idea of how past times were experienced in remembrance—namely, in just the same way.
> —Walter Benjamin, "Theses on the Philosophy of History"

> What is happening in the world more and more is that people are attempting to decolonize their spirits. A crucial act of empowerment, one that might return reverence to the Earth, thereby saving it, in this fearful-of-Nature, spiritually colonized age.
> —Alice Walker, "Clear Seeing Inherited Religion and Reclaiming the Pagan Self"

In 1976, during the national enactments of the Bicentennial, Jay Wright published *Dimensions of History* (Corinth) and *Soothsayers and Omens* (Seven Woods Press), two independent sequences of poems dealing with the cultural and aesthetic imperative to construct an enlarged historical path into the cultural geographies of the diaspora. Like Ezra Pound's *Cantos*, these collections are more than poems "containing history"; they are active attempts to reconstruct the very method and modes of the aestheticized historical, the energized field of narrative threads: storytelling and national (de)construction.[1] For Wright, national*isms* serve as oppositional sponsors of an emerging aesthetic of history. Such efforts require more than the invention or discovery of new historical certainties: they necessitate the deconstruction of received history itself. And what better time than the Bicentennial to investigate the problematic boundaries of nationality, modernity, and reason in this historically suspect construction: the United States of America.

Wright's poetry, seeking "imaginative dissolution and reconstruction of its material" (Rowell 1983:4), responds not simply to the miscarried extensions of Enlightenment dicta, historical revolutionary manifestos, and received national identity; it seeks to escape the oppression of reason and national coherence embedded in even more recent countercultural stirrings such as black nationalism.[2] Recalling Frederick Douglass's determination to authenticate the Centennial celebration through an honest appraisal of the promise and fulfillment of life in America, Wright's aestheticized history moves to supplant the temporal, inherited, and brittle constellation of the founding fathers with a centering pan-African patriarchy[3] curiously akin in impulse to Alice Walker's decentering, womanist rift with mediated history in her Bicentennial novel, *Meridian*. Wright, as if responding to Pound's lament that "*le personnel manqué* . . . we have not men for our times" (1995:344), invents a postnational[4] narrative in which his "founding fathers" actually dissolve national corridors, boundaries, and chronology to construct an ephemeral, transactional tale.

Like the Centennial, which followed and apotheosized the Civil War, the Bicentennial was a postwar, mercantile ode to *Pro*gress as well as a subtextual charge to pro*gress* through national cohesion and ambitions.[5] Such epochal celebrations are anathema to Wright, who believes that their sole function is the sheer obliteration of the living consciousness of historical and cultural trace memories. The Bicentennial was an enactment of what Homi Bhabha defines in "DissemiNation" as "the construction of a discourse on society that *performs* the problem of totalizing the people and unifying the national will" (1994:160–61). Bhabha further remarks that "this breakdown in the identity of the will is another instance of the supplementary narrative of nationness that 'adds to' without 'adding up'" (1994:161). Inadequate constructions of history serve no one, least of all a poet who seeks authentic and vital commemorative linguistic structures.

Although his aesthetic deliberations are born out of Vietnam-era cynicism and Bicentennial tawdriness, Wright owes much of his antihistoricism to the broader historical tide of the twentieth century.[6] No writer has better captured the elegiac note of humanity's loss of history and the leisure of historical time sounded by Walter Benjamin in his 1936 disquisition on narrative, history, community, and solitude, "Der Erzähler" ("The Storyteller"). Written in the late 1920s, it laments an aesthetic and *historical* concern: "the art of telling stories is coming to an end" (1968:83). And with that simple assertion Benjamin displaces the very meanings of "story," "experience," and "history" as he reinscribes that which began with the First World War: "a process began to become apparent which has not halted since then. Was it not noticeable at the end of the war that men returned from the battlefield grown silent—not richer, but poorer in communicable experience? . . . A generation that had gone to school on a horse-drawn streetcar now stood under the open sky in a countryside in which nothing remained unchanged but the clouds, and beneath these clouds, in a field of force of destructive torrents and explosions, was the tiny, fragile human body" (1968:84). Unwilling to fetishize the emblematic ruins of the past and unable to presume attachment to the received history of Pound and Eliot, Wright, adapting and extending the tradition of Emerson, makes a commitment to what Wallace Stevens called, in "Notes toward a Supreme Fiction," "this invention, this invented world" (1954:380). Stevens's "major man," an example of the exemplary figure thought to be essential to historical constructions, will undergo a startling subordination as Wright creates a decentered counterdiscourse to a national epic. Stridently postnational and aggressively transnational, he posits a new (w)hole: a poetic of history that attempts utter effacement of a mediating force, either in the person of the poet or in the presence of the text. History, stripped of its numbing informational qualities, demographic insistence, and subservience to pastness and nationalisms, will thrive in the fluid immediacy of a story being told. "Mean egotism" will vanish, as Emerson's and Whitman's poet-priests are effaced by an experiential elder, the patriarch-storyteller, who fades into the story being told.

Suggestive of what Bhabha identifies as the "postcolonial passage through modernity . . . in [which] the past [is] projective" (1994:253), this chronotropic aesthetic underwrites the historiographical intent of *Soothsayers and Omens*. In this collection, Wright will extend Benjamin's insight that stories represent more than the possibility for experience; they are human history. The figure of the storyteller, which assumes constellatory outline in the opening section of Benjamin's essay, will authorize the potential grandeur and spectacular remove of Wright's poetic of history.

\|\|\|\|

Soothsayers and Omens, a poetic sequence that attempts to provide an opening into discontinuous and simultaneous history, rejects received national and linguistic structures in a lyric alternative to the epic. In its sly echo of Wallace Stevens's "The Comedian as the Letter C" (1954:65),[7] *Soothsayers and Omens* circumscribes a field of poetic resonance that is at once canonical—and therefore recognizable—and foreign. A worldly "pleasure of merely circulating" invests the sequence with a simultaneous familiarity and strangeness (Stevens 1954:149–50). Poems self-reflexively call to mind Eliot, Pound, Stevens, Crane, and Hayden even as they thwart such patterned allusions with echoes of anthropologically summoned texts. Wright enacts Stevens's "Tea at the Palaz of Hoon," creating the very "compass" of these new landscapes in which readers find themselves "more truly and more strange" (1954:65).

Unlike Pound, who trod the accepted path of westerners seeking perceptual extensions through the art and religion of the Orient, Wright investigates the transatlantic prophetic realms of the Western Hemisphere and Africa to emphasize the crux of Westernization as well as its expansiveness. Pound's contributions to the aestheticization of history originate in his ability to fracture and assemble the received European historical script. Wright's appropriation of an earlier modernist text yields a decentered inversion of European literatures and inscribes a startling dependence on African and Western Hemispheric literary artifacts. Revoking Pound's summary of the Enlightenment—

> rights
> diffusing knowledge of principles
> maintaining justice, in registering treaty of peace
> changed with the times (1995:351)

—Wright advances beyond the formal historical landscape to a local, associative geography that relies on the routine, not the spectacular, for effect. As if to answer Pound's revolutionary capsule of national assemblage and cooperative cohesion—"not a Virginian / but an American Patrick Henry" (1995:363)—Wright asks: "not an American but . . . ?"[8] In sounding this cultural ambiguity, Wright thwarts the nationalist ends of continuous narrative with the possibilities inherent in the open silences of a discontinuous narrative.

A historically informed poetic, retrieved from the stagnation of chronology and fact associated with history and news, necessitates an enlarged aesthetic, one that embraces the sense of storytelling that Walter Benjamin had associated with "the ability to exchange experiences" in the "realm of living speech" (1968:83, 87). Benjamin's "The Storyteller" asserts that the evolution of the novel and "information" in modern society are the primary means by which the life of experience, culture, and history is nullified in favor of a stable and isolating product. Recalling Thoreau's hostile ambivalence toward the invention of the telegraph, Benjamin deplores the subversion of narrative by news: "Every morning brings us the news of the globe, and yet we are poor in noteworthy stories. This is because no event any longer comes to us without already being shot through with explanation" (1968:89). Such information, anticipating the mediated and isolating depletion of television news, surrenders to its immediate, mediated context and dies into history. The spiritual and aesthetic lapses in such constructions were rooted, Benjamin thought, in the difference between "the writer of history, the historian, and the teller of it, the chronicler" (1968:95). And it is in this conjoined spirit of orality and textuality in the "act of the poem" (Rowell 1983:4) that Wright locates his progressively unmediated, historically charged aesthetic. Explanation, if it is to come at all, comes through the grander, suggestive history of the shared experience of a poetry (curiously reminiscent of Stevens's) "in the service of a new and capable personality at home and in the transformative and transformed world" (Rowell 1983:9).

The four-part, architectonic structure of *Soothsayers and Omens* is at once a reconstruction and a resituation of the Romantic poet in the landscape. Wright frustrates a pattern of mere imitation by shuttling between the Emersonian and the transcendental conjurers of many cultural traces. Three sequences detail a grounding and departure, historically and socially, before fulfilling their aesthetic and cultural promise in a concluding, bold-titled excursion into simultaneous discontinuity, "Second Conversations with Ogotemmêli."

The untitled opening sequence progresses from a declamatory initiation of birth and its attendant installation of an alternative patriarchy through a sequence of mythological potential and shifting chronologies (indebted to Hart Crane) and ends with paired portraits of the exemplary and historical. Poetry inverts history into "a livable assertion" (1976b:11), insisting on what Wright calls "spiritual resonance" (Rowell 1983:4).

"The Charge" initiates Wright's subversion of the chronological in history by means of its ritual-centered, rigidly present-tense installation of patriarch and storyteller. The earlier, foreboding structure of "death as history" yields to its cultural inverse, "history as birth," a dying into a new narrative sequence and coherence:

This is the morning.
There is a boy,
riding the shadow of a cradle,
clapping from room to room
as swift as the memory of him. (1976b:11)

The faint disjunction between the present-tense, gestural insistence of these opening lines—"This is," "There is"—establishes the sequence's attitude toward temporal and spatial ideas of order. Like Benjamin's soothsayers, Wright's personae will not "experience time as either homogeneous or empty." Through the confluence of memory, history, preexistence, and death, "The Charge" begins the work of the sequence: the denial of death as history.

Suffused with a Blakean and Emersonian insistence of "infant sight," the five-part sequence displaces English lyrical conventions into a startling and strange reconfiguration. From Vaughan and Milton to Whitman and Thoreau, Wright culls a lexicon that denies the conventional distinctions of life and death. Whitman's "Out of the Cradle" and Vaughan's "They Are All Gone into the World of Light!" shrug off their shrouds and don the unexpected raiment of life:

> Now,
> I hear you whistle through the house,
> pushing wheels, igniting fires,
> leaving no sound untried,
> no room in which a young boy,
> at sea in a phantom cradle,
> could lurch and scream
> and come and settle in the house.
> You are so volubly alone,
> that I turn,
> reaching into the light for the boy
> your father charged you to deliver. (11)

The denial of presence and time, of reference and sequential continuities, persists throughout the poem. Generational superiority fades into a Wordsworthian simultaneity at the transitional moment of the birth of a child who resembles Moses in his circumstance and presence: "where the women will hold the boy, / plucked from the weeds, / a manchild, discovered" (12). Pronouns, in their seemingly logical array, realign into suspect, logic-thwarting reference, until the I's, we's, and you's forge a collective and cross-referential community of ill-determined genealogy. Even what appears to be the familiar punning of "sun" and "son"—"where the sun forever enters this circle. / Fathers and sons sit"—fails to assume its conventional duality, as the poem advances toward a binary-resistant, structural integrity that departs from lyric and semantic convention.[9]

Enlarging the realm of circumspection and locution to include the finite and infinite tasks the poet to "prepare a place" of history-nullifying, timeless continuities "where the sun forever enters this circle" (12). Wright extends Blakean "particulars" to create a "whole" where "All things here move / with that global rhythm" (13). What began as a descent into birth ritual has concluded as a startling revision of a death-defying, liberation narrative: "This is the moment / when all our unwelcome deaths / charge us to be free" (13).

Such an imperative insinuates itself into Wright's originary "Sources."[10] Evocative of Crane's "Voyages" in *White Buildings,* another six-poem excursion into "time and the elements," "Sources" bridges the immediate and individual world of "The Charge" with the exemplary and historical realms of the concluding Benjamin Banneker poems. Wright embarks on an epical journey of vast interiority as he plumbs the potential depths of historical narrative. The sequence moves beyond that which Crane found "answered in the vortex of our grave" to a moment of communicative display of communion and grace (1966:36). A nourishing rain replaces Crane's tempestuous sea, instilling a certainty and cycle in the consecrated ground.

Orphean strains mix with alien modalities to stress the complexities of cultural weave and historical moment in these poems. The familiar is rendered strange, as allusions drift into tangential relation with barely perceived scripts and recombine into an apparent whole. "Sources" offers an elemental reweaving of the received and intuited histories. Ecclesiastical proffering sustains and restores—"I lift these texts, / wanting the words / to enter my mind like pure wind" (1976b:16)—even as the sequence evokes poems as distant as Stevens's "To the Roaring Wind."

The revolutionary passage from source to moment, from ancestor to poet, necessitates both the "life / and death of all our fathers" if history is to assume what James Baldwin called its "literal presence" (1985:410). The reanimated historical moment for Wright is one in which liberated ancestral moments are praised and carried in the living descendants. Such freedom resides in the ability of the living to fetch history from the dead, the "new and capable imagination" that refuses to fossilize the exemplary dead into memorial history. As Eliot explains in "Little Gidding":

> This is the use of memory:
> For liberation—not less of love but expanding
> Of love beyond desire, and so liberation
> From the future as well as the past. (1971:142)

The incipient cosmology of the first section solidifies around the arrested figures of Benjamin Banneker and Thomas Jefferson to form constellations of apparent national coherence and construction—apt characters for deconstructive poetics in the season of Bicentennial celebration.[11] In these paired poems, storytelling becomes the means by which Wright creates poems out of history, not poems of history. Remote, historical substrata establish Baldwin's present-tense notion of history. Prefiguration and historical spectacle constitute an enactment, not a reenactment, of encounter and speculation. An extension of the birth ritual of "The Charge," "Benjamin Banneker Helps to Build a City" and "Benjamin Banneker Sends His 'Almanac' to Thomas Jefferson" invoke historical motifs to impose structure on the flux of the present.

Constellatory, like the figure of a poem, the city enlarges beyond its vision; its design escapes the logic of reason to enter into an aesthetic realm with its own spatial order.[12] Just on the secular side of Saint Augustine's City of God, Banneker's realm is at once celestial and earthly, thematizing the Enlightenment projection of attainable, worldly—"heavenly"—cities.[13] The creativity doubles as history, "moving as though it knew its end, against death" (1976b:22). History succumbs to a world of consuming plans and "prefigurations." To shed the confines of either inspiration, the poet forces an encounter:

> I call you into this time,
> back to that spot,
> and read these prefigurations
> into your mind,
> and know it could not be strange to you
> to stand in the dark and emptiness
> of a city not your vision alone. (22)

"This time" and "that spot" form the nexus, "that spot / where the vibration starts" (22–23). As a descendant of Pound and Eliot, Wright must search "the texts / and forms of cities that burned, / that decayed, or gave their children away" (22). Histories and offspring yielded or were lost.

The juxtaposition of an alternate mode of perception, an aestheticized history that accommodates the irrational in speech and actions, requires the displacement of the ideational constructs and informational models of culture by the astrological force of the metaphysical and mythological. Reason, chronology, and national identity must retire in the face of an enhanced cultural logic. A superimposition of a simultaneous, sanctifying presence serves to redeem and transport the reason-stranded poet and astronomer:

> Over the earth,
> in an open space,
> you and I step to the time
> of another ceremony.
> These people, changed,
> but still ours,

shake another myth
from that egg. (23)

Such betweenness epitomizes the hybridity of the black Atlantic cultures in which imposed, culture-severing boundaries stranded lives from their mythic structures and historical context.[14] Alternative theologies sustain competing cosmologies and lead to a potential sanctification upon rebaptism: "A city, like a life, / must be made in purity" (23).

Crane's sonorities and Pound's textualities inspired Wright's reconstruction of the historical path by which personage and place are known. Yet Wright's renewing script cannot make use of Pound's syntactical and historical disruptions. A retraction into the "stillness" before genesis—

Image of shelter, image of man,
pulled back into himself,
into the seed before the movement,
into the silence before the sound
of movement, into stillness (24)

—allows for an inspired new story, for restorative annals. Skirting the allure of myth, that protean antagonist of history, Wright advances into a stylized recapitulation of call-and-response that will allow the documentary presence of Banneker to thrive within an aestheticized frame:

Recall number.
Recall your calculations,
your sight, at night,
into the secrets of stars. (24)

Banneker's epistle to Jefferson, unorchestrated by Wright, serves as the authentic excursion into the rational and purposeful models of history. Unheeded in his time, Banneker slips within the broader compass of prophetic utterance and invocation, challenging the Promethean and Protestant order of this inherited cosmology and spawning the poem's rhetorical challenge to "the movement, / the absence of movement, the Prefiguration of movement" in this place (25). The astronomer becomes the very incarnation of the Enlightenment, a transformative cosmology. The authentication of Enlightenment pledges of liberty resides in a historical inversion:

So they must call you,
knowing you are intimate stars;
so they must call you,
knowing different resolutions. (25)

Instead of the modernist clock that drives the collating impulse of Stevens's "souvenirs and prophecies," impelling time into anterior and posterior space, Banneker posts "calculations and forecasts" by which to realign "the small, / imperceptible act, which itself becomes free" (25). Attuned to celestial harmonies and earthly disjunctions, the astronomer represents the unease with which the ideological legacy of the Rights of Man was received by African Americans:

> Free. Free. How will the lines fall
> into that configuration?
> How will you clear this uneasiness,
> posting your calculations and forecasts
> into a world you yourself cannot enter? (25)

The proximate "configuration" of lyric space and transtemporality allow this poem to seek a counterdiscourse, one in which "vision" traverses the boundaries of "the city a star, a body" (26) into that still-potential space of aestheticized history, the province of the poem.

When Thomas Jefferson received Benjamin Banneker's *Almanac*, he responded instantly to its synecdochic force: "Sir,—I thank you sincerely for your letter of the 19th instant and for the Almanac it contained. No body wishes more than I do to see such proofs as you exhibit, that nature has given to our black brethren, talents equal to those of the other colors of men" (1984:982). "Benjamin Banneker Sends His 'Almanac' to Thomas Jefferson" countermands Jefferson's presidential approbation with its own lyrical reinvestment of speculative reason and prophetic vision. Though it lacks the intense communion of the earlier poem, it nonetheless collaborates in Wright's evolving historical display.[15] For here, the poet visits the astronomer, not in some interstitial space, but rather "in mind," in historical setting. At once a colloquy and a dialogue, the poem necessitates a larger view of "calculation," "language," and "form"—the things that submit to reason and those that do not. Verifications of celestial truths, those of Banneker's purview—"Solid, these calculations / verify your body on God's earth"—give way to mythological extractions, those of Wright's aesthetic:

> I, who know so little of stars,
> whose only acquaintance with the moon
> is to read a myth, or to listen
> to the surge
> of the songs the women know. (1976b:27)

The celestial order posited by Banneker's science is one that conducts a historically sound and metaphysically charged dialogue:

> So you look into what we see
> yet cannot see,
> and shape and take a language
> to give form to one or the other,
> believing no form will escape,
> no movement appear, nor stop,
> without explanation,
> believing no reason is only reason,
> nor without reason. (27)

The prophetic realm of the soothsayer or seer is one that both formalizes and accepts an utter lack of formality in the perceived order of things. The aesthetic gaps or "silences" that Wright requires for his interventions into history are to be found in the "crack of the universe" of the previous poem or the "flaw" of this one. Beyond the compass of the perfect number, the numerical whole forwarded by Banneker, beyond the reach of "the perfect line," the lyrical snare offered by Wright, rest the "omissions" of the historical and the aesthetic. Within this silenced realm lurks the quarrel between "the man and the God," the free and the captive.

Banneker becomes the mediating force between the genealogical and historical imperatives that order the received texts. The challenge of Banneker's *Almanac* is more than one of cognitive display: it is one of justified existence. To argue with reason in the person of Jefferson is to quarrel with the ordering principle of the nation itself: "Your letter turns on what the man knows, / on what God, you think, would have us know" (28). Wright inverts the cosmological relationship into one where Banneker scrutinizes the order of being itself:

> All stars will forever move under your gaze,
> truthfully, leading you from line to line,
> from number to number, from truth to truth,
> while the man will read your soul's desire,
> searcher, searching yourself,
> losing the relations. (28)

"Losing the relations" is an encumbered line, resonant with the promise of calculations as well as the frailty of transactions even as it suggests the ultimate sacrifice of a stabilizing genealogy. Like the one "so volubly alone" in "The

Charge," Banneker moves beyond the barely perceptible relations to assume the potential charge of a space of silence and imperfection.

The transient arc from the "livable assertion" to "losing the relations" is one that guides both poet and reader to a cunning instability, a moment and place of irrationality and aesthetic crisis. Within part 1, Wright has succeeded in moving in and through history in such a way that even the most mundane occurrence has become one of speculative poise and abiding uncertainty. Part 2 requires an application of this emerging knowledge, an unseating of domestic ordinariness in the light of this newly found celestial turbulence.

Readers of *Soothsayers and Omens* have expressed relief upon reaching the collection's middle sections, mistaking them for familiar, confessional, anecdotal lyrics "grounded in 'personal' experience" (Rowell 1983:6). The Baedeker surface of familiar detail obscures the restless lines of call-and-response, false seculars and spirituals, Catholic and Protestant rituals—the unsettled logistics of history surging beneath the surface. Ceremonies of possession and rituals of sacrifice fail to quiet the dead of many cultures, lost inhabitants of the once-named and noble New Mexican landscape. What Adrienne Rich has called "contraband memories" suffuse the history emergent in this shifting landscape that is "still untouched by the step and touch / of the sons of slaves, / where no slave could ever go" (1976b:32).[16] In "Entering New Mexico," one does not know what might be summoned from the depths of local or national histories.

> Call,
> and some pantalooned grandfather may come,
> with the leisure of Virginia still on his tongue,
> and greet you uneasily.
> Here, he holds uneasy land
> from which he pistols out intrusions (32)

Naming itself assumes unpredictable and prophetic powers; in "The Master of Names," it summons "A history that is none, / that may never be written, / nor conceived again" (34). Within the proper name resides "a power / ... almost forgotten" (36).

Extending Walter Benjamin's reflection that "Counsel woven into the fabric of real life is wisdom" (1968:86), Wright surmounts the difficulty of his predetermined landscape—one in which reason and order have been disabled—by weaving his determinations into local historical and genealogical sites in order to discover the matrix of historical wisdom. "The Albuquerque Graveyard" and "Family Reunion" may be seen as application sites for his evolving aesthetic structures of history.

At once an excursion and an incursion into the borderland of grief and remembrance, "The Albuquerque Graveyard" occasions an aesthetic debate on memory, literacy, and history.[17] The incremental advance into the scene of commemoration—

> take three buses,
> walk two blocks,
> search at the rear
> of the cemetery (38)

—echoes grander historical slights, as "buses" and "rear" metonymically realign into "the back of the bus." "The pattern of the place" anticipates a deeper historical disquisition:

> I am going back
> to the Black limbo,
> an unwritten history
> of our own tensions. (38)

This apparent historical act of recovery is balanced by the tugging immediacy of "our." Steeped in the catholicity of the place, the poem toys with its racial and cultural inversions of Dante as well as its hemispheric soundings. History expresses itself in the silence of the ruins; Wright discovers himself in the volatile "tensions" of the buried "curse[s] and rage."

If history is to be extracted from this fossilized underlayer of neglect,[18] Wright must turn beyond the evidential to a correspondence between the exemplary and the collective:

> of one who stocked his parlor
> with pictures of Robeson,
> and would boom down the days,
> dreaming of Othello's robes. (38)

Dreaming here has a nearly astrological force as it locates the individual within a commemorative historical sweep of potential realized. In reminiscence, the recognition scenes of "small heroes" resonate locally and nationally, as the poet fades into the persona of Frederick Douglass:

> Here, I stop by the simple mound
> of a woman who taught me
> spelling on the sly,
> parsing my tongue
> to make me fit for her own dreams. (38–39)

The ordered summoning of "unwritten history" produces discontent. The quest yields to an enactment of a modest call-and-response in which the poet "search[es] the names / and simple mounds [he] call[s] [his] own / . . . and turn[s] for home" (39). "Home," having acquired an internal and external voice in Wright's canon, recalls the historical cascade of the title poem of *The Homecoming Singer*:

> her voice shifting
> and bringing up the Carolina calls,
> the waterboy, the railroad cutter, the jailed,
> the condemned, all that had been forgotten
> on this night of homecomings. (1971:31)

To "turn for home" is to position oneself in direct relation to the genealogical site of history itself. If history is to be rescripted into a living and inclusive form, it must be superimposed on its recognizable origins: the family. Home is where Wright will reacquaint himself with Benjamin's "source" for storytelling, the place of "the securest among our possessions . . . the ability to exchange experiences" (1968:83).

Unlike "the hierarchy of small defeats" populating "The Albuquerque Graveyard," "the elders and saints" of "Family Reunion" confront the traces of that earlier, "unwritten history." Semblance becomes resemblance as "an unfamiliar relative's traces" are confronted (39). Cropped and candid, the snapshots aestheticize lives into glimpsed, historical extensions. Images engender familiar narratives, exchanged experiences, and recognition scenes. Graveyard ruins surrender to the always spontaneous, genealogical accord with the living:

> of hearing a voice, and being able to coax
> the speaker into echoes of himself, his selves,
> his forgotten voices, voices he had never heard:
> of calling your own name, and having it belled
> back in tongues, being changed and harmonized
> until it is one name and all names. (40)

Historical recognition depends on individuation, which must then evolve into a harmonious whole, *recognition* insisting initially on cognition. Because authentication of his aesthetic demands the restorative sound of a vox humana without, as Benjamin Banneker knew, "losing the relations," Wright must open his discontinuous narrative to the hemispheric pulse of historical antecedent.

Readers of *The Homecoming Singer* will recall Wright's initial fascination with the Mexican fortress Chapultepec: "This is the castle where they lived,

/ Maximilian and Carlotta, / and here is where Carlotta slept" (1971:40). What may be seen as the primary historical grounding of that earlier collection has slipped into duplicitous aesthetic service in part 3 of *Soothsayers and Omens,* as the recurrent sounding of Chapultepec recalls the euphonious slopping of Stevens's "November off Tehuantepec" in "Sea Surface Full of Clouds" (1954:98–102). The preparatory path to Wright's new history lies along abbreviated recapitulations of "The Comedian as the Letter C," in which tone and circuit shift to include "The Sense of Comedy: I" (roman numeral or personal pronoun?) in hope of circumventing Crispin's "faint, memorial gesturings" (1954:29).

Unlike Stevens's "introspective voyager," Wright's persona in "The Museums of Chapultepec" prefers "Moore's concrete apples, / Giacometti's daggers" to Crispin's porpoises and apricots (1976b:49). And yet he, like Crispin, is drawn by "A sunken voice, both of remembering / And of forgetfulness, in alternate strain" (Stevens 1954:29). So enmeshed is this section of *Soothsayers and Omens* in the aesthetic web of Stevens that the poetic sequence seems proximate to its ancestor, steadily moving toward Crispin's discovery: "*The Idea of a Colony* / Nota: his soil is man's intelligence" (Stevens 1954:36). Wright, like Crispin, writes "his prolegomena, / And, being full of caprice, inscribe[s] / Commingled souvenirs and prophecies" (Stevens 1954:37).

The confluence of history and literature occurs in the announcement of "The Birthday." Shuttling between the Emersonian and Blakean contraries of temporal and spatial logic, Wright seeks a fixed and fluid identity for the historical. The speaker is as focused as Benjamin Banneker:

> and my eyes kept focussed
> at one point in the light,
> as though I would fix
> the face and name of a friend
> absent even from my memory. (1976b:52)

Caught "between one day and another, / between one age and another," the poet seeks to resolve an apparent conundrum at the center of his debate: "a chosen point to celebrate / the fact of moving still" (52). The definitional instability of "still" has troubled the entire collection, nagging the lines into an uncertain correspondence; but here, it offers the promise of reflection and endurance: the promise of history itself.

The prophetic trajectory of desire and reminiscence coalesces in "Jason Visits His Gypsy." This poem of agitated display attempts to define history linguistically. Even as the gypsy's spectacle draws one simultaneously into and away from the unraveling truth, it becomes the very celebration of "the fact of moving still":

> [she] moves,
> raveling the sand into her sleeve,
> past your still body,
> past your stilled desires. (1976b:54)

Nomadic, nationless, the gypsy seems the ideal simulacrum for Wright's emerging transhistorical and transnational identity:

> The gypsy knows what you have forgotten,
> . . . .
> knows the rhythm of raveling
> the sand into the dark and closeness
> of a space, where only she can live. (54)

The section comes to a rest with another "Homecoming: *Guadalajara-New York, 1965,*" a bifurcated tradition and hemispheric ellipsis that reannunciates as well as terminates the earlier sequential debates of reason, history, identity, and narrative. The disembarkation, to use the language of Gwendolyn Brooks, necessitates a conceptual and linguistic pastiche: syntax and diction strain to accommodate competing visions, and allusions collide as architect and poet debate the structural integrity of inheritance. Insistent on its lineage, the poem echoes Stevens's "The Worms at Heaven's Gate," noting that "The strange and customary turns / of living may coincide" (58).

In a different city, at a different time, the poet transgresses the boundaries of language, nation, history, and time. The Enlightenment constructions so in favor during the Bicentennial have lost even their oppositional, aesthetic value for Wright:

> From line to line,
> from point to point,
> is an architect's end of cities.
>
> But I lie down
> to a different turbulence
> and a plan of transformation. (58)

The *dis*ease between "turbulence" and "plan" intensifies the undetermined path to come. Suspension of the defining boundaries of individual and collective identity will enable Wright to proceed into a history tolerant of "the strange and customary turns / of living" (58).

"Second Conversations with Ogotemmêli," the final section, is doubly estranged from the text proper in that it bears the only subtitle and commits wholeheartedly, and perhaps unexpectedly (to those who neglected the note on the verso of the half-title page), to structures and silences inherent in Marcel Griaule's version of Dogon tribal cosmology. Though previous historical, geographical, and biographical references may have been unfamiliar to the reader, they were inevitably assimilated and accommodated by the overlap of the poems. "Second Conversations," with alienating familiarity, presumes an antecedent, a "first" that signals Wright's dependence on Griaule; "Ogotemmêli" becomes the *named* initiator, the medium through which disclosure (if it is to come at all) will come. Unlike *Dimensions of History*, *Soothsayers and Omens* offers neither "cautionary remarks" nor explanation; except for the prefatory notes, it insists on the aesthetic self-sufficiency of its materials. Wright's cautionary and sly modernist introduction to the notes appended to *Dimensions of History*, on the other hand, shares his expectations for readers of this collection: "The notes are offered as an aid in reading the poem, not as the poem itself, nor a substitution for it. The notes could have been more extensive, and more detailed. I have given only so many because I must, ultimately, rely on the good will and intelligence of the reader. If the reader trusts the poem as much as I trust him or her, he or she should have no difficulty with my exploration of these dimensions of history" (1976a:105).[19] The acute intimacy of these extended poetic explorations in *Soothsayers and Omens* transfers responsibility for coherence and vitality to the reader. In this final, elaborate response to Stevens's Western world of "inconstancy," Wright pilots an excursion into the deepest recesses of transatlantic narrative literatures and histories, allusions and mythologies, in the hope of grasping the weave of the design.

Reading initiates this conversation: Wright's reading of a translation of Griaule's *Conversations with Ogotemmêli: An Introduction to Dogon Religious Ideas* (1962). Poetic invention, the mind creating, closes the silences between poet, who is alienated by successive mediation and remove—stories "heard" through the scrim of translator, text interposed, allusive field (Emerson, Stevens, Pound, Crane, Hayden, Derrida, Bloom)—and experience; it also bridges the gap between the poet and the Dogon storyteller. The anthropological study sponsors the radical subversion of texts inherent in the collection as a whole, extracting poetry in recital. Wright has acceded to Benjamin's situational definition of storytelling—"A man listening to a story is in the company of a storyteller; even a man reading one shares this companionship" (1968:100)—and, in doing so, has relinquished poetic authority to the patriarchal storyteller in the act of disclosure. Emblematic discontinuities abound as conversations, auditorily ephemeral, evade the structures of time and reason and create a momentarily reciprocal aesthetic. Anxious to move beyond the totalizing fields of myth or history, Wright locates coherence and correspondence in that space where poetic and epistemology are one.

Although scholarly attention to the source reveals the imitative array of poems and descriptive language, received diction, and gloss, it does little to disclose the aesthetic of Wright's evolving cosmology. As Hugh Kenner cautions: "It is hard alone to wring song from philology" (195). Immersion in the contextual source leads to an informational gloss that is counterproductive to the revealed revisionary attitude toward aesthetic form and history. This overlapping series reinscribes as it reanimates the lost voice—and the silences—of Ogotemmêli on the accreted, Western canonical context of Wright's experience. Polyphony and polyvocality display the syncretic instability of history and biography under erasure.

"Ogotemmêli" originates the concluding sequence through an intimate dialogue between speaker and storytelling mediator—described by Griaule as one with an "eagle mind and considerable shrewdness" (14)—that is at once instructive and obfuscating. The three-part poem startles with its patterned and excluding repetitions; it is, indeed, a series of "second conversations," exchanges with a history at once textual and informal, European and African, "civilized" and "primitive," historical and simultaneous. The stanzas resemble reliquaries, storing barely contained allusions, artifacts, and utterances as they threaten to sound a tide of discontinuous meanings. Even as the image of Ogotemmêli begins to take visual and linguistic form in parallels and transmutations of its textual origin, it shades into a dimly perceived auditory presence—"But your voice comes clearly / only where I found you" (61)—insisting on the phenomenological instability of the poetic record. If this "you" grows in familiarity—

> You tilt your head like a bird,
> and wait until my step stops.
> You squint and sniff,
> as though you would brush away
> some offensive smell or movement (61)

—it does so in its tangential and immediate relationship to antecedent visions. Recalling earlier, ambiguously aligned descriptions—"These others stand with you, / squinting the city into place, / yet cannot see what you see" (22)—these actions coalesce to form an enlarged and enlarging series of qualities associated with the historical and eternal in Wright's world.

The second stanza's clustered reduplications of the original force an immediacy and contrariness that spirals into arch parodies of the pastoral—"trace the fat, wet sheep"—and startling inversions of Miltonic atmosphere: "when no light comes, / you will lead me into the darkness" (61). These lines then resolve into aversions and reversals of Cotton Mather's patriarchal speculations on an invisible world: "Father, your eyes have turned / from the tricks of our visible world" (62). The display of correspondences, far from insisting on relation and wholeness, advances the poem into a provisional world of displacement and disjunction. Closure of this final history can be achieved only through a tolerance of what Walter Benjamin has termed *Stillstand* (1968:84), a gap in temporality itself:

> So I arrive,
> at the end of this, my small movement,
> moving with you, in the light you control,
> learning to hear the voice in the silence,
> learning to see in the light
> that runs away from me. (62)

That moment of static, enduring immediacy of "reaching into the light for the boy" (11) or "learning to see in the light" is the time of Benjamin's storytelling, the moment of Wright's history.

The figure of the named Dogon elder reinscribes and decenters the collection's originating patriarchal figure, the poet-patriarch of "The Charge," prompting a regenesis and realignment of the phenomenal world. The open yet culminating sequence—from "Beginning" to "The Dead"—articulates the newness of Wright's transcultural diasporic aesthetic. Semantic and linguistic disjunction denies the verifiable and informational qualities of the history embedded in this discontinuous narrative of postnational consciousness. Emerson's poet-priest and Wright's own poet-patriarch dissolve into Benjamin's storyteller as patriarch, one who (as Benjamin concludes) "has borrowed his authority from death" (1968:94).

"Beginning" appears to dismantle the raiment and facades of received cultural hierarchy and to establish a modernist tableau relative to the "dung and death" of Eliot's "East Coker" or the dust swirling about Pound's cage at the U.S. Army's Detention Training Center north of Pisa:

> Alive again,
> you wait in the broken courtyard.
> Oblivious of its dungheap and ashes,
> you sit once more,
> near the main façade,
> and listen for this unfamiliar footstep. (63)

The historicity of Maximilian and Carlotta, essential to the poems of *The Homecoming Singer,* fractures into the postmodernist shards of this "broken courtyard," an abandoned system of figuration. The discontinuity of "arrive, / at the end of this, my small movement" extends this celebratory, posited continuum: "Alive again." The return signaled is more complex than being to origins; it cycles through a temporality as yet unannounced—or at least unclear. Movement, life's linear creep or history's expected chronological order, meets with immediate status: the weight of "wait." All of this seems to echo Benjamin's "Ur-history of the 19th Century," in which truth was found in the "garbage heap" of modernity, the "rags, the trash" of commodity production.

And yet readers of the antecedent text will recall more than the atmospheric sponsor of these descriptions: they will recognize clusters of the details themselves. The essential confrontation is not with the prefigured storyteller but with his linguistic trace, fossilized in Griaule's "Conversations." The inspiration of that unmediated, original space will come not from the figure but from the word—"Facing you, / I cannot tell what word, / or form of that word, I shall face" (63)—or soundings of the exchange. The word, the thread that Robert Duncan called "The Torn Cloth" (1984:137–39), initiates the "reaving" of Wright's aesthetic.

If the epistemologically charged aesthetic is to redeem history, it must offer an unmediated space of enactment or realization that is at once provisional and whole. Nathaniel Mackey sees such constructions, in the light of Griaule, as "fabrications": "What this means is not only that our purchase on the world is a weave but also that the word is a rickety witness, the telltale base on which our sense of the weave sits. *Fabric* echoes *fabrication,* as both go back to a root that has to do with making. The creaking of the word calls attention to the constructedness of the hold on the world fabrication affords" (1993:180). Such "purchase" affords little if it fails to secure trust. For Wright, trust responds to dependency and cultural reversals as he relinquishes history to conversation, word to silence. "Lurking near the borders of speech" in "The First Word," Wright succumbs to "the craft of the first word, / weaving speech into spirit" (64).

The evanescence of form thematizes the perceived cosmography of the Dogon tribe, its "world system associated with constellations" (Griaule 1965:32), as well as the canonical tide of poems under erasure. "The Third Word"—

> this seed
> being broken there
> on the smithy's anvil
> will burst to stars,
> design a man (67)

—reduplicates a system of parallels expansive enough to claim Griaule, the Stevens of "The Auroras of Autumn," Ogotemmêli, and Eliot. Decipherings yield analogues that share a global urge for the construction of provisional structures to define and stabilize the existential mysteries of being human.

Ogotemmêli incarnates the problematic of Wright's evolving, historical poetic: the denial of the emblematic, the effacement of the authorial self. Ogotemmêli's ego inheres in the story. From the Poundian personae—"these masks, / with a place at last" (73)—Wright posits an essential emancipation: "Living, we free them; / dying, we learn / how we are freed ourselves" (73). No longer is the Emersonian equation of poet as seer applicable:

> I come here,
> .... attuned to some animal's
> tentative step,
> ... the design
> that escapes my eyes. (74)

The New World extension of this ancient, received covenant will be "to design / your own prefiguration" (76).

The Dogons' supernatural fear of naming, a "marked reluctance, arising from respect and fear, to mention the names or picture the forms of supernatural powers" (Griaule 1965:113), denies the possibility of narrative or lyric coherence in the Western sense. The simultaneous weaving and unweaving of Ogotemmêli's conversations result in the absence of an aesthetic construction; the story exists only in the telling. The "reluctance" to name refuses linguistic access to the Emersonian poet as "namer" but not to the poet as "language-maker" or as "the only teller of news." If, as Benjamin asserts, "a man's knowledge or wisdom, but above all his real life—and this is the stuff that stories are made of—first assumes transmissible form at the moment of his death" (1968:94), then the unresisted lines of "The Dead" initiate the transmission of the sequence's discontinuities and disjunctions. Epistemology and poetic come under erasure in this final telling.

Movement subordinates death in a progressive distancing from Western aesthetics and traditions. Silence (and silences) animate the internal path of allusion to the Banneker poems and their attendant histories and cosmologies, as well as to the forlorn and fetishized dead in "The Albuquerque Graveyard." The indeterminate silence of the animistic and ill-defined displaces the beginnings and endings, the linearity and logic of the articulate, creating a space where contraries embrace—"moves still," "living dead." Poundian masks and Yeatsian dances fail to unify perceptions and resolve disjunction; so the poems slip:

into the rhythm
of emptiness and return,
into the self
moving against itself,
into the self
moving into itself,
the word, and the first design. (78)

"Design," the province of the creator, yields to self-designation as Wright advances into the ultimate, because self-determined, liberation narrative—"Now, / I designate myself your child" (78)—in which covenant and circumstance "will have their place" and the poet, now subservient to the patriarch, will "learn these relations." The transmutation of "design" from nominal to verbal status reduplicates the pattern of this provisional, and often self-negating, collection. The progressive disabling of the textual field intensifies Wright's earlier judgment on Thomas Jefferson, "the man [who] read [Banneker's] soul's desire, / . . . / losing the relations" (28).

The linguistic trace of "The Dead" restlessly echoes from Governor John Winthrop of the Massachusetts Bay Colony to Ogotemmêli, from religious predestination to aesthetic prefiguration. If Wright's cultural inversions constitute a temporizing, postnational, postmodern aesthetic, they do so with an ironic, solipsistic imperative: Trust the telling, not the tale. The split pairing of death and freedom advances a new "covenant" of admitted contraries: "a sign, / that your world moves still" (78). Wright has invented a simultaneous historical field in which language, culture, and nation are subsumed by the *telling* of the tale of the tribe.

With his invention of a historical consciousness independent of nation and narration, Jay Wright evolves beyond the chaotic "carnival of gods, customs, and arts . . . the alien and disconnected" that Nietzsche had most feared (1980:10, 28) into the uncharted ambivalence of the "cultural space . . . [of] the nation with its transgressive boundaries and its 'interruptive' interiority" (Bhabha 1994:5). The discrete representational strategies of race rhetoric that once had underwritten the narrative of black America resolve in Wright's poetry into a simultaneous field of textual orality, a site of critical memory in which the postnational and postmodern continue to write America black.

Notes

1. Seeking to foreground Wright's aesthetic confrontation with national narratives, I risk invoking "America" as a received (desig)nation for the United States. See Kut-

zinski (1987:49–50) for a rationale for its de-emphasis: "Wright's territory is the New World, and I am employing this term very self-consciously to de-emphasize as much as possible the nationalistic connotations the term 'America' has acquired as a result of being used as a shorthand expression for the United States. If 'America' in any way suggests a potentially unified area of study, it does so, as we have already seen, only by subordinating all cultural elements of a non-European origin to the claims of the so-called Anglo-North American cultural establishment."

2. For further discussion of the political field of the Black Arts movement, see the contemporaneous criticism included in the following anthologies: Redmond (1976); Baraka/Neal (1968); Henderson (1972). For contemporary assessment of the aesthetic consequences of these nationalist stirrings, see C. K. Doreski (1992), Gates (1987), Nielsen (1994), and Mackey (1993).

3. See, for example, Hollander (1981:n.p.), a review of Wright's *The Double Invention of Komo*, in which he identifies among the book's "subsidiary quests": "mythologies of the manly." See Mullen (1992:37) for a terse overview of "threatened black masculinity" in African-American letters, specifically Nathaniel Mackey's *Bedouin Hornbook*.

4. For a justification of this problematic term, see Bhabha (1994:4): "If the jargon of our times—postmodernity, postcoloniality, postfeminism—has any meaning at all, it does not lie in the popular use of the 'post' to indicate sequentiality—*after*-feminism; or polarity—*anti*-modernism. These terms that insistently gesture to the beyond, only embody its restless and revisionary energy if they transform the present into an expanded and ex-centric site of experience and empowerment."

5. See Benjamin's "The Storyteller," "The Image of Proust," and "Theses on the Philosophy of History" (1968: 83–110, 201–15, 253–64) for discussions of Enlightenment notions of progress in historical materialism; see Foner (1976) for documentary evidence of alternative declarations of independence; see Bhabha (1994:142) for the ultimate question of nation as narration: "How do we plot the narrative of the nation as narration that must mediate between the teleology of progress tipping over into the 'timeless' discourse of irrationality?"

6. See White (1978:36): "The First World War did much to destroy what remained of history's prestige among both artists and social scientists, for the war seemed to confirm what Nietzsche had maintained two generations earlier. History, which was supposed to provide some sort of training for life . . . had done little to prepare men for the coming of the war."

7. Although Wright was obviously responding to Wallace Stevens's "The Comedian as the Letter C," not Holly Stevens's *Souvenirs and Prophecies*, it is interesting to note that her project was also published during the Bicentennial.

8. See Bhabha (1994:246) regarding de Certeau's formulation of the "non-place from which all historiographical operation starts, the lag which all histories must encounter in order to make a beginning."

9. See Wilson Harris (1967:10) for an expanded discussion of the "sun" and its "terrible" reality in the West Indian world and its metaphorical weight "in the American world [where] energy is the sun of life."

10. See Griaule (1965) and Turner (1974) for the cosmological ground of this partially shared system that underwrites the ontology of these earlier poems.

11. See Kutzinski (1987:54–72) for a compelling discussion of the Banneker poems as they serve to foreground her study of myth and history in Wright's *Dimensions of History*. All readers of Wright's poetry should be grateful to this model exercise in philology. Though I often take issue with her insistent readings that facilitate the "history as myth" equation (substituting one fixity for another), I am throughout this chapter indebted to her research.

12. Banneker's urban sophistication continues to inspire. See, for example, Rita Dove (1983:36–37) for her curatorial reading of "Banneker": "At nightfall he took out / his rifle—a white-maned / figure stalking the darkened / breast of the Union—and / shot at the stars, and by chance / one went out. Had he killed? / *I assure thee, my dear Sir!* / Lowering his eyes to fields / sweet with the rot of spring, he could see / a government's domed city / rising from the morass and spreading / in a spiral of lights."

13. For consideration of Benjamin's "readings" of cities, see Bahti (1992:183–204); Buck-Morss (1989); Benjamin (1986).

14. Gilroy (1993) and Bhabha (1994) provide essential readings of postcolonial transatlantic culture.

15. I strongly disagree with Kutzinski's reading of "Benjamin Banneker Sends His 'Almanac' to Thomas Jefferson," which subordinates the poem to "a shorter version . . . a kind of double which revoices most of the important aspects of the former poem" (1987:55). Such an interpretation ignores the metaphysical and metaphoric vitality of the thing itself: the almanac.

16. See Rich (1993:130): "Africans carried poetry in contraband memory across the Middle Passage to create in slavery the 'Sorrow Songs.'"

17. In many ways, Wright's poem extends a genre familiar to readers of Allen Tate's "Ode for the Confederate Dead" and Robert Lowell's "For the Union Dead" (see William Doreski [1990:24–25, 78–80, 139–45]). Wright's elegiac response addresses not the failure to commemorate but the inability to do so.

18. See Alice Walker (1975:93–118).

19. See Rowell (1983:4), where Wright defines the collectivity of the poetic enterprise: "The *we* is the corporation of human beings who require and accept poetry's charter within it."

Works Cited

Bahti, Timothy. 1992. *Allegories of History: Literary Historiography after Hegel*. Baltimore, Md.: Johns Hopkins University Press.

Baldwin, James. 1985. "White Man's Guilt" (1968). In *The Price of the Ticket: Collected Nonfiction, 1948–1985*. New York: St. Martin's Press. 409–14.

Baraka, Amiri, and Larry Neal, eds. 1968. *Black Fire: An Anthology of Afro-American Writing*. New York: William Morrow.

Benjamin, Walter. 1968. *Illuminations: Essays and Reflections.* Trans. Harry Zohn. New York: Schocken Books.

———. 1986. "Paris, Capital of the Nineteenth Century" (1955). In *Reflections: Essays, Aphorisms, Autobiographical Writings.* Trans. Edmund Jephcott. New York: Schocken Books. 146–62.

Bhabha, Homi K. 1994. *The Location of Culture.* New York: Routledge.

Buck-Morss, Susan. 1989. *The Dialectics of Seeing: Walter Benjamin and the Arcades Project.* Cambridge, Mass.: MIT Press.

Crane, Hart. 1966. *White Buildings* (1926). In *The Complete Poems and Selected Letters and Prose of Hart Crane.* New York: Liveright Publishing. 3–44.

Doreski, C. K. 1992. "Kinship and History in Sam Cornish's *Generations.*" *Contemporary Literature* 33:663–86.

Doreski, William. 1990. *The Years of Our Friendship: Robert Lowell and Allen Tate.* Jackson: University Press of Mississippi.

Dove, Rita. 1983. *Museum.* Pittsburgh: Carnegie-Mellon University Press.

Duncan, Robert. 1984. *Ground Work: Before the War.* New York: New Directions.

Eliot, T. S. 1971. "Little Gidding" (1942). In *The Complete Poems and Plays, 1909–1950.* San Diego, Calif.: Harcourt Brace Jovanovich. 138–48.

Foner, Philip, ed. *We, the Other People: Alternative Declarations of Independence by Labor Groups, Farmers, Women's Rights Advocates, Socialists, and Blacks, 1829–1975.* Urbana: University of Illinois Press, 1976.

Gates, Henry Louis, Jr. 1987. *Figures in Black: Words, Signs, and the "Racial" Self.* New York: Oxford University Press.

Gilroy, Paul. 1993. *The Black Atlantic: Modernity and Double Consciousness.* Cambridge, Mass.: Harvard University Press.

Griaule, Marcel. 1965. *Conversations with Ogotemmêli: An Introduction to Dogon Religious Ideas.* Trans. Ralph Butler, Audrey Richards, and Beatrice Hooke. New York: Oxford University Press.

Harris, Wilson. 1967. *Tradition: The Writer and Society—Critical Essays.* London: New Beacon Publications.

Henderson, Stephen E. 1972. *Understanding the New Black Poetry: Black Speech and Black Music as Poetic References.* New York: William Morrow.

Hollander, John. 1981. "Tremors of Exactitude." Review of *The Double Invention of Komo,* by Jay Wright. *Times Literary Supplement,* 30 January, n.p.

Jefferson, Thomas. 1984. "Letter to Benjamin Banneker" (1791). In *Writings: Autobiography, Notes on the State of Virginia, Public and Private Papers, Addresses, Letters.* New York: Library of America. 982.

Kenner, Hugh. 1971. *The Pound Era.* Berkeley: University of California Press.

Kutzinski, Vera M. 1987. *Against the American Grain: Myth and History in William Carlos Williams, Jay Wright, and Nicolás Guillén.* Baltimore, Md.: Johns Hopkins University Press.

Mackey, Nathaniel. 1993. *Discrepant Engagement: Dissonance, Cross-Culturality, and Experimental Writing.* Cambridge: Cambridge University Press.

Mullen, Harryette. 1992. "'Phantom Pain': Nathaniel Mackey's *Bedouin Hornbook.*" *Talisman* 9:37–43.
Nielsen, Aldon Lynn. 1994. *Writing between the Lines: Race and Intertextuality.* Athens: University of Georgia Press.
Nietzsche, Friedrich. 1980. *On the Advantage and Disadvantage of History for Life.* Trans. Peter Preuss. Indianapolis: Hackett.
Pound, Ezra. 1995. *The Cantos of Ezra Pound* (1972). New York: New Directions.
Redmond, Eugene B. 1976. *Drumvoices: The Mission of Afro-American Poetry—A Critical History.* Garden City, N.Y.: Doubleday-Anchor.
Rich, Adrienne. 1993. "History Stops for No One." In *What Is Found There.* New York: W. W. Norton. 128–44.
Rowell, Charles H. 1983. "'The Unravelling of the Egg': An Interview with Jay Wright." *Callaloo* 6.3: 3–15.
Stevens, Wallace. 1954. *The Collected Poems of Wallace Stevens.* New York: Alfred A. Knopf.
———. 1966. *Letters of Wallace Stevens.* Ed. Holly Stevens. London: Faber and Faber.
———. 1976. *Souvenirs and Prophecies: The Young Wallace Stevens.* Ed. Holly Stevens. New York: Alfred A. Knopf.
Turner, Victor. 1974. *Dramas, Fields, and Metaphors: Symbolic Action in Human Society.* Ithaca, N.Y.: Cornell University Press.
Walker, Alice. 1975. "Looking for Zora." In *In Search of Our Mothers' Gardens: Womanist Prose.* San Diego, Calif.: Harcourt Brace Jovanovich. 93–118.
———. 1997. "Clear Seeing Inherited Religion and Reclaiming the Pagan Self." *On the Issues* 6 (Spring): 16–23, 54–55.
White, Hayden. 1978. *Tropics of Discourse: Essays in Cultural Criticism.* Baltimore, Md.: Johns Hopkins University Press.
Wright, Jay. 1967. "Death as History." In *Death as History.* New York: Poets Press. N.p.
———. 1971. *The Homecoming Singer.* New York: Corinth Books.
———. 1976a. *Dimensions of History.* Santa Cruz, Calif.: Kayak.
———. 1976b. *Soothsayers and Omens.* New York: Seven Woods Press.

9

From Gassire's Lute:
Robert Duncan's Vietnam War Poems

Nathaniel Mackey

The tale of Gassire's lute, taken from an ancient epic known as the *Dausi*, comes into Western literature via the first of Ezra Pound's *Pisan Cantos*. Pound got it from the writings of Leo Frobenius, who heard it among the Soninke of Mali toward the end of the first decade of the twentieth century. Douglas Fox, who along with Frobenius edited *African Genesis*, a book of myths, legends, and folktales out of Africa, suggests that the *Dausi* dates back to around 500 B.C. and that the story of Gassire's lute as Frobenius gives it comes from the period between the fourth and the twelfth centuries A.D., during which time it was sung by griots. The tale is one I am continually intrigued by and attracted to. Not only is it one of the "dreams of the race" that, as William Carlos Williams warns us, make poetry "a dangerous subject"; it is also a poem that alerts us to the dangers of poetry.

I use the story of Gassire's lute here as a point of entry into Robert Duncan's "great theme of War" (*Bending* 114). It is a tale that fits his theme well, one to which he himself refers in "Orders" and "The H.D. Book." An unsettling, highly suggestive piece of myth, the tale works as something of a primer for the concerns at work in Duncan's Vietnam War poems as well as for the concerns those poems give rise to in my response to them. The story itself runs something like this: There was once a city known as Wagadu, which was destroyed four times, once through vanity, once through dishonesty, once through greed, and once through strife. Each time it was destroyed, it was rebuilt, and each of its earthly manifestations took a different name—first Dierra, then Agada, Ganna, and finally Silla. But Wagadu was essentially immaterial, "the strength which lives in the hearts of men" (Fox and Frobenius 97). The first destruction of Wagadu, brought about by the vanity of Gassire and his lute's playing of the *Dausi*, ushered in the songs of the griots. A fierce warrior and the son of Nganamba, king of Wagadu, Gassire awaits the death of his father so that he can become king. Nganamba is very old, as is Gassire, whose eight sons are all grown and have children of their own. Nganamba hangs on, though; and, out of impatience, Gassire goes to an old wise man to ask when his father will die and bequeath to him his sword and shield. The wise man answers: "Ah, Gassire, Nganamba will die, but he will not leave you his sword and shield. You will carry a lute. Shield and sword shall others inherit. But your lute shall cause the loss of Wagadu" (Fox and Frobenius 100).

The old wise man goes on to tell Gassire that his way will lead him to the partridges in the field, whose language he will understand. The next evening, following a battle in which Gassire outdoes all his earlier heroics, he hears a partridge singing the *Dausi* to a group of younger partridges. The bird sings of its battle with a snake and brags of the immortality of the *Dausi,* its ability to outlive heroes and kings. Gassire goes back to the wise man, tells him what he has heard, and asks if humans can know the *Dausi,* too. The wise man warns him again that since he cannot become king, he will become a griot—and that this is why Wagadu will perish. "Wagadu can go to blazes!" (Fox and Frobenius 102). Gassire answers and goes to the smith, whom he orders to make him a lute. The smith says that he will do it, but it will take the blood of Gassire's sons to make the lute sing: "This is a piece of wood. It cannot sing if it has no heart. You must give it a heart. Carry this piece of wood on your back when you go into battle. The wood must ring with the stroke of your sword. The wood must absorb down-dripping blood, blood of your blood, breath of your breath" (Fox and Frobenius 103). He, too, warns that this is why Wagadu will perish; and again, Gassire says in anger: "Wagadu can go to blazes!" For the next seven days Gassire goes into battle, with the lute slung over his shoulder and one of his sons at his side. Each day a son is killed, and his blood drips down onto the lute. On the eighth day, the men of the city gather and tell Gassire that the killing must cease. They banish him from Wagadu; he leaves with his family, some friends, his servants, and his cattle, and goes into the Sahara. One night he has trouble getting to sleep; and when he finally does doze off, he is awakened by a voice. The voice turns out to be that of the lute singing the *Dausi*. On hearing it, Gassire falls to his knees weeping; at that moment, his father back in Dierra dies, and Wagadu disappears for the first time.

Presumably, other parts of the *Dausi* deal with the second, third, and fourth disappearances of Wagadu; but no such accounts appear in either *African Genesis* or the sixth volume of Frobenius's *Atlantis,* where we find the tale of Gassire's lute. A story called "The Rediscovery of Wagadu" follows that of Gassire's lute in both books, and it tells us that Wagadu disappeared for seven years, was found again, and then was lost for 740 years. Nothing is said about dishonesty, greed, or strife causing this disappearance, and the tale has wholly to do with the getting back of a great war drum known as Tabele from the devils who have stolen it and tied it to the sky. Once Tabele is recovered and beaten, Wagadu reappears. So what is available to us is an enigmatic picture of a spectral city that is both of the earth and not of the earth, visible at times and at other times invisible. Both tales suggest that war has something to do with making Wagadu visible. Only after the great war drum is beaten does the city reappear in the second tale; and in the first, we read that Wagadu "is sometimes visible because eyes see her and ears hear the clash of swords and ring of shields" (Fox and Frobenius 109). The first tale attributes the disappearance of Wagadu to "the indomitability of men"—or, in another translation, "the lack of human restraint" (Fox and Frobenius 97, 140)—and the second describes at least one disappearance as the work of devils, the Djinns who steal Tabele and tie it to the sky. These may well be different ways of saying the same thing. The Djinns might be the embodiment of a human susceptibility to the daimonic.

There is also reason to see warfare as having to do with daimonic inspiration. The day after Gassire's first consultation with the wise man, he goes into battle against the Burdama and outdoes himself. "Gassire was greater than Gassire" (Fox and Frobenius 101) is how it is put in the tale. The shocked Burdama call him a Damo, which a note in one of the translations describes as "a terrifying creature unknown to the singer" (Fox and Frobenius 143). The separation the tale makes between what makes Wagadu visible ("the clash of swords and ring of shields") and what causes it to disappear ("the indomitability of men") is, perhaps, too easy, almost naive. If Wagadu is "the strength which lives in the hearts of men," it cannot help but be their "indomitability," too. Both the availability and the invisibility of Wagadu have to do with a rendezvous with vertical powers—the war drum, remember, is tied to the sky—a rendezvous that makes for unruliness. The capacity for invasion alive in the human heart is the openness to an otherness that cuts both ways. Our inspiration is also our peril, a risk of inflation whose would-be rise can take us down into hell. The singer of the tale is caught between cosmology (the claim that for better or worse this is how it is) and morality (the claim that were it not for human vices, things would turn out well). The loss of Wagadu gets told in terms of human failings, while these failings are shown to be crucial to the destined order of things. "Gassire," the old wise man says, "you are hastening to your end. No one can stop you" (Fox and Frobenius 102).

The splendor of Wagadu and the loss of Wagadu are variations on a single theme of inspiration. Wagadu is lost because of human vanity, and Wagadu is itself a conceit of the human mind. Pound, in "Canto LXXIV," invokes it as a mental construct, "now in the mind indestructible." When we look at the beginning of the canto and see the fascist tyrant Mussolini, hung by his heels in Milan, mourned as the first in history to be "twice crucified," we recognize the truth of Duncan's warning that "in every event of his art man dwells in mixed possibilities of inflation or inspiration" ("Day Book" 35). Just as Gassire's vanity overlaps with his inspiration, Wagadu in *The Cantos* is a projection of Pound's vanity, the risk of inflation his inspiration takes and the stubbornness with which he dwells in that risk.

> I believe in the resurrection of Italy   quia impossible est
>   4 times to be the song of Gassir
>   now in the mind indestructible (442)

The indictment of the artist made by the tale of Gassire is a haunting one, so much so that Pound, if for no other reason than to acquit himself, directly addresses the content of his Wagadu projection in "Canto LXXXI." Not one to buckle easily, Pound repeats the admonition "Pull down thy vanity" seven times, only to end by denying the charge.

> Pull down thy vanity
>   How mean thy hates
> Fostered in falsity,
>   Pull down thy vanity,
> Rathe to destroy, niggard in charity,
> Pull down thy vanity,
>   I say pull down.
>
> But to have done instead of not doing
>   this is not vanity
> To have, with decency, knocked
> That a Blunt should open
>   To have gathered from the air a live tradition
> or from a fine old eye the unconquered flame
> This is not vanity
>   Here error is all in the not done,
> all in the diffidence that faltered (521–22)

One of the conditions of vanity is that it does not recognize itself, just as one of the terms of poetic inspiration is that the poet in its grips does not brood over its possible defects. The risk of inspiration may well be inflation, but the risk of brooding is one of inertia, not doing. However, Pound's gravitation toward the Soninke tale acknowledges, albeit subliminally, the grain of truth in its unflattering portrait of the artist.

Like Pound, Duncan in his appropriation of the tale vacillates between acknowledgment and self-acquittal, between confession and aggrandizement, with affirmation winning out in the end. He makes two references to the tale in "Orders," a poem prompted in part by the U.S. Marines' invasion of the Dominican Republic in 1965. The poem in a sense heralds his poetry of the Vietnam War, being followed in *Bending the Bow* by "Up Rising," probably the most well-known and certainly the most angry of his Vietnam poems. It is notably a poem in which he appears to question his calling as a poet, coming close to disowning the kind of poetry he is most given to. The exaltedly mythic, rhapsodic vein he so masterfully works all but comes under fire. The poem begins almost like an oath of office, as if he were being sworn in as a more public, more political poet.

>   For the Good,
> il ben dello intelletto,   the good of the people,
>   the soul's good.
>
>   I put aside
>
> whatever I once served of the poet, master
>   of enchanting words and magics (*Bending* 77)

Is it a repudiation of poetry or the activation of a thwarted desire to rule that enters the picture here? Gassire does not come in till further on in the poem; but in this resolve to speak for "the good of the people," we already hear the song of the would-be king. What we may tend to overlook about Gassire is that he wants to rule, that becoming a griot is something of an act of sublimation, an attempt at compensation. Duncan himself, as far back as "The Venice Poem," has spoken of poetry as a vain substitute for kingship:

> I no longer know the virgin mirror.
> Sometimes the diadems of poetry
>   —mock gold glories cut out from paper
> of an afternoon—
>   —turn until my head turns, inflate
> a bulbous image of a world, a vulgar empire.
> And I can sit upon a throne,
>   cross-eyed king of one thousand lines.
> In the mirror of poetry I conjure
>   luxuries I can ill afford. (*First Decade* 88)

Is it the unfulfilled desire to rule that indicts the mirror? Could the same desire have inflated it? Here, as in the opening of "Orders," the desire to put aside the vanity of poetry mingles with the vanity of the desire to be king. Why else would we get such lordly music from a poem that claims to disown music? Further along in "Orders," Duncan talks of putting music aside, though all the majesty of his music is still there.

> I thought to come into an open room
> where in the south light of afternoon
> one I was improvised
> passages of changing dark and light
> a music dream and passion would have playd
> to illustrate concords of order in order,
> a contrapuntal communion of all things
>
>   but Schubert is gone
>   the genius of his melody
> has passt, and all the lovely marrd sentiment
> disownd I thought to come to (*Bending* 78)

We look at Pound, and we see a poet hankering to get into government, wanting to dictate policy, to wield decision-making power, to sit in smoke-filled rooms. In Duncan, we see not so much an eye to the actual grind of political authority but a kind of Shelleyan sense of the poet as actual, though unacknowledged, king. He is also close to Williams, who in "The Basis of Faith in Art" insists: "Poetry is a rival government always in opposition to its cruder replicas" (180). Senses of rivalry and opposition run freely in Duncan's poems of the Vietnam War, and the figural meaning he gives to Wagadu in "The H.D. Book" clearly carries both. He writes there of the writers from whom he draws his poetic lineage, taking heart in his objection to the war from a sense of them having likewise opposed the warfare state. At one point, he evokes Wagadu as the "city... that those who are devoted to Beauty remember" ("H.D. Book" 48); later, he refers to it as something of a rival government in the hearts of his poetic elders:

> Pound, Lawrence, Joyce, H.D., Eliot, have a black voice when speaking of the contemporary scene, an enduring memory from this First World War that had revealed the deep-going falsehood and evil of the modern state. These had from their earliest years as writers a burning sense of the "they" that ran the war and that accepted its premises and of the "we" whose allegiance belonged to a Wagadu hidden in their hearts.... Their threshold remains ours. The time of war and exploitation, the infamy and lies of the new capitalist war-state, continue. And the answering intensity of the imagination to hold its own values must continue. ("H.D. Book" 50, 53)

Here, Wagadu is what Duncan elsewhere calls "the commune of Poetry" (*Bending* vi); and in his next mention of it, we notice a tension that troubles his use of the tale in "Orders." He suggests that "the Wagadu of the *Cantos* is the lost city not of a tribe but of a kindred among all men, 'an aristocracy of emotion' Pound called it" ("H.D. Book" 55). The communalist assertion, however, is belied by the elitist ring of Pound's phrase, with inclusiveness ("a kindred among all men") at odds with exclusivity ("an aristocracy of emotion"). Only the assertiveness of Duncan's poetics holds the two together. (He writes a bit further on, probably with a sense of the irony involved: "The very heightened sense of the relatedness of everything sets poets apart" ["H.D. Book" 58].)

We see something of the same split in "Orders," where Wagadu is more or less identified with the lute that destroys it. Referring to the U.S. Marines in the Dominican Republic, Duncan writes:

From house to house the armd men go,

   in Santo Domingo hired and conscripted killers
   against the power of an idea, against

     Gassire's lute,   the song
       of Wagadu, household of the folk,
     commune of communes
   hidden seed in the hearts of men
     and in each woman's womb   hidden. (Bending 77)

Thinking back to the tale itself, we might balk at this yoking together of Wagadu and Gassire's lute. We are at least suspicious of the poetic conceit that wants to attribute a communal impulse—"the good of the people," "household of the folk," "commune of communes"—to Gassire, since we have heard him tell Wagadu to go to hell, watched him sacrifice his sons for his personal glory (having drafted them just as a government does), and seen him kicked out of Wagadu. Is this a case of unconscious distortion, Duncan altering a truth he cannot face? Or is he consciously presenting a reformed Gassire, a symbolic projection of his "putting aside" of a certain poetic stance? In either case, the inappropriateness of Gassire's lute as a symbol of "the folk" is a symptom of something else going on in the poem, something that the "putting aside" he announces both addresses and aggravates. Duncan is not what we tend to think of as a populist poet. When he names a number of his poetic masters further on in the poem, we do not find—nor do we expect to find—Carl Sandburg or Langston Hughes, for example, among them. We do find an admirer of Mussolini and a self-proclaimed monarchist on the list:

> Down this dark corridor, "this *passage*," the poet reminds me
>
> and now that Eliot is dead, Williams and H.D. dead,
> Ezra alone of my old masters alive,   let me
>   acknowledge Eliot was one of them, I was
>   one of his,   whose   "History has many
>   cunning passages, contrived corridors"
>
> comes into the chrestomathy. (Bending 78)

(Is the earlier line "From house to house the armd men go," with its faint echo of "In the room the women come and go," an added homage to Eliot, who had recently died when the poem was written?)

By announcing what appears to be a populist intent at the beginning of "Orders," Duncan leaves himself open to the sort of rebuke Charles Olson aims at Pound for his opening lines in "Canto LXXIV" ("The enormous tragedy of the dream in the peasant's bent / shoulder").

> And with no back references, no
> floating over Asia arrogating
> how a raiding party moves in advance of a nation, thereby eventually
> giving a language the international power
> poets take advantage of. As they also,
> with much less reason, from too much economics speak
> of the dream
> in a peasant's bent shoulders, as though it were true
> they cared a damn
> for his conversation (Olson, Distances 38)

The pull between what I will roughly call "populist" and "elitist" impulses gives a telling quiver to Duncan's poem. We hear it in the slight note of apology—edged with a tinge of defiance—in his acknowledgment of Eliot. We hear it more expressly toward the beginning of the poem, where Duncan goes on to qualify his "putting aside" of an oracular, possibly inflated sense of his role as poet:

> not to disown the old mysteries, sweet
>   muthos   our mouths telling
>
> and I will still tell the beads, in the fearsome
>   street I see glimpses of   I will pray again
>   to those great columns of moon's light,
>   "Mothering angels, hold my sight steady

>   and I will look this time as you bid me   to see
>   the dirty papers, moneys, laws, orders
>   and corpses of people and people-shit." (*Bending* 77)

We see that the "putting aside" he announces does not so much repudiate as enlarge his art, bringing with it added rather than diminished risks of inflation. Acknowledging himself to be something of an ivory-tower poet, Duncan strikes out into new terrain, stepping into the world of current events, assuming a public, more oratorical, voice. But he is at the same time digging more deeply into the oracular, rhapsodic vein. Olson noted this in 1968 at Beloit College, where he said of some then-recent Duncan poems (apparently some or all of the *Passages* that later appeared in *Tribunals*): "Unbelievable, these new *Passages*. . . . I mean where Duncan . . . I mean he's moved into a—almost a status or something, if I may use that word—a condition of status. . . . He's become a BIG poet, like Yeats. . . . he put on the robe" (*Muthologos* 79).

In spite of the split that Duncan apparently acknowledges with his "putting aside," the overall push of the poem is to have it both ways. The charge the poem is given is not one of abdicating the exalted mode but of bringing it to bear on more resistant matters. "Orders" continues Duncan's insistence on the relevance of myth and a sense of historical recurrence, in whose light he now looks at events on the six o'clock news. The lines preceding his acknowledgment of Eliot put into practice the sense of historical resonance and interconnectedness that he uses the term "passages" to evoke. With its intervention in the Dominican Republic, the United States reminds him of Herod and of the Abbé of Citeaux.

>   They do not know where It is   at Béziers
>   the Abbé of Citeaux orders   *Kill them all—*
>   *the Lord will know His own!*
>   Pillars I saw in my dream last year, stand
>   in my heart and hold the blood,
>   my pulse rises and beats against its walls.
>   In the streets of Santo Domingo Herod's hosts again
>   to exterminate the soul of the people go (*Bending* 77–78)

In the course of the poem, the communal feeling entered into at its beginning increasingly shows itself to open onto something other than a simple populist proposition. A mingling of vertical and horizontal inclinations inflates the words "commune" and "household." The oracular mode, Duncan's urge to become a mouthpiece for cosmic truth, is such that his "household of the folk" gives way to or turns out to be "the great household," the cosmos itself. The "commune of communes" likewise inclines toward the "It" of the passage just quoted. What Duncan means by "It," his introduction to *Bending the Bow* tells us, is the "striving to come into existence" of a cosmogonic Spirit, the sense of the world he roots his poetics in: "This configuration of It in travail: giving birth to Its Self, the Creator, in Its seeking to make real . . . this deepest myth of what is happening in Poetry moves us as it moves words" (*Bending* vii).

No simple humanism holds sway over "Orders." The poem's cosmic insistences border on misanthropy, a kind of masochism at times, as at the poem's conclusion:

> There is no
> good a man has in his own things except
> it be in the community of every thing;
> no nature he has
> but in his nature hidden in the hearts of the living
> in the great household.
> The cosmos will not
> dissolve its orders at man's evil.
> "That which is corrupted is corrupted with reference to
> itself but not destroyd with reference to the universe;
> for it is either air or water"
> Chemistry having its equations
> beyond our range of inequation.
> There must be a power of an ambiguous nature
> and a dominion given to choice: "For the
>
> electing soul alone is transferred
> to another and another order[.]" (*Bending* 79–80)

Here, "community" has more an ecological—with whose etymology his use of the word "household" has to do—than a populist ring, and the passage's assurance of the imperviousness of the cosmos repeats Duncan's conviction that "the universe is faithful to itself" (*Bending* v). Like the teller of the tale of Gassire's lute, Duncan is caught between morality and cosmology, between outrage at human evil and a "higher" understanding of evil's place in the scheme of things. As Duncan states in a passage that also explains the title of the poem: "The moralist must always be outraged by what God finds good; for God works, as the creative artist works, not with a sense of rewards and punishments, but to fulfill the law that he creates. He seeks in His Creation intensifications of Its orders. In the plenitude of His powers, He works always upon the edge of arbitrary alternatives; He could, we know, change the work if He would. But first among His powers is His Oneness in creation, the universe is faithful to itself" (*Bending* vii–viii). The "orders" to which the poem's title refers, then, are "Its," "a power of an ambiguous nature."

The capitulation of what seems at first a political or an ideological imperative to a status quo conceived as cosmic, a sense of serving "It" or "What Is" (*Bending* vii)—"my thoughts are servants of the stars, and my words . . . / come from a mouth that is the Universe," Duncan writes in one of the later *Passages* (*Bending* 120)—seems to confirm the split between ideology and poetry that Roland Barthes writes of in *Mythologies*:

> It seems that this is a difficulty pertaining to our times: there is as yet only one possible choice, and this choice can bear only on two extreme methods: either to posit a reality which is entirely permeable to history, and ideologize; or, conversely, to posit a reality which is *ultimately* impenetrable, irreducible, and, in this case, poetize. In a word, I do not yet see a synthesis between ideology and poetry (by poetry I understand, in a very general way, the search for the inalienable meaning of things). (158–59)

This capitulation, however, is only one moment, though a recurrent one, in Duncan's work, and it can also be said that his sense of "What Is" is dialectical, evolutional enough not to be caught postulating an "inalienable meaning." Barthes's formulation offers a way of looking at two poles between which Duncan dances, particularly in the war poems, where he both objects to the U.S. assault on Indochina and accepts—even all but embraces—the war as a revelatory, epiphanic event, a showing forth of "What Is": "In a blast, the poem announces the Satanic person of a president whose lies and connivings have manoeuvred the nation into the pit of an evil war. What does it mean? It is a mere political event of the day, yet it comes reveald as an eternal sentence" (*Bending* x).

The tug between morality and cosmology, between ideology and poetry, bears the brunt of the troublesome impact that the notion of inspiration makes on humanistic assumptions. The ages-old sense of inspiration as an inspiriting, an invasion of a human vessel by a nonhuman daimon or spirit, carries the danger of a loss of touch with human realities and feelings. Taken seriously, the notion complicates and unsettles what we mean by "human," since if we are subject to such invasions, our susceptibility has to be a factor of what being human means. Ideology and morality tend to posit fixed notions of what is properly to be regarded as human, notions to which the otherness of inspiration may pose a threat. We see Duncan caught in this complication. He will make a morally inflected use of the terms "human" and "dehumanization" in his denunciations of Lyndon Johnson: "I have been criticized for dehumanizing Johnson in the poem *Up Rising,* but such men have dehumanized themselves, removed themselves from the human consequences of their acts and from the disorders that underlie their ratiocinations. Did they not have the immunity to the reality of what they are doing that the dehumanization of official identity and idealism gives, they would come into the full obsessional sickness of soul of the human state" ("Man's Fulfillment" 248). Duncan will also, as if to deny this removal the possible rationalization of having been prompted by inspiration, write in "The Soldiers": "Johnson now, no inspired poet but making it badly, / amassing his own history in murder and sacrifice / without talent" (*Bending* 113). But what if Johnson *were* inspired? Would the destruction of Vietnam be justified?

In the tale of Gassire's lute, it appears to be the artist who is dehumanized. Gassire becomes a Damo in battle before turning to his lute, and the appetite that the lute has for blood might imply the more sinister, vampirish aspect of inspiration. Gassire does weep once the lute finally sings the *Dausi,* though, so there has not been a total removal from the possibility of a human response. In "Orders," it is exactly the human response, a mix of rage, grief, and dismay, that the blood shed by Gassire's sons—and by the people of the Dominican Republic—serves to further. The blood may well have inspired Duncan's song, but the song despairs of its inspiration. Duncan walks a tightrope, and his exulting in the "lure for feeling" (to use Whitehead's phrase) that is provided by that blood has to keep clear of celebrating beauty, the song, as though the blood were justified by it:

>   a poetry
>   having so much of beauty
>   that in whose progressions   rage,
>   grief, dismay transported—but these
>   are themselves transports of beauty!   The blood
>
>   streams from the bodies of his sons
>   to feed the voice of Gassire's lute. (*Bending* 78–79)

The risk of inflation is also, as Duncan points out in his indictment of Johnson, the risk of insulation. Duncan in the office of poet—"BIG poet," no less—runs a risk analogous to that of Johnson in the office of president, the risk Duncan speaks of as ossification in his play on the word "office" in "The Multiversity."

> In this scene   absolute authority
>   the great dragon himself so confronted
>   whose scales are men officized—ossified—conscience
>   no longer alive in them,
>   the inner law silenced (*Bending* 70)

The poetic office's investment in whatever feeds it might become a kind of callous, a smugness in which the poet's "faithfulness in the poetry he creates" (*Bending* viii)—the delight he takes in "transports of beauty"—does not adequately respond to the human misery those transports report. It is in acknowledgment of this risk that Duncan talks of "putting aside" the office.

The problem of inflation tells in the voice itself, in the rhetorical ring we hear in lines like: "There is no / good a man has in his own things except / it be in the community of every thing." Weary of high-sounding cant, of idealizations and preachments from public officials, are we ready for such a sermon coming from a poet? The mode is problematic—and sufficiently so that Ian Reid, who quotes from a letter Duncan had written him, can write: "Duncan himself is aware of it, remarking that in them [the war poems] he seems unable to move outside the almost hypnagogic high tone" (Bertholf and Reid 181). It is a problem Duncan has acknowledged elsewhere in relation to another poem in the *Passages* series, one that even more directly relates the problem of an oracular, oratorical mode to the question of inspiration (or daimonic impersonation). In "Moving the Moving Image," the sermonizing voice of Hermes, forecasting the day when "this Vision of the Cosmos in which the Greatest Good is / will be in danger of perishing" (*Bending* 61), takes over half the poem. Duncan has written about the difficulty this takeover presents in performing the poem:

> In "Moving the Moving Image," as Hermes speaks, delivering here his "Perfect Sermon," as it is called in the Hermetic Tradition, the poet performing must move into the high priesthood in which the official speaks in the god's person. My voice must move now in musical pitches so severely represst in every training our American speech lays upon us that, properly, each time, I dread my attempt. The mode itself is heretical; banned by the Puritans of the modernist movement as long before it had been banned by their Puritanical ancestors opposing the music of Papist incantations.
>
> Could I improve my delivery by rehearsing, initiating myself into the alien order of god's voice? But the speech of this persona of the poem must come each

time out of the total ground of the poem in the presence of its auditors. The voice of the man falters and must brave the heart in which he fails to give himself over, inept as he is, to the sublimity of the concept. For this is the drama the poem projects. ("Preface" 54–55)

This faltering of the voice, which in its coming down cracks the possible hardening into "high priesthood," restores a sense of human proportion. The faltering is true to the condition the Perfect Sermon describes, wherein we "no longer cherish or abide in the Mind of the Universe / Nor take manhood in the music of its many powers" (*Bending* 66), a state in which talk of these things is problematic.

The artist (as opposed, perhaps, to the office), however much he or she might opt for insulation or exemption, cannot help but suffer the content of the art. This is partly the meaning of the blood feeding Gassire's lute, something like García Lorca's *duende*. The faltering of Duncan's voice, which David Bromige calls "the broken chant of yearning to be that other, of the will to be one with what is nearly forgotten" (105), speaks from the heart of the condition it laments, tellingly fails to rise above that condition. We hear the pathos of an upward aspiration that we both identify with and are put off by, hearing the echo of our own resistance in Duncan's inability to keep the godly voice aloft. The aspiration caves in on itself as if to confess to what it wants immunity from. If poetry is a rival government, if it has a more compelling claim to our allegiance than its cruder replicas, it would have to be because of just such a capacity for confession, the acknowledgment of a richer play of response than etiquettes of office allow. It is in the richer play that the outlawed or unacknowledged pathos reasserts itself, that the passion of it, its keeping close to the *heart* of the matter, troubles all entrenchment, any dwelling in the security of an attitude.

Works Cited

Barthes, Roland. *Mythologies.* Trans. Annette Lavers. New York: Hill and Wang, 1975.
Bertholf, Robert J., and Ian W. Reid, eds. *Robert Duncan: Scales of the Marvelous.* New York: New Directions, 1979.
Bromige, David. "Beyond Prediction." *Credences* 2 (1975): 105.
Duncan, Robert. *Bending the Bow.* New York: New Directions, 1968.
———. *The First Decade: Selected Poems, 1950–1956.* London: Fulcrum Press, 1969.
———. "From the Day Book—Excerpts from an Extended Study of H.D.'s Poetry." *Origin* 2d ser., 10 (1965): 35.
———. "The H.D. Book." In *A Caterpillar Anthology.* Ed. Clayton Eshelman. Garden City, N.Y.: Doubleday, 1971. 48–53.

———. "Man's Fulfillment in Order and Strife." *Caterpillar* 8–9 (1969): 248.
———. "Preface to a Reading of Passages 1–22." *Maps* 6 (1974): 53–55.
Fox, Douglas C., and Leo Frobenius. *African Genesis*. New York: Stackpole Sons, 1937.
Frobenius, Leo. *Leo Frobenius, 1873–1973: An Anthology*. Ed. Eike Haberland. Trans. Patricia Crampton. Wiesbaden: F. Steiner, 1973.
Olson, Charles. *The Distances*. New York: Grove Press, 1960.
———. *Muthologos: The Collected Letters and Interviews*. Vol. 2. Ed. George F. Butterick. Bolinas, Calif.: Four Seasons Foundation, 1979.
Pound, Ezra. *The Cantos of Ezra Pound*. New York: New Directions, 1970.
Williams, William Carlos. *Selected Essays*. Norfolk, Conn.: New Directions, 1954.

Contributors

Charles Bernstein is the David Gray Professor of Poetry and Letters at the State University of New York at Buffalo. His books include *The Sophist, Islets/Irritations, Controlling Interests, Poetic Justice, Disfrutes, Content's Dream,* and *A Poetics.* Bernstein was coeditor of the legendary small press magazine *L=A=N=G=U=A=G=E.*

Rachel Blau DuPlessis is a professor of English at Temple University. Her books of criticism include *The Pink Guitar: Writing as Feminist Practice, H.D.: The Career of That Struggle,* and *Writing beyond the Ending: Narrative Strategies of Twentieth-Century Women Writers.* Among her many books of poetry are *Drafts, Tabula Rosa,* and *Wells.*

C. K. Doreski has taught at Daniel Webster College, the University of Massachusetts, Emmanuel College, and Boston University. She is the author of *Elizabeth Bishop: The Restraints of Language* and *Writing America Black: Race Rhetoric and the Public Sphere* and is completing *Citizenship and Its Discontents: Americans at Home in the Second World War* with the assistance of a National Endowment for the Humanities fellowship.

Kathryne V. Lindberg, an associate professor at Wayne State University, has been on the faculties at Harvard University, Columbia University, and the University of California at Los Angeles. Among her many works of criticism is *Reading Pound Reading: Modernism after Nietzsche.*

Nathaniel Mackey, who teaches at the University of California at Santa Cruz, is the author of *Eroding Witness, School of Udhra, Whatsaid Serif, Bedouin Hornbook,* and

Djbot Baghostus's Run. His most recent collection of critical essays is *Discrepant Engagement: Dissonance, Cross-Culturality, and Experimental Writing*.

Maria K. Mootry directs the African-American Studies Program at the University of Illinois at Springfield, where she also is a member of the faculty in English. She is the coeditor of *A Life Distilled: Gwendolyn Brooks, Her Poetry and Fiction*.

Aldon Lynn Nielsen, Fletcher Jones Chair of Literature and Writing at Loyola Marymount University, has taught at San Jose State University, Howard University, George Washington University and the University of California at Los Angeles. His collections of poetry are *Heat Strings, Evacuation Routes: A User's Guide, Stepping Razor*, and *Vext*. His books of criticism include *Reading Race: White American Poets and the Racial Discourse in the Twentieth Century, Writing between the Lines: Race and Intertextuality, Black Chant: Languages of African-American Postmodernism*, and *C. L. R. James: A Critical Introduction*.

Felipe Smith is an associate professor of English at Tulane University and has taught at the University of New Orleans and Louisiana State University. He is the author of *American Body Politics: Race, Gender, and Black Literary Renaissance*.

Lorenzo Thomas is a member of the English department faculty at the University of Houston. He published his first volume of poems, *A Visible Island*, in 1967. Since that time, his books of poetry have included *Fit Music, Dracula, Framing the Sunrise, Chances Are Few*, and *The Bathers*.

Name Index

Abbott, Craig S., 85, 95
Adamic, Louis, 13
Adorno, Theodor W., 128
Agard, John, 117, 130n
Aiken, Conrad, 89–90, 91–92, 103
Alcoff, Linda Martín, 16–17, 19
Aldrich, Thomas Bailey, 96
Alexander, Will, 154
Allen, Donald, 149
Andrews, Bruce, 111, 126, 129n
Apollinaire, Guillame, 78n, 172
Arens, William, 15
Armistead, W. S., 8
Arnold, Matthew, 95
Art Ensemble of Chicago, 156, 157
Ashbery, John, 155
Askenasy, Hans, 15
Auden, W. H., 155
Augustine, Saint, 190

Bahti, Timothy, 206n
Bailey, William Edgar, 150
Baker, Houston A., Jr., 25, 26, 41, 118
Bakhtin, Mikhail, 113
Baldwin, James, 41, 168, 189
Balzac, Honoré de, 103
Banneker, Benjamin, 189–94, 196, 197, 203, 204, 206n
Baraka, Amiri, 1, 5–7, 25, 149, 153, 163, 172, 173, 178n, 181n

Barber, J. Max, 96, 100, 102
Barnes, Djuna, 77n
Barthes, Roland, 219
Baudelaire, Charles, 152
Baum, Joan, 9
Bellitt, Ben, 158
Benét, William Rose, 77n, 87
Benjamin, Walter, 8, 10, 183, 184–85, 186–87, 194, 196, 199, 201, 202, 203, 205n, 206n
Bennett, Gwendolyn, 72
Bennett, Louise, 112, 115–16, 119, 122, 130n
Bernstein, Charles, 20, 179n
Berryman, John, 19
Bérubé, Michael, 102
Bhabha, Homi, 184, 205n, 206n
Biarujia, Javant, 126–27, 131n
Blake, William, 128, 188, 197
Blaser, Robin, 113
Blesh, Rudi, 142, 147n
Bloom, Harold, 199
Bloom, Valerie, 130n
Bogan, Louise, 98
Bone, Robert, 5, 6
Bontemps, Arna, 5
Boyce, Sonia, 152
Bracques, Georges, 142
Braithwaite, William Stanley, 16–18, 20, 84–106
Branch, Anna Hempstead, 92
Brathwaite, Kamau, 112, 113, 114, 117, 118, 119, 120, 121, 179n

Brawley, Benjamin, 97, 100–101, 102
Breeze, Jean Binta, 130n
Breton, André, 178n
Brodhead, Richard, 48
Bromige, David, 222
Brooks, Gwendolyn, 5–6, 7, 75n, 133–47, 198
Brossard, Nicole, 111
Brown, Edmund R., 91, 112
Brown, Sterling, 18, 47, 113, 118, 119, 123, 124
Bruce, Lenny, 169
Buck-Morss, Susan, 206n
Bunting, Basil, 112, 114–15, 119, 123, 126, 130n
Bynner, Witter, 87
Byrnes, Lillian, 73–74

Caen, Herb, 178
Canaan, Gilbert, 98
Carlotta (empress), 197, 202
Carlyle, Thomas, 2
Carroll, Charles, 7–8
Cassuto, Leonard, 15
Cavell, Stanley, 110
Césaire, Aimé, 10, 148, 150, 154, 177
Cha, Theresa Hak Kyung, 129n
Chametsky, Jules, 6
Charters, Ann, 171
Chatfield-Taylor, H. C., 90
Chessman, Caryl, 171, 176, 181n
Christian, Barbara, 164
Churchill, Winston, 136, 137
Clarkson, Thomas, 9
Cleaver, Eldridge, 25–26, 27, 31, 41
Clemenceau, Georges, 139–40
Clemens, Samuel. *See* Twain, Mark
Clement, Rufus, 97
Colbert, Claudette, 19
Coleman, Ornette, 6–7
Coles, Robert, 65–66
Collins, Merle, 130n
Columbus, Christopher, 2, 3, 9, 18, 19
Conneau, Theophilus, 9
Conner, Charles H., 150
Conrad, Joseph, 3, 75n
Coolidge, Clark, 111
Cooper, James Fenimore, 90
Costello, Bonnie, 79n
Crane, Hart, 119, 169, 171, 172, 186, 187, 189, 191, 199
Crowley, Tony, 112–13
Cullen, Countee, 47, 58, 71–72, 73, 76n, 113, 118, 119

cummings, e. e., 14, 59, 134
Cuney, Waring, 74

Damas, Leon, 12–13
Damon, Maria, 19, 178–79n, 180n
Dante Alighieri, 136
Darwin, Charles, 122
Davidson, Michael, 179n
Davies, Mary Carolyn, 97
Dean, James, 152
de Certeau, Michel, 120, 125, 205n
Dekoven, Marianne, 75n
Depestre, René, 10
Derrida, Jacques, 171, 199
de Zayas, Marius, 64, 78n
Dett, V. R. Nathaniel, 150
Deveaux, Alexis, 149
Dewdney, Christopher, 111
Diawara, Manthia, 152
Dickinson, Emily, 96, 129n, 174
Dijkstra, Bram, 49
Di Prima, Diane, 164
Dixon, Thomas, 50, 157
Donahue, Joseph, 178
Donne, John, 139, 153
Douglas, Frederick, 184, 195
Dove, Rita, 206n
Doolittle, Hilda (H.D.), 14, 111, 209, 214, 216
Doreski, Carole, 20
Doreski, William, 206n
Dos Passos, John, 63
Du Bois, W. E. B., 16–17, 25–42, 46, 47, 52, 61, 75n, 97, 98, 99, 102, 103, 113, 118, 142, 150, 157
Dumas, Alexandre, 103
Dumas, Henry, 149
Dunbar, Paul Laurence, 99, 100–101, 112, 118, 119, 120, 133, 156
Duncan, Robert, 4–5, 7, 15, 20, 202, 209–23
DuPlessis, Rachel Blau, 20

Earle, Ferdinand Phinny, 87, 89
Edwards, Ken, 130n
Eliot, T. S., 2, 3, 4, 9, 14, 15, 50, 74n, 77n, 92, 110, 111, 129n, 180n, 185, 186, 189, 190, 201, 203, 214, 216, 217
Ellington, Edward Kennedy "Duke," 169, 170, 173
Ellis, George W., 97
Ellison, Ralph, 11, 14, 33, 41, 135
Emerson, Ralph Waldo, 110, 176, 185, 187, 188, 197, 199, 201, 203

NAME INDEX

Evans, Steve, 19
Everett, Anna, 2

Fabre, Michel, 33
Fanon, Frantz, 153–54, 164–65, 176, 177
Farber, James, 153
Farnsworth, Robert, 135
Ferguson, Deanna, 111
Ferlinghetti, Lawrence, 174–75, 179n
Ferris, William H., 99, 103
Ficke, Arthur Davison, 87
Fields, Julia, 149, 153
Fish, Stanley, 10
Fishkin, Shelley Fisher, 17, 19, 44
Fitzgerald, F. Scott, 79n
Fitzhugh, George, 1, 2, 4, 8–9, 10, 11, 13, 14
Fletcher, John Gould, 92
Foch, Marshall Ferdinand, 97
Foner, Jack D., 134
Foner, Philip, 205n
Foster, Ed, 178
Foster, Hal, 62, 66
Fox, Douglas, 209
Franco, Francisco, 158
Fredman, Stephen, 149–50
Freud, Sigmund, 168
Friedlander, Ben, 19
Frobenius, Leo, 209, 210
Frost, Robert, 85, 93
Fry, Roger, 65, 67

García Lorca, Federico, 157–59, 222
Garrison, William Lloyd, 8
Garvey, Marcus, 98, 99, 154
Gauguin, Paul, 51
Genette, Gerard, 142
Giacometti, Alberto, 197
Gershwin, George, 77n
Gillespie, Abraham Lincoln, 119, 125–26, 131n
Gioia, Dana, 85
Gilroy, Paul, 206n
Goldberg, Isaac, 96, 97
Goldman, Emma, 87
Graham, Billy, 152
Gramsci, Antonio, 119, 120
Grant, Ulysses S., 158
Griaule, Marcel, 199–204, 206n
Griffith, D. W., 15, 56, 100, 157
Grossman, Ernesto, 129
Gubar, Susan, 18–19, 76n
Guignon, Henri, 136

Haldeman-Julius, Emmanuel, 97
Hale, Edward Everett, 96
Hall, Stuart, 179n
Hamsun, Knut, 98
Handlin, Oscar, 99–100
Harmon, Judith E. B., 100
Harper, Frances Ellen Watkins, 133
Harris, Joel Chandler, 54
Harris, Wilson, 13, 205n
Haweis, Stephen, 68
Hawthorne, Nathaniel, 11–12, 15, 160
Hayden, Robert, 186, 199
H.D. *See* Doolittle, Hilda
Hearst, William Randolph, Jr., 170
Hegel, Georg Wilhelm Friedrich, 165
Hejinian, Lyn, 111, 129n
Hemingway, Ernest, 63, 77n
Henderson, Alice Corbin, 93–94
Henderson, David, 149, 180n
Henry, Paget, 153–54
Henry, Patrick, 186
Hentoff, Nat, 5
Hernton, Calvin, 37–38
Herrnstein, Richard, 7–8
Higginson, Thomas Wentworth, 96
Hitler, Adolph, 136
Höch, Hannah, 62–63
Holiday, Billie, 160, 172, 175
Hollander, John, 205n
Hollings, Ernest F., 2–3
Holmes, Oliver Wendell, 101
Honour, Hugh, 31
Hoover, J. Edgar, 167
Hope, John, 96–97
Hopkins, Pauline, 96
Howe, Julia Ward, 96
Howe, Susan, 111
Howells, William Dean, 95–96
Huggins, Nathan, 65
Hughes, Langston, 41, 45, 47, 53–54, 71, 73, 96, 112, 113, 119, 123, 215
Hunt, Erica, 149
Hurston, Zora Neale, 163, 166
Huxley, Aldous, 122

Inman, P., 125
Isaacs, Diane, 65–66
Isherwood, Christopher, 176

Jackson, Murray, 178
James, C. L. R., 154

NAME INDEX

Jameson, Roscoe, 75n
Janis, Harriet, 142, 147n
Januzzi, Marisa, 79n
Jeckyll, Walter, 120, 130n
Jeffers, Robinson, 13, 14
Jefferson, Thomas, 8, 13, 189–94, 204
Jesus Christ, 8, 171, 172
Joan of Arc, 136
Joans, Ted, 173, 178n
Johns, Orrick, 87–89
Johnson, Fenton, 47, 72, 73, 94, 97
Johnson, Georgia Douglas, 47, 71
Johnson, Helene, 47, 71
Johnson, James Weldon, 14, 25–42, 45, 47, 76n, 99, 100–101, 102, 112, 129n, 130–31n
Johnson, Linton Kwesi, 112, 117, 119, 130n
Johnson, Lyndon, 220
Johnson-Rouillier, Cyraina, 79n
Jolson, Al, 15, 129n
Jonas, Stephen, 149
Jones, LeRoi. *See* Baraka, Amiri
Joyce, James, 68, 111, 125, 173, 214
Judd, Denis, 134, 136

Kallen, Horace, 98
Kaplan, E. Ann, 179n
Kaufman, Bob, 10–11, 19, 21, 149, 152, 157–59, 160, 163–82
Kaufman, Eileen, 179n, 180n
Kaufman, George, 180n
Keats, John, 171
Kennedy, John F., 171
Kenner, Hugh, 200
Kerlin, Robert T., 150–51
Kerouac, Jack, 164, 169, 170, 171, 175–76, 179n
Khlebnikov, Velimer, 125, 126
Kilmer, Joyce, 87
Knight, Brenda, 180n
Knowles, Frederic Lawrence, 96
Kraus, Karl, 8
Kreyemborg, Alfred, 46, 92
Kutzinski, Vera, 204–5n, 206n

Lacan, Jacques, 165, 176
Larsen, Nella, 76n
Lawrence, D. H., 43, 47–48, 63, 64, 78n, 214
Lawrence, Nick; 130n
Leadbelly. *See* Ledbetter, Huddie
Ledbetter, Huddie, 174
Leland, Christopher T., 178
Lemke, Sieglinde, 12
Leonard, Tom, 111

Levinger, E. E., 77n
Levy, Eugene, 33
Lewis, Ida, 146n
Lincoln, Abraham, 2, 136, 138, 140
Lindberg, Kathryne V., 20–21
Lindsay, Vachel, 1, 2, 4, 5, 9, 14, 15, 77n, 87, 92
Livingstone, David, 9
Lloyd George, David, 136, 139–40
Locke, Alain, 39, 52, 99, 102
Loftin, Elouise, 12
Loftis, N. J., 148, 155, 158, 160
Logan, Rayford, 85
Longfellow, Henry Wadsworth, 85, 86, 96
Lowell, Amy, 91
Lowell, Robert, 134, 206n
Loy, Mina, 47, 67–69, 75n, 79n, 129n, 130n

Macaulay, Thomas, 9
Mac Cormack, Karen, 111
MacDiarmid, Hugh, 112, 114–15, 119, 123, 126, 130n
Mackey, Nathaniel, 12, 20, 130n, 149, 156–57, 180n, 202
Mailer, Norman, 99, 166, 168, 179n, 180n
Major, Clarence, 149
Markham, Edwin, 87, 88
Marsden, Dora, 44
Marshall, Paule, 159–60
Martí, José, 180n
Marx, Karl, 130n
Mather, Cotton, 201
Matibag, Eugenio, 13
Matisse, Henri, 78n
Maximilian (emperor), 197, 202
McCaffery, Steve, 111
McKay, Claude, 25–42, 73, 99, 112, 118–24, 130n
Mearns, Hughes, 95
Melnick, David, 125, 126
Melville, Herman, 121
Mercer, Kobena, 179n
Michaels, Walter Benn, 16–17, 18, 52, 79n
Mighty Sparrow, the, 1, 3, 4
Millay, Edna St. Vincent, 87–89
Miller, Adam David, 6
Miller, Cristanne, 79n, 80n
Miller, Kelly, 97, 150
Milton, John, 188, 201
Mitchell, Angelyn, 18
Mitchell, Roscoe, 156
Mohanty, Chandra, 179n
Monroe, Harriet, 18, 57, 78n, 84–106
Monroe, Jonathan, 150

NAME INDEX

Moore, Marianne, 43–47, 69–71, 74n, 75n, 76–77n, 79n, 197
Mootry, Maria, 20
Morrison, Toni, 46, 50, 58, 77n
Moses, 152, 188
Mottram, Eric, 130n
Moulton, Louise Chandler, 96
Moynihan, Daniel Patrick, 27, 99
Mozart, Wolfgang Amadeus, 6
Mullen, Harryette, 111, 129n, 159–61, 205n
Murphy, Margueritte, 150, 153
Murray, Charles, 7–8
Mussolini, Benito, 212, 215

Nadel, Ira B., 94
Natambu, Kofi, 178n
Neal, Larry, 149
Neihardt, John G., 90
Newsome, Effie Lee, 53–54, 77n
Nicholls, Peter, 110–11
Nichols, Grace, 130n
Nielsen, Aldon Lynn, 18, 20, 61, 78n, 94, 121
Nietzsche, Friedrich Wilhelm, 204, 205n
North, Michael, 14, 15, 18, 20, 54, 61, 76n, 129n, 130n

Ogotemmêli, 187, 199–204
O'Hara, Frank, 19
Olson, Charles, 154, 216, 217
Oppenheim, James, 103
O'Sullivan, Maggie, 111

Page, L. C., 16, 96
Peabody, Josephine Preston, 87
Perednik, Jorge Santiago, 107, 108, 109, 111
Perry, Bliss, 96
Perry, Gill, 66
Petain, Henri Phillipe, 139
Petrarch, 139, 144
Petry, Ann, 41
Picasso, Pablo, 62, 64, 78n, 142
Pitcher, Oliver, 149, 154–55
Plessy, Homer, 44, 45
Postell, Tom, 149
Poston, Robert L., 98–99
Pound, Ezra, 17–18, 43–47, 50, 69, 70, 74n, 75n, 77n, 87, 90, 92, 93–94, 110, 111, 152, 166, 179n, 183, 184, 185, 186, 190, 191, 199, 201, 203, 209, 211–16

Quatermain, Peter, 112, 129–30n

Rainey, Lawrence S., 151
Ransome, John Crowe, 4–5
Raworth, Tom, 111
Rawson, Claude, 15
Ray, Man, 62–63
Redding, J. Saunders, 5, 102
Reid, Ian, 221
Rexroth, Kenneth, 5–7
Rich, Adrienne, 150, 194, 206n
Richardson, Joan, 48, 49–50, 75n, 76n
Rimbaud, Arthur, 166, 169, 178n, 179n
Rittenhouse, Jessie Belle, 88–89, 91, 92, 96
Roberson, Ed, 10
Robertson, Lisa, 111
Robeson, Paul, 195
Roosevelt, Theodore, 97
Rosenberg, Ethel, 172
Rosenberg, Julius, 172
Rothenberg, Jerome, 67
Russell, Bertrand, 98, 154

Said, Edward, 51, 56, 58
Sanday, Peggy, 15
Sandburg, Carl, 76n, 93, 94, 215
Scalapino, Leslie, 111
Schelling, Andrew, 5
Schiller, Johann Christoph Friedrich von, 177
Schmitz, Neil, 118
Schnittkind, Henry Thomas, 96, 97, 98
Schopenhauer, Arthur, 122
Schwartz, Daniel R., 72n
Scott, Randolph, 143
Shakespeare, William, 9, 103, 137, 144
Sheeler, Charles, 78n
Shelley, Percy Bysshe, 214
Smedman, Lorna J., 19
Smith, Felipe, 20
Smith, Michael, 112, 116–17, 119, 130n
Spahr, Juliana, 129n
Spencer, Herbert, 122
Spicer, Jack, 5, 7, 15
Spingarn, Joel E., 87, 93
Spinoza, Baruch, 122
Stallybrass, Peter, 38
Starkweather, Charles, 152
Stavros, George, 146n
Stedman, Edmund Clarence, 85, 91, 96
Stein, Gertrude, 14, 15, 43, 47, 53–54, 61, 64–65, 67, 75n, 78n, 111, 112, 113, 129n, 159–61, 174
Stepto, Robert Burns, 147
Stevens, Elsie, 76n

Stevens, Holly, 78n, 205n
Stevens, Wallace, 43, 47, 48–60, 75n, 76n, 77n, 78n, 79n, 87, 103, 125, 157, 185, 186, 187, 189, 192, 197, 198, 199, 203, 205n
Stewart, Maria, 35–36
Stoddard, Lothrop, 79n
Strang, Catrina, 111
Sundquist, Eric, 58, 131n

Tafari, Levi, 130n
Tagore, Rabindranath, 98
Tate, Allen, 15, 206n
Taussig, Michael, 15
Tchaikovsky, Pëtr Ilich, 177
Teasdale, Sara, 87
Temple, Shirley, 15
Thomas, Lorenzo, 12–13, 20, 130–31n, 149, 152–53
Thoreau, Henry David, 186, 188
Till, Emmett, 26, 154
Tolson, Melvin B., 102, 112, 113, 119, 124, 131n, 133–47, 149, 150, 154, 157
Toomer, Jean, 77n, 102, 119, 149
Torgovnick, Marianna, 65–66, 78n
Torrance, Ridgley, 87
Trotter, William Monroe, 96, 100, 102
Turner, Patricia, 4, 9
Turner, Victor, 147, 206n
Twain, Mark, 95

Untermeyer, Louis, 87, 97
Urbina, Luis C., 98

Van Gogh, Vincent, 177
Van Vechten, Carl, 63
Vaughan, Henry, 188
Vicuna, Cecilia, 111

Wagner, Jean, 85
Walcott, Derek, 179n
Walker, Alice, 183, 184
Waller, Fats, 6
Warren, Kenneth, 76–77n
Washington, Booker T., 36, 45–46, 47, 113, 118
Washington, George, 152
Waters, John, 180n
Wattles, Willard, 93
Wayne, John, 143
Wells-Barnett, Ida B., 26–27, 102
Wheatley, John, 16
Wheatley, Phillis, 13, 16, 17, 133
Wheeler, Edward, 87
Wheelock, John Hall, 87
White, Hayden, 205n
White, Walter, 63
Whitehead, Alfred North, 154, 220
Whitman, Walt, 86, 87, 88, 166, 176, 185, 188
Whittier, John Greenleaf, 86, 96
Williams, Bert, 14
Williams, Kenny J., 85
Williams, Raymond, 134
Williams, William Carlos, 14, 46, 47, 60–62, 75n, 77n, 108, 112, 129n, 152, 159, 173, 179–80n, 209, 214, 216
Wilson, Woodrow, 100, 139–40, 157
Winthrop, John, 204
Witekind, Herman, 30
Woodward, C. Vann, 45
Wordsworth, William, 188
Wright, Jay, 183–208
Wright, Richard, 41
Wylie, Elinor, 78–79n

Yarborough, Richard, 148
Yeats, William Butler, 74n, 203, 217

Zukofsky, Louis, 112, 113, 119, 124–25

Typeset in 10.5/13 Minion
with Minion display
Designed by Dennis Roberts
Composed by W. L. Ridenour
for the University of Illinois Press
Manufactured by Versa Press, Inc.

University of Illinois Press
1325 South Oak Street
Champaign, IL 61820-6903
www.press.uillinois.edu